HENRY IV
Part I

The RSC Shakespeare

Edited by Jonathan Bate and Eric Rasmussen

Chief Associate Editors: Héloïse Sénéchal and Jan Sewell

Associate Editors: Trey Jansen, Eleanor Lowe, Lucy Munro,
Dee Anna Phares

Henry IV Part I

Textual editing: Eric Rasmussen

Introduction and Shakespeare's Career in the Theater: Jonathan Bate

Commentary: Jan Sewell and Héloïse Sénéchal

Scene-by-Scene Analysis: Esme Miskimmin

In Performance: Karin Brown (RSC stagings), Jan Sewell (overview)

The Actor's Voice and the Director's Cut

(interviews by Jonathan Bate and Kevin Wright): Michael Pennington,
Adrian Noble, Michael Boyd

Editorial Advisory Board

The RSC Shakespeare

William Shakespeare

HENRY IV
PART I

Edited by Jonathan Bate and Eric Rasmussen

Introduction by Jonathan Bate

The Modern Library
New York

CONTENTS

INTRODUCTION

TRAGICAL-COMICAL-HISTORICAL-PASTORAL

Shakespeare's art of mingling comedy, history, and tragedy reached its peak in the two parts of *Henry IV*. As history, the plays paint a panorama of England, embracing a wider social range than any previous historical drama as the action moves from court to tavern, council chamber to battlefield, city to country, Archbishop and Lord Chief Justice to whore and thief. As comedy, they tell the story of a prodigal son's journey from youth to maturity and an old rogue's art of surviving by means of jokes, tall tales, and the art of being not only witty in himself, but the cause that wit is in other men. As tragedy, they reveal the slow decline of a king who cannot escape his past, the precipitate demise of an impetuous young warrior who embodies both the glory and the futility of military heroism, and the heartbreaking dismissal of a substitute father who has loved a prince with a warmth of which his true father is incapable.

The action begins some time after the events that ended Shakespeare's earlier play, *Richard II*. Henry Bullingbrook has usurped the throne of King Richard, who has been murdered. But now the rebels who helped Henry to the throne have turned against him. Whereas *Richard II* conformed to the traditional structure of tragedy—the story of the fall of a powerful man—the *Henry IV* plays adopt a wider perspective. *Richard II* had been written entirely in verse, the medium of royal and aristocratic characters, whereas long stretches of the *Henry IV* plays are in prose, the medium of the common people. The little scene with the Carriers at the tavern just before the highway robbery is a miniature of ordinary working-day life and common speech: "This house is turned upside down since Robin the ostler died."

The deep structure of the two parts of *Henry IV* is that not of tragedy but of pastoral comedy. They were written around the same time as *Much Ado About Nothing* and *As You Like It*, when Shakespeare's comic muse was at its zenith. They are his most enjoyable history plays because they are his funniest—and in the figure of Sir John Falstaff they introduce his greatest comic character—but they also share with the comedies a technique of counterpointing the intrigue of court and power politics against what has been called the "green" or "festive" world.

The traditional comic pattern turns on the successful effort of a young man to outwit an opponent and possess the girl of his choice. The girl's father, or some other authority figure of the older generation, resists the match, but is outflanked, often thanks to an ingenious scheme devised by a clever servant, perhaps involving disguise or flight (or both). The union of the lovers brings a renewed sense of social integration, expressed by some kind of festival at the climax of the play—a marriage, a dance, or a feast. All right-thinking people come over to the side of the lovers, but in Shakespearean comedy there is usually a party pooper, a figure who refuses to be assimilated into the harmony—Malvolio in *Twelfth Night*, Don John in *Much Ado About Nothing*, Jaques in *As You Like It*, Shylock in *The Merchant of Venice*. The key to the two parts of *Henry IV* is that they take the comic structure and apply it to Prince Harry—with the difference that, instead of his courtship (which ends up being tacked on very briefly at the end of *Henry V*), the action turns on his maturation from wild youth to exemplary warrior prince and statesman. And, in a brilliant reversal, the figure who is isolated at the end is not the party pooper but the embodiment of the festive spirit: Falstaff. Comedy is thus placed in opposition to the march of history. The necessity to reject Falstaff in the name of historical destiny and social order is why the final resolution is tinged with the feeling of tragedy.

The distinctive feature of pastoral comedy is that the action develops by means of a shift of location from the everyday world of work, business, politics, patriarchy, and power to a "green" or "festive" place of play, leisure, anarchy, feminine influence, and love—the wood in *A Midsummer Night's Dream*, Belmont in *The Merchant of Venice*, the Forest of Arden in *As You Like It*, rural Bohemia in *The Winter's Tale*. After the comic resolution is achieved, there has to be a return to the normative world, but recreative change has been effected by the values of the festive world. In *Henry IV Part I*, a tavern in Eastcheap plays the part of the festive world. In *Part II*, there is a reprise of that setting, but also a rural green world. As in the comedies, the shuttle between contrasting worlds and contradictory value systems creates the dialectic of the drama. But because of the calling of the prince to power, there can be no reconciliation between the value systems. Prince Hal announces in his first soliloquy that his time of "playing holidays" and "loose behaviour" will be but an interlude before he takes upon himself the mantle of historical duty.

HARRY TO HARRY

Richard II had followed the tragic pattern of a mismatch between the character of a man of high estate and the demands of his position as a ruler. It juxtaposed the fall of King Richard to the rise of Henry Bullingbrook, comparing them to a pair of buckets on a pulley, one descending into a well as the other ascends. Once Bullingbrook has become King Henry IV, the pattern is reasserted and reversed in the next generation. Henry sees his son seeming to become another Richard, a time waster surrounding himself with unsuitable companions and allowing the country to run to seed. He sees himself— a soldier, a man of decision and action—not in his son, but in Hotspur, child of the Percy family who had helped him to displace Richard from the throne.

Historically, Henry Percy, known as Hotspur, was more than twenty years older than Prince Henry (usually called Harry and, by Falstaff alone, Hal), the future King Henry V, victor of Agincourt. With his habitual dramatic license, Shakespeare altered history and made them rival youths of the same generation. Henry IV's nightmare of history repeating itself is that Hotspur will play his own role to his son's Richard. He wishes that "some night-tripping fairy" had exchanged the two Harries in their cradles "And called mine Percy, his [i.e. Northumberland's] Plantagenet." But this time it is the rebel who falls and the true heir who succeeds. *Henry IV*, a doubleheader of a play, is full of doubles. There are paired fathers and sons: the king and the prince, Northumberland and Hotspur in *Part I*. There are surrogate fathers to the young hero: Sir John Falstaff and, in *Part II*, his antithesis, the Lord Chief Justice. There are brothers in blood (in

Part I, Northumberland and Worcester, Hotspur and his brother-in-law Mortimer; in *Part II*, Prince Harry and Prince John, the aged kinsmen Shallow and Silence) and brothers in jest (Hal's "sworn brethren" among the tavern crowd, Ned Poins chief among them).

One of the questions that fascinates Shakespeare in these plays is, what is the appropriate education for a future king? The Tudor view was that the ideal king should combine the qualities of soldier, scholar, and courtier. Fencing, jousting, and hunting offered training in the chivalric arts of the medieval aristocracy, but a learned humanist tutor was also required to drill the prince in languages, literature, history, ethics, law, and theology. And at the same time it was necessary to imbibe the elaborate codes of behavior, the conventions of propriety and deference, upon which courtship depended.

Hotspur is the embodiment of an old-style chivalric warrior. He would rather be astride his horse than engaging in courtly parley with his wife. He lives by the code of honor and is deliciously scornful of the courtly manners embodied by the trimly dressed, clean-shaved lord who comes with "pouncet-box" in hand to demand Hotspur's prisoners: the clash of styles between battlefield and court is enough to turn him into a rebel. Hotspur has boundless courage and energy, but his desire "To pluck bright honour from the pale-faced moon" is susceptible to parody: his own wife teases him and Prince Hal mocks him as "the Hotspur of the north, he that kills me some six or seven dozen of Scots at a breakfast, washes his hands, and says to his wife 'Fie upon this quiet life! I want work.'" His impulsiveness means that he cannot calculate, he is never the politician. "[A] plague upon it, / I have forgot the map!" he says during a council of war. A more politic customer would be most unlikely to have forgotten it—and would never admit as much if he had.

As Hotspur embodies the old chivalric code, his fellow warrior, the Welshman Glendower, stands for an equally antiquated mode of being: magical thinking. He boasts of portents at his birth—fiery shapes in the air and goats running from the mountains—but this kind of talk is ridiculed. When he claims that he can call spirits from the vasty deep, Hotspur wryly asks, "But will they come when you do call for them?" Talk of dragons and finless fish is "skimble-skamble stuff" which does nothing to advance the cause of the rebellion. In the end, the consequence of Glendower's desire to listen to prophecies is that he fails to turn up for the battle.

HONOR VERSUS INSTINCT

Part I shows Prince Harry playing "truant" from "chivalry," but returning to it when the time is ripe. Even as he proves himself on the battlefield, the critique of honor continues with Falstaff's mock "catechism": "Can honour set to a leg? No . . . Who hath it? He that died o'Wednesday." Falstaff's philosophy is a simple "give me life": never mind about ethical and political codes of behavior. "I am not a double man," he says to Hal, putting down the dead Hotspur, whom he has been carrying on his back. Yet he is double the size of anyone else in the play and he has a double life, rising from feigned death on the battlefield of Shrewsbury so that he can return in *Part II*. It will be altogether harder to get rid of cowardly Falstaff than to defeat brave Hotspur. "Thou art not what thou seem'st," remarks Hal: in seeming to have killed Hotspur, Falstaff is not the coward he has appeared to be. But he has not slain Hotspur, merely stabbed him when he is already dead—a supremely dishonorable deed. And yet, what is honor? A mere word, an empty code. It is the trickster, the chancer, who survives, not the honorable man.

Falstaff is at once the great deceiver and the great truth-teller, who reduces war to its bottom line: common foot soldiers are but "food for powder." One of the reasons why Shakespeare made him fat was to remind the audience of the solidity of the human body: Falstaff's girth is a way of saying that history is made not only of big speeches and dramatic events, but also of the daily lives of people who eat, drink, sleep, and die: "Rare words! Brave world! Hostess, my breakfast, come! / O, I could wish this tavern were my drum!"

A key word is "instinct." Hotspur has instinctive courage and Falstaff an instinctive sense of self-preservation. The king thinks that his son is instinctively idle and irresponsible. The aim of a sixteenth-century royal humanist education was to overcome such innate

propensities by developing the ethical, linguistic, and political facul-
ties of the pupil prince. For Hal, the King's Tavern in Eastcheap
serves as a parody of the schoolroom at court. Falstaff is explicitly
identified as his "tutor" and a central part of his education is to learn
a new language—not, however, Latin, Greek, or the rhetorical elaboration of courtly speech, but the language of the people. This is a
Harry who develops the art of speaking with every "Tom, Dick and
Francis." He learns their jargon—"They call drinking deep, dyeing
scarlet"—and he becomes "so good a proficient in one quarter of an
hour" that he will be able to "drink with any tinker in his own language" for the rest of his life.

Henry IV believes that one of the failings of his predecessor
Richard II had been to seek to make himself popular, thus eroding
the necessary distance that creates awe and gives mystique to the
monarchy. But King Henry's own distance from public life—he is
nearly always seen surrounded by an inner circle of courtiers or
closeted alone in his chamber—causes power to ebb from him. His
son, by contrast, comes to know the common people, developing a
rapport that will enable him to inspire and lead his army in *Henry V*.
The point is made through the very linguistic medium of the drama:
all Shakespeare's other English kings speak entirely in verse,
whereas Prince Hal has command of a flexible prose voice, with
which he reduces himself to the level of his people, an Eastcheap
trick that he repeats when he goes in disguise among his men on the
night before the battle of Agincourt.

The prince works according to the principle articulated by the cunning politician Ulysses in *Troilus and Cressida*: a man "Cannot make
boast to have that which he hath, / Nor feels not what he owes, but by
reflection, / As when his virtues shining upon others / Heat them and
they retort that heat again / To the first giver." That is to say, we can
only make value judgments through a process of comparison. "Percy
is but my factor, good my lord, / To engross up glorious deeds on my
behalf": by temporarily ceding glory to Henry Hotspur, Henry Monmouth will seem all the more glorious when he eventually triumphs
over him. His whole strategy is revealed in the imagery of his first
soliloquy: the sun seems brighter after cloud and a jewel on a dull
background will "show more goodly and attract more eyes / Than

that which hath no foil to set it off." The offsetting of the prince against his various foils is the structural key to the drama.

THE PRINCE AS MACHIAVEL?

What is the basis of political rule? Orthodox Tudor theory propounded that kings and magistrates were God's representatives on earth, their authority sanctioned by divine law. But the Elizabethan stage had another possible answer. Christopher Marlowe's tragedy *The Jew of Malta*, written about 1589 and well known to Shakespeare, has an extraordinary opening. The prologue is spoken by an actor pretending to be the Florentine political theorist Niccolò Machiavelli. He voices a series of deeply subversive suggestions about the nature of sovereignty. His riposte to political orthodoxy is that the only basis of effective government is raw power:

> I count religion but a childish toy,
> And hold there is no sin but ignorance . . .
> Many will talk of title to a crown:
> What right had Caesar to the empery?
> Might first made kings, and laws were then most sure
> When, like the Draco's, they were writ in blood.

Religion as an illusion; the idea that human knowledge does not require divine sanction; the notion that it is "might" not "right" that decides who rules; the proposition that the most effective laws are those based not on justice but on the severity exemplified by the ancient Greek lawgiver Draco (from whose name we get the word "draconian"). French and English thinkers of Shakespeare's time demonized Machiavelli for holding these views, but for Christopher Marlowe the act of thinking the unthinkable made Machiavelli a model for his own overreaching stage heroes.

Shakespeare's history plays are steeped in the influence of Marlowe, but politically he was much more cautious—he would never have risked suffering Marlowe's end, stabbed to death by a government spy while awaiting questioning in a heresy investigation. But that did not stop Shakespeare from recognizing the theatrical charisma of the

Marlovian machiavel. He created a string of such characters himself—Aaron the Moor in *Titus Andronicus*, Richard III, Iago in *Othello*, Edmund in *King Lear*. What attracted him to the type was not so much the subversive politics as the stage panache of the unapologetic villain. Political orthodoxy is staid and solemn. The machiavel is nimble and witty. But is he necessarily brutal and irreligious?

Prince Harry is a man of the future; his father is haunted by the past. Both parts of *Henry IV* are suffused with the memory of the "by-paths and indirect crooked ways" by which Bullingbrook "met" (or rather took) the crown. The king is revealed at his most vulnerable halfway through *Part II*, in a scene that may have troubled the censor: sick and sleepless, he meditates on the cares of state, the fragility of office, and the weight of his past sin. A usurper himself, Henry IV has no ground on which to base his authority over the rebels who were once his allies. The only basis of his power is victory on the battlefield. In each part, this is achieved by means of a trick. At Shrewsbury in *Part I*, the device consists of dressing several different men as the king in order to confuse the enemy. Having slain one of the impersonators, Douglas assumes that he is addressing another of them: "What art thou, / That counterfeit'st the person of a king?" This time, however, it is the king, not a counterfeit—which beautifully dramatizes the point that the king *is* a counterfeit because of his usurpation. In *Part II*, the king is too sick to fight his own battle, so at Gaultree Forest the Machiavellian strategy of reneging upon the terms of a negotiated truce is carried out by his second son, Prince John of Lancaster. Does that make Prince Harry into the true follower of Machiavelli, who advised that the effective prince is one who gets someone else to do his dirty work for him?

At the beginning of *Part I*, the king says that he must postpone his Crusade to the Holy Land because of the new civil broils at home, the fresh wound upon the earth of England. His dream of expiating his sins by liberating Jerusalem from the heathen is never translated into action. The prophecy that he would end his life there is only realized ironically: he dies in the "Jerusalem chamber" of Westminster Abbey. Henry IV's fear, apparently borne out by the bad company that Prince Harry keeps, is that the sin of the father will be visited upon the reign of his son:

For the fifth Harry from curbèd licence plucks
The muzzle of restraint, and the wild dog
Shall flesh his tooth in every innocent.
O my poor kingdom, sick with civil blows!
When that my care could not withhold thy riots,
What wilt thou do when riot is thy care?
O, thou wilt be a wilderness again,
Peopled with wolves, thy old inhabitants!

He imagines that the "riot" of the wayward prince will be translated into civil disorder when he becomes king. That is also Falstaff's hope on hearing that his beloved Hal is now Henry V: "the laws of England are at my commandment . . . and woe unto my Lord Chief Justice!" But he is in for a shock: Hal immediately adopts Falstaff's adversary, the Lord Chief Justice, as his new surrogate father. As in *Part I* he had startled the rebels by transforming himself from tavern idler to armed warrior on horseback, so in *Part II* he will prove that he has learned the civic virtues as well as the military ones.

The prince's self-revelatory soliloquy early in *Part I* began with the words "I know you all." The newly crowned king's rejection of Falstaff late in *Part II* begins with the words "I know thee not, old man." The verbal echo is unmistakable: he has ceased to be Hal, he is now delivering on his promise that the time would come when he would throw off the companions and misleaders of his youth. As predicted in the soliloquy, Harry has succeeded in falsifying men's hopes. His reformation glitters over his fault. Falstaff and company suddenly seem to be no more than instruments in a princely conjuring trick, a theatrical act of self-transformation designed to impress a public audience.

Radically opposing interpretations thus become possible. By one account, the politic march of history stands in violent contrast to the humane virtues of friendship, loyalty, good humor, sociability, verbal inventiveness, self-mockery, and love. Humanity gives way to what the Bastard in *King John* called "commodity." History is a Machiavellian nightmare of violence and self-interest. The alternative view is that Falstaff embodies the temptations of the flesh. He scores highly for at least three of the seven deadly sins—gluttony, lust, and sloth.

He is the Vice figure of the old tradition of morality plays and his rejection is accordingly Hal's final step on the path toward political and moral redemption. So it is that Hal can be played equally persuasively as a young man going on a journey toward maturity but still enjoying his departures from the straight and narrow path, or as one of Shakespeare's Machiavellian manipulators—energetic and intellectually astute, a brilliant actor, but intensely self-conscious, emotionally reined in.

We may perhaps reconcile the opposing readings by supposing that, in the character of Prince Hal, Shakespeare—perhaps as his own riposte to Marlowe—set out to create a new and distinctive kind of "good machiavel": a political realist who is prepared to take difficult, even brutal, decisions when it is necessary, but who, instead of being atheistic and self-interested, always tries to do what he takes to be God's will and so to serve the best interests of his nation and his people. Still, though, the dilemma remains: even as Falstaff uses Hal for his own advancement, he is always a truer father than the cold and politic King Henry IV can ever be. The point is made with beautiful clarity by the contrast between Falstaff's heated engagement in the scene in which he and Hal act out the prodigal prince's forthcoming interview with his father and the king's chilly detachment in the interview itself.

REFORMATION AND REJECTION

It is not known whether Shakespeare always intended Henry IV to be a two-part play or whether he discovered at some point in the writing or production of Part I that it would be dramatically unsatisfying to contain a double climax in a single play, to have Prince Harry prove himself a chivalric hero by defeating Hotspur on the battlefield and then immediately dissociate himself from Falstaff and the other thieves. Instead, the rejection of Falstaff is withheld until Part II, but anticipated in the play-within-the-play in Part I, where the prince's return to his father is pre-enacted in the tavern.

The scene is a glorious piece of improvised theater, with the actors changing roles and parodying different linguistic registers. Thus, for instance, when Falstaff plays King Henry he apes the affected courtly prose style of the once fashionable writer John Lyly: "for though the camomile, the more it is trodden the faster it grows, yet youth, the more it is wasted the sooner it wears." It is a mark of Shakespeare's attention to detail that when Falstaff is playing the king he calls the prince "Harry" instead of his pet name, "Hal." Though the language of the mock play is intricate and varied, the staging is simple: "This chair shall be my state, this dagger my sceptre and this cushion my crown." The meta-theatrical effect reminds the audience that they are in a theater, and at the same time suggests that power is itself a form of theater. There is no intrinsic reason why a golden crown is sacred and a stuffed cushion anarchic; whether in a theater or a palace, a throne may represent a "chair of state," but it is still a mere chair.

A chair is a chair and, as Gadshill puts it, "*Homo* is a common name to all men." Falstaff may be "that reverend Vice, that grey Iniquity, that father Ruffian, that Vanity in years," but he is also the embodiment of the shared frailty of all humanity: "If sack and sugar be a fault, heaven help the wicked: if to be old and merry be a sin, then many an old host that I know is damned." To banish plump Jack is to banish "all the world." "I do," says Hal, playing the role of his father the king. "I will," he adds, anticipating what he will do when he becomes king himself. As so often when Shakespeare's art is working in its most concentrated form, judgment is left suspended. Is Hal "essentially made," with or without knowing it? And is it possible to be a true friend and a true prince? At the end of the "play extempore," he is friend more than prince, lying to an authority figure, the sheriff, in order to protect Falstaff. So is he—as some editors emend—"essentially mad," fundamentally as opposed to temporarily a "madcap"? "The true prince may, for recreation sake, prove a false thief," says Falstaff: is the playtime of "recreation" a space for a brief interlude of misrule or a crucible in which the self is re-created?

There is little historical warrant for the story of Henry V's riotous youth. A "prodigal son" narrative was attached to him in the chronicles and the anonymous play *The Famous Victories of Henry the Fifth* in order to highlight the change he undergoes when he becomes king, submits to the rule of law, and so unifies and brings to order the nation that his father divided. The rejection of Falstaff and company is part and parcel of Harry's symbolically becoming a new person at the moment of his coronation. The notions of "reformation" and the washing away of past iniquities clearly have strong religious connotations. Each time the prince returns to the court, he speaks a language of "fall" and "pardon." When he fights well, his father tells him, "Thou hast redeemed thy lost opinion."

The rhythm of Prince Hal's life is that of providential history, leading to his "reformation" and his assumption of the roles which attracted Queen Elizabeth to him: unifier of the body politic, victor over a rival kingdom, heroic leader of a great and independent nation. The rhythm of Falstaff's life is that of the body and the seasons. In *Part II* he will journey into the deep England of Justice Shallow's Gloucestershire orchard. We learn from Shallow that Falstaff began his career as page to Thomas Mowbray, Duke of Norfolk. This appears to be a Shakespearean fancy without source: it is true of neither the historical Sir John Falstaff, who flees the battlefield in *Henry VI Part I*, nor the historical Sir John Oldcastle, of whom the character of Falstaff was originally an irreverent portrait. Why did Shakespeare give his fictional Falstaff a past that began in the service of Mowbray? At one level, it links him with opposition to the Lancastrian ascendancy represented by King Henry IV and his son. Mowbray was Henry IV's opponent when the latter was still Bullingbrook, back at the beginning of *Richard II*. Like father, like son: as Bullingbrook's accusation of treachery was instrumental in the banishment of Mowbray from the land, so Hal will banish Falstaff from his presence. Mowbray departs with a moving farewell to his native land and language; the effect of his words is to suggest that love of the English earth and the English word goes deeper than dynastic difference. We do not hear similar patriotic sentiments in the mouth of the self-interested Bullingbrook; he does nothing to bring back the old England idealized in the deathbed speech of his father, John of Gaunt (whose name and whose England will also be remembered by Shallow).

In Shakespeare's own time, those who suffered banishment because of ideological difference, but who claimed that they were nevertheless loyal to England, were predominantly Catholics. And this suggests another level to the allusion that binds Falstaff to the Duke of Norfolk. To an Elizabethan audience, the name of Norfolk—

the only surviving dukedom in the land—was synonymous with overt or suspected Catholic sympathy. The old Catholic ways persisted in the country long after the official change of religion inaugurated by Henry VIII's break from Rome. The Catholic liturgy's integral relationship with the agricultural calendar and the cycles of human biology could not be shattered overnight. There may, then, be a sense in which Falstaff's journey into deep England is also a journey into the old religion of Shakespeare's father and maternal grandfather. One wonders if it is a coincidence that, in fleshing out the skeletal character of the prince's riotous companion that he inherited from the old play *The Famous Victories of Henry the Fifth*, Shakespeare retained and made much of his own father's name, John. It is ironic that Falstaff's original surname, Oldcastle, had to be changed because the character was regarded as an insult to the memory of the proto-Protestant Lollard of that name: "for Oldcastle died martyr," says the epilogue to *Part II*, "and this is not the man."

Indeed, it is not the man, for Falstaff is if anything an embodiment of those ancient Catholic rhythms which were suppressed in the name of Reformation. Vestiges of Oldcastle litter the text: "Falstaff sweats to death" suggests a martyr burning on a bonfire, and "if I become not a cart as well as another man" could suggest a religious dissident on the way to the stake as well as a criminal being taken to the gallows. Protestants, especially in the extreme form of Puritans, were traditionally lean; fat monks were symbolic of the corruptions of Catholicism. By making Sir John fat and not calling him Oldcastle, Shakespeare raises the specter of Catholic as opposed to Protestant martyrdoms. Falstaff is Malvolio's opposite: he stands for cakes and ale, festival and holiday, all that was anathema to Puritanism. At the beginning of *Henry V*, the Archbishop of Canterbury confirms that Prince Harry's transformation was completed with the rejection of Falstaff: "Never came reformation in a flood, / With such a heady currance, scouring faults." If there is a proto-Protestant or embryonic Puritan in the plays, it is King Harry V, newly washed of his past, casting off his old companions, turning away England's former self.

ABOUT THE TEXT

Shakespeare endures through history. He illuminates later times as well as his own. He helps us to understand the human condition. But he cannot do this without a good text of the plays. Without editions there would be no Shakespeare. That is why every twenty years or so throughout the last three centuries there has been a major new edition of his complete works. One aspect of editing is the process of keeping the texts up to date—modernizing the spelling, punctuation, and typography (though not, of course, the actual words), providing explanatory notes in the light of changing educational practices (a generation ago, most of Shakespeare's classical and biblical allusions could be assumed to be generally understood, but now they can't).

But because Shakespeare did not personally oversee the publication of his plays, editors also have to make decisions about the relative authority of the early printed editions. Half of the sum of his plays only appeared posthumously, in the elaborately produced First Folio text of 1623, the original "Complete Works" prepared for the press by Shakespeare's fellow actors, the people who knew the plays better than anyone else. The other half had appeared in print in his lifetime, in the more compact and cheaper form of "Quarto" editions, some of which reproduced good quality texts, others of which were to a greater or lesser degree garbled and error-strewn. In the case of a few plays there are hundreds of differences between the Quarto and Folio editions, some of them far from trivial.

If you look at printers' handbooks from the age of Shakespeare, you quickly discover that one of the first rules was that, whenever possible, compositors were recommended to set their type from existing printed books rather than manuscripts. This was the age before mechanical typesetting, when each individual letter had to be picked out by hand from the compositor's case and placed on a stick (upside down and back to front) before being laid on the press. It was an age of murky rushlight and of manuscripts written in a secretary hand that had dozens of different, hard-to-decipher forms. Printers' lives were a lot easier when they were reprinting existing books rather than struggling with handwritten copy. Easily the quickest way to have created the First Folio would have been simply to reprint those eighteen plays that had already appeared in Quarto and work from manuscript only on the other eighteen.

But that is not what happened. Whenever Quartos were used, playhouse "promptbooks" were also consulted and stage directions copied in from them. And in the case of several major plays where a reasonably well printed Quarto was available, the Folio printers were instructed to work from an alternative, playhouse-derived manuscript. This meant that the whole process of producing the first complete Shakespeare took months, even years, longer than it might have done. But for the men overseeing the project, John Hemings and Henry Condell, friends and fellow actors who had been remembered in Shakespeare's will, the additional labor and cost were worth the effort for the sake of producing an edition that was close to the practice of the theater. They wanted all the plays in print so that people could, as they wrote in their prefatory address to the reader, "read him and again and again," but they also wanted "the great variety of readers" to work from texts that were close to the theater life for which Shakespeare originally intended them. For this reason, the *RSC Shakespeare*, in both *Complete Works* and individual volumes, uses the Folio as base text wherever possible. Significant Quarto variants are, however, noted in the Textual Notes.

Henry IV Part I is one of the plays where the Folio text was printed from a Quarto, though with reference to a playhouse manuscript, in which a large number of oaths had been removed in accordance with the 1606 Parliamentary "Act to Restrain the Abuses of Players," whereby theater companies were prohibited from taking God's name in vain. Most modern editors use the First Quarto of 1598 as their copy text but import stage directions, act divisions, and some corrections from Folio. Our Folio-led editorial practice follows the reverse procedure, using Folio as copy text, but deploying the First Quarto as a "control text" that offers assistance in the correction and identification of compositors' errors in the Folio, of which there are many. The traditional notion of fidelity to Shakespeare's first Quartos, on the grounds that they represent the texts closest to "what the author wrote," is sometimes more an ideal than a reality. Early Quartos have errors too. And later Quartos made good corrections as well as introducing new errors. The lesson of textual transmission is the same as that of the theater: the Shakespearean text was mobile in its own time and remains ever mobile. Each time one of the plays is performed, whatever the "copy text," the words will be slightly different, thanks to the tricks of actors' memories. So, too, each time the play is edited, there will be dozens of differences of punctuation, emendation, and interpretation. Textual mobility is an essential part of Shakespeare's evolving creative afterlife. Our text is a modernized version of one moment in that life—the moment of the Folio, when all Shakespeare's history plays were gathered and put in sequence for the first time.

In order to respect the integrity of the Folio text, we have not reinserted the Quarto oaths that were removed from it. They are, however, listed at the end of the text and we recommend classroom discussion of the effect of their removal and rehearsal room reinsertion of them for the purposes of contemporary performance.

The following notes highlight various aspects of the editorial process and indicate conventions used in the text of this edition:

Lists of Parts are supplied in the First Folio for only six plays, not including *Henry IV Part I*, so the list here is editorially supplied. Capitals indicate that part of the name which is used for speech headings in the script (thus "Sir Richard VERNON").

Locations are provided by the Folio for only two plays. Eighteenth-century editors, working in an age of elaborately realistic stage sets, were the first to provide detailed locations. Given that Shakespeare wrote for a bare stage and often an imprecise sense of place, we have relegated locations to the explanatory notes at the foot of the page, where they are given at the beginning of each scene where the imaginary location is different from the one before.

Act and Scene Divisions were provided in the Folio in a much more thoroughgoing way than in the Quartos. Sometimes, however, they were erroneous or omitted; corrections and additions supplied by editorial tradition are indicated by square brackets. Five-act division is based on a classical model, and act breaks provided the opportunity to replace the candles in the indoor Blackfriars playhouse which the King's Men used after 1608, but Shakespeare did not necessarily think in terms of a five-part structure of dramatic composition. The Folio convention is that a scene ends when the stage is empty. Nowadays, partly under the influence of film, we tend to consider a scene to be a dramatic unit that ends with either a change of imaginary location or a significant passage of time within the narrative. Shakespeare's fluidity of composition accords well with this convention, so in addition to act and scene numbers we provide a *running scene* count in the right margin at the beginning of each new scene, in the typeface used for editorial directions. Where there is a scene break caused by a momentary bare stage, but the location does not change and extra time does not pass, we use the convention *running scene continues*. There is inevitably a degree of editorial judgment in making such calls, but the system is very valuable in suggesting the pace of the plays.

Speakers' Names are often inconsistent in Folio. We have regularized speech headings, but retained an element of deliberate inconsistency in entry directions, in order to give the flavor of Folio.

Verse is indicated by lines that do not run to the right margin and by capitalization of each line. The Folio printers sometimes set verse as prose, and vice versa (either out of misunderstanding or for reasons of space). We have silently corrected in such cases, although in some instances there is ambiguity, in which case we have leaned toward the preservation of Folio layout. Folio sometimes uses contraction ("turnd" rather than "turned") to indicate whether or not the final "-ed" of a past participle is sounded, an area where there is variation for the sake of the five-beat iambic pentameter rhythm. We use the convention of a grave accent to indicate sounding (thus "turnèd" would be two syllables), but would urge actors not to overstress. In cases where one speaker ends with a verse half line and the next begins with the other half of the pentameter, editors since the late eighteenth century have indented the second line. We have abandoned this convention, since the Folio does not use it, nor did actors' cues in the Shakespearean theater. An exception is made when the second speaker actively interrupts or completes the first speaker's sentence.

Spelling is modernized, but older forms are occasionally maintained where necessary for rhythm or aural effect.

Punctuation in Shakespeare's time was as much rhetorical as grammatical. "Colon" was originally a term for a unit of thought in an argument. The semicolon was a new unit of punctuation (some of the Quartos lack them altogether). We have modernized punctuation throughout, but have given more weight to Folio punctuation than many editors, since, though not Shakespearean, it reflects the usage of his period. In particular, we have used the colon far more than many editors: it is exceptionally useful as a way of indicating how many Shakespearean speeches unfold clause by clause in a developing argument that gives the illusion of enacting the process of thinking in the moment. We have also kept in mind the origin of punctuation in classical times as a way of assisting the actor and orator: the comma suggests the briefest of pauses for breath, the colon a middling one, and a full stop or period a longer pause. Semicolons, by contrast, belong to an era of punctuation that was only just coming in during Shakespeare's time and that is coming to an end now: we have accordingly used them only where they occur in our copy texts (and not always then). Dashes are sometimes used for parenthetical interjections where the Folio has brackets. They are also used for interruptions and changes in train of thought. Where a change of addressee occurs within a speech, we have used a dash preceded by a period (or occasionally another form of punctuation). Often the identity of the respective addressee is obvious from the context. When it is not, this has been indicated in a marginal stage direction.

Entrances and Exits are fairly thorough in Folio, which has accordingly been followed as faithfully as possible. Where characters are omitted or corrections are necessary, this is indicated by square brackets (e.g. "[*and Attendants*]"). *Exit* is sometimes silently normalized to *Exeunt* and *Manet* anglicized to "remains." We trust Folio positioning of entrances and exits to a greater degree than most editors.

Editorial Stage Directions such as stage business, asides, indications of addressee and of characters' position on the gallery stage are used only sparingly in Folio. Other editions mingle directions of this kind with original Folio and Quarto directions, sometimes marking them by means of square brackets. We have sought to distinguish what could be described as *directorial* interventions of this kind from Folio-style directions (either original or supplied) by placing them in the right margin in a different typeface. There is a degree of subjectivity about which directions are of which kind, but the procedure is intended as a reminder to the reader and the actor that Shakespearean stage directions are often dependent upon editorial inference alone and are not set in stone. We also depart from editorial tradition in sometimes admitting uncertainty and thus printing permissive stage directions, such as **Aside?** (often a line may be equally effective as an aside or as a direct address—it is for each production or reading to make its own decision) or **may exit** or a piece of business placed between arrows to indicate that it may occur at various different moments within a scene.

Line Numbers in the left margin are editorial, for reference and to key the explanatory and textual notes.

Explanatory Notes at the foot of each page explain allusions and gloss obsolete and difficult words, confusing phraseology, occasional major textual cruces, and so on. Particular attention is given to nonstandard usage, bawdy innuendo, and technical terms (e.g. legal and military language). Where more than one sense is given, commas indicate shades of related meaning, slashes alternative or double meanings.

Textual Notes at the end of the play indicate major departures from the Folio. They take the following form: the reading of our text is given in bold and its source given after an equals sign, with "Q" indicating that it derives from the First Quarto of 1598, "Q5" that it derives from the Fifth Quarto of 1613, "Q7" from the Seventh Quarto of 1632, "F" from the First Folio of 1623, "F2" a correction introduced in the Second Folio of 1632, "F3" a correction introduced in the Third Folio of 1663–64, and "Ed" one that derives from the subsequent editorial tradition. The rejected Folio ("F") reading is then given. Selected Quarto variants and plausible unadopted editorial readings are also included. Thus, for example, "**1.2.80 for . . . it** = F. Q = for wisedome cries out in the streets and no man regards it" indicates that we have retained the Folio reading "for no man regards it," but that "for wisedome cries out in the streets and no man regards it" is an interestingly different reading in the First Quarto of 1598.

KEY FACTS

MAJOR PARTS: (with percentage of lines/number of speeches/ scenes on stage) Falstaff (20%/151/8), Prince Henry (18%/170/10), Hotspur (18%/102/8), King Henry (11%/30/6), Worcester (6%/35/7), Poins (3%/36/3), Glendower (3%/23/1). Several characters speak between 15 and 30 of the play's 3,000 lines: Douglas, Hostess Quickly, Gadshill, Vernon, Mortimer, Lady Percy, Bardolph, Blunt, Northumberland, Westmorland, Francis.

LINGUISTIC MEDIUM: 55% verse, 45% prose.

DATE: Probably written and first performed 1596–97; registered for publication February 1598. Falstaff's name was originally Oldcastle; it was probably changed to Falstaff either during the months when William Brooke, Lord Cobham (an indirect descendant of the historical Sir John Oldcastle), was Lord Chamberlain (August 1596 to March 1597) or following the suppression of playing (July–October 1597) caused by a politically inflammatory play called *The Isle of Dogs*.

SOURCES: Based on the account of the reign of Henry IV in the 1587 edition of Holinshed's *Chronicles*, with some use of Samuel Daniel's epic poem *The First Four Books of the Civil Wars* (1595). Thus, for instance, the historical Hotspur was twenty years older than Hal, but Daniel made them contemporaries for dramatic effect. The intermingling of historical materials and comedy, in the context of the prince's riotous youth, is developed from the anonymous Queen's Men play *The Famous Victories of Henry the Fifth* (performed late 1580s), which includes characters who may be regarded as crude prototypes of Falstaff and Poins.

TEXT: Quarto 1598 (text probably based on a scribal transcript of Shakespeare's manuscript; two printings, one of them lost save for a few sheets), reprinted 1599, 1604, 1608, 1613, 1622 (indicating that this was one of Shakespeare's most popular plays). The Folio text was set from the Fifth Quarto, correcting some but nowhere near all of its mistakes. Oaths were systematically removed in accordance with the 1606 Parliamentary "Act to Restrain the Abuses of Players": since the Act applied to stage performances, not printed books, this suggests that a theatrical manuscript also lay behind the Folio text. There is therefore good reason to regard Folio as an autonomous text, with its own authority. Our text is based on Folio, but where there are manifest errors, either derived from the Quarto tradition or introduced by the Folio compositors, we restore readings from the First Quarto.

THE FIRST PART OF HENRY THE FOURTH,
with the Life and Death of Henry Surnamed Hotspur

LIST OF PARTS

KING HENRY IV, formerly Henry Bullingbrook, Duke of Lancaster

PRINCE HENRY, Prince of Wales, Hal or Harry Monmouth

PRINCE JOHN, his younger brother, Lord of Lancaster

Earl of WESTMORLAND

Sir Walter BLUNT

Sir John FALSTAFF

Edward or Ned POINS

PETO

BARDOLPH

Earl of NORTHUMBERLAND, Henry Percy

Earl of WORCESTER, Thomas Percy, his younger brother

HOTSPUR, Sir Henry (or Harry) Percy, Northumberland's son

Lord Edmund MORTIMER, Earl of March, Hotspur's brother-in-law

Owen GLENDOWER, Welsh lord, Mortimer's father-in-law

Earl of DOUGLAS, a Scots Lord

Sir Richard VERNON

ARCHBISHOP of York, Richard Scroop

SIR MICHAEL, member of Archbishop's household

LADY PERCY (Kate), Hotspur's wife, Mortimer's sister

LADY MORTIMER, Mortimer's wife, Glendower's daughter

FIRST CARRIER (Mugs)

OSTLER

SECOND CARRIER (Tom)

GADSHILL

CHAMBERLAIN

FIRST TRAVELLER

SECOND TRAVELLER

FRANCIS, an apprentice drawer or tapster

VINTNER

HOSTESS QUICKLY, landlady of a tavern

SHERIFF

SERVANT

MESSENGER

Lords, Soldiers, other Travellers, and Attendants

Act 1 Scene 1

Enter the King, Lord John of Lancaster, [the] Earl of Westmorland,
with others

KING HENRY IV   So shaken as we are, so wan with care,
     Find we a time for frighted peace to pant,
     And breathe short-winded accents of new broils
     To be commenced in strands afar remote.
5   No more the thirsty entrance of this soil
     Shall daub her lips with her own children's blood.
     No more shall trenching war channel her fields,
     Nor bruise her flow'rets with the armèd hoofs
     Of hostile paces. Those opposèd eyes,
10   Which, like the meteors of a troubled heaven,
     All of one nature, of one substance bred,
     Did lately meet in the intestine shock
     And furious close of civil butchery
     Shall now, in mutual well-beseeming ranks,
15   March all one way and be no more opposed
     Against acquaintance, kindred and allies.
     The edge of war, like an ill-sheathèd knife,
     No more shall cut his master. Therefore, friends,
     As far as to the sepulchre of Christ —
20   Whose soldier now, under whose blessèd cross
     We are impressèd and engaged to fight —

1.1 Location: the royal court. Henry Bullingbrook had usurped the English crown in 1399 when he forced his cousin, Richard II, to abdicate. Richard died shortly afterward in mysterious circumstances. The early years of Henry's reign were dominated by a determination to justify and consolidate his claim to the throne and by a number of insurrections. As the play opens, Henry voices his anxiety about civil unrest   **1 we** i.e. the king/the nation as a whole   **wan** pale, sickly   **2 Find we** let us find   **frighted** frightened   **3 breathe short-winded accents** speak while out of breath   **broils** quarrels, fighting   **4 strands afar remote** distant shores   **5 entrance** mouth   **6 daub** smear, plaster   **7 trenching** plowing   **8 flow'rets** small flowers   **armèd** iron-shod/armored   **9 paces** (horse's) tread/gallop   **opposèd** hostile, malevolent   **10 meteors** regarded as bad omens   **12 intestine shock** internal, domestic military encounter   **13 close** hand-to-hand fighting   **14 mutual well-beseeming** united and ordered   **19 sepulchre of Christ** Christ's tomb (at Jerusalem; Henry is planning a crusade to the Holy Land)   **21 impressèd** conscripted   **engaged** pledged, committed

Forthwith a power of English shall we levy,
Whose arms were moulded in their mother's womb
To chase these pagans in those holy fields
25 Over whose acres walked those blessèd feet
Which fourteen hundred years ago were nailed
For our advantage on the bitter cross.
But this our purpose is a twelvemonth old,
And bootless 'tis to tell you we will go:
30 Therefore we meet not now.— Then let me hear
Of you, my gentle cousin Westmorland,
What yesternight our council did decree
In forwarding this dear expedience.

WESTMORLAND My liege, this haste was hot in question,
35 And many limits of the charge set down
But yesternight, when all athwart there came
A post from Wales loaden with heavy news;
Whose worst was that the noble Mortimer,
Leading the men of Herefordshire to fight
40 Against the irregular and wild Glendower,
Was by the rude hands of that Welshman taken,
And a thousand of his people butcherèd,
Upon whose dead corpse there was such misuse,
Such beastly shameless transformation,
45 By those Welshwomen done as may not be
Without much shame retold or spoken of.

KING HENRY IV It seems then that the tidings of this broil
Brake off our business for the Holy Land.

---

22 power army **levy** raise, muster **23 arms** upper limbs/weapons **mother's** natural
mother's/England's **24 fields** lands/battlefields **25 blessèd feet** i.e. Christ's **27 bitter**
painful/pitiable **29 bootless** pointless **31 gentle** kindly/noble **cousin** kinsman
32 yesternight last night **33 dear** important/urgent/noble/costly **expedience** expedition
34 liege lord, superior to whom feudal service was due **hot in question** hotly debated
35 limits . . . charge responsibilities relating to the undertaking **36 But** only, as recently as
athwart adversely, at odds with our business **37 post** messenger **loaden** weighed down
heavy sad/weighty **40 irregular . . . Glendower** uncivilized guerrilla fighter (Glendower was
leader of the Welsh rebels) **41 rude** rough **43 corpse** corpses **44 transformation**
mutilation **47 tidings** news **48 Brake** archaic past tense of "break"

WESTMORLAND   This matched with other like, my gracious lord.
50   Far more uneven and unwelcome news
Came from the north and thus it did report:
On Holy Rood day, the gallant Hotspur there,
Young Harry Percy, and brave Archibald,
That ever-valiant and approvèd Scot,
55   At Holmedon met, where they did spend
A sad and bloody hour,
As by discharge of their artillery,
And shape of likelihood, the news was told,
For he that brought them, in the very heat
60   And pride of their contention did take horse,
Uncertain of the issue any way.
KING HENRY IV   Here is a dear and true industrious friend,
Sir Walter Blunt, new lighted from his horse,
Stained with the variation of each soil
65   Betwixt that Holmedon and this seat of ours,
And he hath brought us smooth and welcome news.
The Earl of Douglas is discomfited,
Ten thousand bold Scots, two and twenty knights,
Balked in their own blood did Sir Walter see
70   On Holmedon's plains. Of prisoners, Hotspur took
Mordake, Earl of Fife, and eldest son
To beaten Douglas, and the Earl of Athol,
Of Murray, Angus, and Menteith.

---

49 matched with together with, accompanied by   50 uneven rough, unsettling   52 Holy
Rood day 14 September, dedicated to the cross (rood) of Christ   Hotspur Henry Percy's
nickname suggests that he is vigorous, hasty, and hotheaded   54 approvèd tried and tested
(in battle)   55 Holmedon the Northumberland site of the battle   56 sad serious/leading to
sorrow   58 shape of likelihood likely conjecture   59 heat . . . contention middle of the
fiercest fighting   61 issue outcome   any either   62 Here either "here at court" or a line
indicating Blunt's presence among the "other" lords in attendance onstage   63 new lighted
only just dismounted   64 variation of each different types of   65 Betwixt between   seat
residence/throne   66 smooth pleasant, welcome   67 discomfited defeated   69 Balked
heaped up (in "balks," i.e. ridges)   71 Mordake . . . Douglas Mordake was Earl of Fife but not
Douglas' son—Shakespeare misread Holinshed's Chronicles, his main source   73 Menteith not
in fact another earl, but one of Mordake's titles

And is not this an honourable spoil?
75   A gallant prize? Ha, cousin, is it not?
WESTMORLAND   In faith, it is a conquest for a prince to boast of.
KING HENRY IV   Yea, there thou mak'st me sad and mak'st me sin
In envy that my Lord Northumberland
Should be the father of so blest a son:
80   A son who is the theme of honour's tongue;
Amongst a grove, the very straightest plant,
Who is sweet Fortune's minion and her pride,
Whilst I, by looking on the praise of him,
See riot and dishonour stain the brow
85   Of my young Harry. O, that it could be proved
That some night-tripping fairy had exchanged
In cradle-clothes our children where they lay,
And called mine Percy, his Plantagenet:
Then would I have his Harry, and he mine.
90   But let him from my thoughts. What think you, coz,
Of this young Percy's pride? The prisoners,
Which he in this adventure hath surprised,
To his own use he keeps, and sends me word
I shall have none but Mordake Earl of Fife.
95 WESTMORLAND   This is his uncle's teaching. This is Worcester,
Malevolent to you in all aspects,
Which makes him prune himself, and bristle up
The crest of youth against your dignity.
KING HENRY IV   But I have sent for him to answer this.
100   And for this cause awhile we must neglect
Our holy purpose to Jerusalem.

---

74 honourable spoil noble gains of war   **75 gallant** fine, splendid   **80 theme** subject, chief topic   **81 straightest plant** most upright tree   **82 minion** favorite   **84 riot** debauchery, corruption   **86 night-tripping** moving nimbly through the night   **fairy** popular belief held that fairies sometimes stole human infants, substituting (troublesome) fairy children for them   **88 Plantagenet** the surname of this royal dynasty   **90 from** go from   **coz** short for "cousin" (i.e. kinsman)   **92 adventure** enterprise, venture   **surprised** captured, ambushed   **97 prune** preen (like a bird)   **bristle** raise, ruffle angrily   **98 dignity** worthiness/kingship   **100 cause** reason

Cousin, on Wednesday next our council we
Will hold at Windsor, and so inform the lords.
But come yourself with speed to us again,
105   For more is to be said and to be done
Than out of anger can be utterèd.

WESTMORLAND   I will, my liege.   *Exeunt*

Act 1 Scene 2   *running scene 2*

Enter Henry, Prince of Wales [and] Sir John Falstaff

FALSTAFF   Now, Hal, what time of day is it, lad?

PRINCE HENRY   Thou art so fat-witted with drinking of old sack
and unbuttoning thee after supper and sleeping upon
benches in the afternoon, that thou hast forgotten to
5   demand that truly which thou wouldst truly know. What a
devil hast thou to do with the time of the day? Unless hours
were cups of sack and minutes capons and clocks the
tongues of bawds and dials the signs of leaping-houses and
the blessed sun himself a fair hot wench in flame-coloured
10   taffeta, I see no reason why thou shouldst be so superfluous
to demand the time of the day.

FALSTAFF   Indeed, you come near me now, Hal, for we that
take purses go by the moon and seven stars, and not by
Phoebus, he, 'that wand'ring knight so fair'. And, I prithee,
15   sweet wag, when thou art king, as God save thy grace —
majesty I should say, for grace thou wilt have none—

---

106 out . . . utterèd can be spoken openly in anger   **1.2 *Location: in London, but***
unspecified; perhaps the prince's apartments   2 fat-witted dull-witted (plays on Falstaff's
physical size)   sack Spanish white wine   4 forgotten neglected/forgotten how   5 demand
that truly ask accurately, rightly   truly genuinely/accurately   7 capons castrated cockerels, a
common dish   8 bawds pimps, procurers of sex   dials sundials/clock faces   leaping-
houses brothels   9 hot lustful   10 taffeta silky material associated with prostitutes
superfluous unnecessarily curious, irrelevant   12 come near me touch the point, begin to
understand me   13 go by travel by the light of/tell the time according to   seven stars
the Pleiades (a group of stars in the constellation Taurus)   14 Phoebus the sun god
'wand'ring . . . fair' probably a phrase from a ballad or popular romance, referring to the sun as
a knight in a tale of romance   15 wag mischievous boy   grace term of address for royalty
(but sense then shifts to "spiritual grace" and then to "prayer before a meal")

PRINCE HENRY   What, none?

FALSTAFF   No, not so much as will serve to be prologue to an egg and butter.

20 PRINCE HENRY   Well, how then? Come, roundly, roundly.

FALSTAFF   Marry, then, sweet wag, when thou art king, let not us that are squires of the night's body be called thieves of the day's beauty. Let us be Diana's foresters, gentlemen of the shade, minions of the moon; and let men say we be men of
25 good government, being governed, as the sea is, by our noble and chaste mistress the moon, under whose countenance we steal.

PRINCE HENRY   Thou say'st well, and it holds well too, for the fortune of us that are the moon's men doth ebb and flow like
30 the sea, being governed, as the sea is, by the moon. As, for proof, now: a purse of gold most resolutely snatched on Monday night and most dissolutely spent on Tuesday morning; got with swearing 'Lay by' and spent with crying 'Bring in', now in as low an ebb as the foot of the ladder and
35 by and by in as high a flow as the ridge of the gallows.

FALSTAFF   Thou say'st true, lad. And is not my hostess of the tavern a most sweet wench?

PRINCE HENRY   As is the honey of Hybla, my old lad of the castle. And is not a buff jerkin a most sweet robe of durance?

19 egg and butter i.e. a very light meal (barely requiring grace to be said as a blessing)
20 roundly plainly, straightforwardly (may play on Falstaff's shape)   21 Marry by the Virgin Mary   22 squires . . . body the night's personal attendants (night's puns on "knight's") thieves . . . beauty i.e. by sleepily wasting the day (beauty puns on "booty")   23 Diana Roman goddess of the moon, patron of hunting and virginity   foresters forest dwellers, servants 24 minions favorites   of good government of good conduct/who live under a good ruler 26 countenance face, appearance/support, authority   27 steal rob/move furtively   28 holds applies, is apt   33 'Lay by' highwayman's command that his victims lay aside their weapons 34 'Bring in' an order for drinks   now . . . gallows one moment one's fortune is as low as the bottom of the ladder leading to the gallows, the next as high as the crossbar at the top of the gallows—i.e. whatever a thief's course, the result (hanging) is the same   36 hostess landlady 38 Hybla Sicilian town famous for its honey   old . . . castle carouser (plays on "Oldcastle," Shakespeare's original name for Falstaff; castle may play on the sense of "stocks," instruments of public punishment in which a thief might be confined; a London brothel called the Castle may also be alluded to, appropriately named given that castle was slang for "vagina") 39 buff jerkin tight leather jacket worn by sheriff's officers (plays on the sense of "naked vagina")   robe of durance long-lasting garment (with sexual connotations; durance plays on the sense of "imprisonment")

40 FALSTAFF   How now, how now, mad wag? What, in thy quips
        and thy quiddities? What a plague have I to do with a buff
        jerkin?

    PRINCE HENRY   Why, what a pox have I to do with my hostess of
        the tavern?

45 FALSTAFF   Well, thou hast called her to a reck'ning many a
        time and oft.

    PRINCE HENRY   Did I ever call for thee to pay thy part?

    FALSTAFF   No, I'll give thee thy due, thou hast paid all there.

    PRINCE HENRY   Yea, and elsewhere, so far as my coin would
50   stretch, and where it would not, I have used my credit.

    FALSTAFF   Yea, and so used it that were it here apparent that
        thou art heir apparent — but, I prithee, sweet wag, shall
        there be gallows standing in England when thou art king?
        And resolution thus fobbed as it is with the rusty curb of old
55   father antic the law? Do not thou, when thou art a king,
        hang a thief.

    PRINCE HENRY   No, thou shalt.

    FALSTAFF   Shall I? O rare! I'll be a brave judge.

    PRINCE HENRY   Thou judgest false already: I mean, thou shalt
60   have the hanging of the thieves and so become a rare
        hangman.

    FALSTAFF   Well, Hal, well, and in some sort it jumps with my
        humour as well as waiting in the court, I can tell you.

    PRINCE HENRY   For obtaining of suits?

65 FALSTAFF   Yea, for obtaining of suits, whereof the hangman

---

41 quiddities quibbles   **What a plague** emphatic form of "what"   **43 pox** venereal disease
45 called . . . reck'ning asked her for the bill/asked her to explain herself/had sex with her
47 pay thy part pay for your share/have sex   **49 coin would stretch** money would go/penis
would grow; **coin** puns on "quoin"—i.e. carpenter's wedge (a euphemism for "penis")
52 heir puns on **here** (which was pronounced in a similar manner)   **54 resolution**
determination   **fobbed** cheated   **curb** restraint (literally, chain passed under a horse's jaw)
old father antic the elderly buffoon (that is)   **58 rare** splendid   **brave** fine, excellent
62 jumps . . . humour fits my disposition   **63 waiting** waiting around/being in attendance
64 suits requests, legal petitions (Falstaff plays on the sense of "suits of clothes"; the hangman
had the right to keep his victims' garments)

hath no lean wardrobe. I am as melancholy as a gib cat or a lugged bear.

PRINCE HENRY   Or an old lion, or a lover's lute.

FALSTAFF   Yea, or the drone of a Lincolnshire bagpipe.

70   PRINCE HENRY   What say'st thou to a hare, or the melancholy of Moorditch?

FALSTAFF   Thou hast the most unsavoury similes and art indeed the most comparative, rascalli'st, sweet young prince. But, Hal, I prithee trouble me no more with vanity. I would

75   thou and I knew where a commodity of good names were to be bought. An old lord of the council rated me the other day in the street about you, sir, but I marked him not. And yet he talked very wisely, but I regarded him not; and yet he talked wisely, and in the street too.

80   PRINCE HENRY   Thou didst well, for no man regards it.

FALSTAFF   O, thou hast damnable iteration and art indeed able to corrupt a saint. Thou hast done much harm unto me, Hal, God forgive thee for it! Before I knew thee, Hal, I knew nothing. And now I am, if a man should speak truly, little

85   better than one of the wicked. I must give over this life, and I will give it over. An I do not, I am a villain. I'll be damned for never a king's son in Christendom.

PRINCE HENRY   Where shall we take a purse tomorrow, Jack?

FALSTAFF   Where thou wilt, lad, I'll make one. An I do not, call

90   me villain and baffle me.

---

66 no lean wardrobe i.e. no small amount (because hangings were common; **wardrobe** may pun on "wardrope," a type of thick rope)   **gib cat** tom cat   67 **lugged bear** baited bear, pulled by the ears and tugged on a chain   68 **lute** the stringed instrument was associated with lovers   69 **bagpipe** musical instrument/tedious, moaning speaker   70 **hare** a proverbially melancholy animal   71 **Moorditch** notoriously filthy drainage ditch outside the northern walls of the City of London   73 **comparative** prone to making comparisons   **rascalli'st** most rascal-like   74 **vanity** foolishness, trifles   75 **commodity** supply   **names** reputations   76 **rated** scolded   77 **marked him not** took no notice of him   80 **no . . . it** biblical allusion, "Wisdom crieth without . . . and no man regarded" (Proverbs 1:20–4), truncated in Folio because of the 1606 Parliamentary "Act to restrain the Abuses of Players"   81 **damnable iteration** a way of constantly quoting Scripture that will lead to damnation   82 **saint** puritan term for a person chosen by God to be saved   86 **An** if   87 **never a** no   88 **Jack** affectionate form of "John"   89 **make one** make up one of the party   90 **baffle** publicly disgrace (a knight)

PRINCE HENRY   I see a good amendment of life in thee, from praying to purse-taking.

FALSTAFF   Why, Hal, 'tis my vocation, Hal: 'tis no sin for a man to labour in his vocation. Poins! Now shall we know if Gadshill have set a watch. O, if men were to be saved by merit, what hole in hell were hot enough for him? This is the most omnipotent villain that ever cried 'Stand' to a true man.

[*Enter Poins*]

PRINCE HENRY   Good morrow, Ned.

POINS   Good morrow, sweet Hal. What says Monsieur Remorse? What says Sir John Sack and Sugar, Jack? How agrees the devil and thee about thy soul, that thou soldest him on Good Friday last for a cup of Madeira and a cold capon's leg?

PRINCE HENRY   Sir John stands to his word, the devil shall have his bargain, for he was never yet a breaker of proverbs: he will give the devil his due.

POINS   Then art thou damned for keeping thy word with the devil.

PRINCE HENRY   Else he had been damned for cozening the devil.

POINS   But, my lads, my lads, tomorrow morning, by four o'clock, early at Gad's Hill, there are pilgrims going to Canterbury with rich offerings, and traders riding to London with fat purses. I have vizards for you all; you have horses for yourselves. Gadshill lies tonight in Rochester. I have bespoke

---

91 amendment reformation   **93 vocation** calling (from God)   **95 Gadshill** named after Gad's Hill in Kent, a notorious place for highway robberies   **set a watch** surveyed the targeted area, conducted a recce (as part of planning a robbery; some editors emend to "set a match"—slang for "plan a robbery")   **saved by merit** had their souls saved through good works and personal desert (as opposed to divine grace)   **97 omnipotent** unparalleled, almighty   **'Stand'** stand and deliver—highwayman's command   **true** honest   **100 Monsieur Remorse** teasing reference to Falstaff   **101 Sir . . . Jack** i.e. Falstaff; another mocking reference, apparently alluding to Falstaff's taste for sweetened wine   **103 Good Friday** the Friday before Easter Sunday, a strict fast day   **Madeira** a strong white wine   **107 give . . . due** proverbial   **110 Else he had** Otherwise he had been   **cozening** cheating   **112 Gad's Hill** the notorious spot for robberies was situated on the Dover road near **Rochester** in Kent; pilgrims traveling to **Canterbury** were often targets   **114 vizards** masks   **115 lies** lodges   **bespoke** ordered

supper tomorrow in Eastcheap; we may do it as secure as
sleep. If you will go, I will stuff your purses full of crowns: if
you will not, tarry at home and be hanged.

FALSTAFF   Hear ye, Yedward, if I tarry at home and go not, I'll
120   hang you for going.

POINS   You will, chops?

FALSTAFF   Hal, wilt thou make one?

PRINCE HENRY   Who, I rob? I a thief? Not I.

FALSTAFF   There's neither honesty, manhood, nor good
125   fellowship in thee, nor thou cam'st not of the blood royal, if
thou dar'st not stand for ten shillings.

PRINCE HENRY   Well then, once in my days I'll be a madcap.

FALSTAFF   Why, that's well said.

PRINCE HENRY   Well, come what will, I'll tarry at home.

130   FALSTAFF   I'll be a traitor then, when thou art king.

PRINCE HENRY   I care not.

POINS   Sir John, I prithee leave the prince and me alone: I
will lay him down such reasons for this adventure that he
shall go.

135   FALSTAFF   Well, mayst thou have the spirit of persuasion and
he the ears of profiting, that what thou speakest may move
and what he hears may be believed, that the true prince may,
for recreation sake, prove a false thief; for the poor abuses of
the time want countenance. Farewell. You shall find me in
140   Eastcheap.

PRINCE HENRY   Farewell, the latter spring! Farewell, All-hallown
summer!

[Exit Falstaff]

---

116 **Eastcheap** London street running from the junction of Cannon and Gracechurch streets
to Great Tower Street   **secure** safely   117 **crowns** gold coins   118 **tarry** stay   119 **Yedward**
dialect form of "Edward"   120 **hang you** i.e. report it and get you hanged   121 **chops** fat
cheeks   125 **blood royal** regal descent (Falstaff goes on to play on the sense of "gold coin
worth **ten shillings**")   126 **stand for** stand and fight for/be worth   135 **Well . . . believed**
Falstaff parodies the language of a Protestant sermon on the power of God's word to move the
congregation   138 **abuses** wrongdoings, sins   139 **want countenance** lack recognition and
support   141 **latter . . . summer** late spring and summer lasting until All Hallows' Eve
(31 October); the suggestion is that Falstaff's youthful behavior is not in keeping with his age

POINS   Now, my good sweet honey lord, ride with us tomorrow. I have a jest to execute that I cannot manage
145   alone. Falstaff, Peto, Bardolph and Gadshill shall rob those men that we have already waylaid: yourself and I will not be there. And when they have the booty, if you and I do not rob them, cut this head from my shoulders.

PRINCE HENRY   But how shall we part with them in setting forth?
150   POINS   Why, we will set forth before or after them, and appoint them a place of meeting, wherein it is at our pleasure to fail; and then will they adventure upon the exploit themselves, which they shall have no sooner achieved, but we'll set upon them.

155   PRINCE HENRY   Ay, but 'tis like that they will know us by our horses, by our habits and by every other appointment, to be ourselves.

POINS   Tut! Our horses they shall not see: I'll tie them in the wood. Our vizards we will change after we leave them. And,
160   sirrah, I have cases of buckram for the nonce, to immask our noted outward garments.

PRINCE HENRY   But I doubt they will be too hard for us.

POINS   Well, for two of them, I know them to be as true-bred cowards as ever turned back. And for the third, if he
165   fight longer than he sees reason, I'll forswear arms. The virtue of this jest will be the incomprehensible lies that this fat rogue will tell us when we meet at supper: how thirty at least he fought with, what wards, what blows, what extremities he endured; and in the reproof of this lies the
170   jest.

---

146 **waylaid** set an ambush for   152 **pleasure** preference, decision   **fail** i.e. to turn up
155 **like** likely   156 **habits** clothes   **appointment** piece of gear   160 **sirrah** sir (familiar form often used to inferiors, jocular here)   **cases of buckram** suits of coarse cloth   **nonce** purpose, occasion   **immask** disguise   161 **noted** well-known   162 **doubt** fear   **hard** tough, powerful   164 **turned back** turned their backs to flee   165 **forswear** swear to give up
166 **incomprehensible** boundless, unlimited   168 **wards** defensive maneuvers (fencing term)
169 **reproof** disproving, refutation/shame, reprimand

PRINCE HENRY   Well, I'll go with thee. Provide us all things
necessary and meet me tomorrow night in Eastcheap. There
I'll sup. Farewell.

POINS   Farewell, my lord.   *Exit Poins*

175 PRINCE HENRY   I know you all, and will awhile uphold
The unyoked humour of your idleness.
Yet herein will I imitate the sun,
Who doth permit the base contagious clouds
To smother up his beauty from the world,
180 That when he please again to be himself,
Being wanted, he may be more wondered at,
By breaking through the foul and ugly mists
Of vapours that did seem to strangle him.
If all the year were playing holidays,
185 To sport would be as tedious as to work;
But when they seldom come, they wished-for come,
And nothing pleaseth but rare accidents.
So, when this loose behaviour I throw off
And pay the debt I never promisèd,
190 By how much better than my word I am,
By so much shall I falsify men's hopes,
And like bright metal on a sullen ground,
My reformation, glittering o'er my fault,
Shall show more goodly and attract more eyes
195 Than that which hath no foil to set it off.
I'll so offend to make offence a skill,
Redeeming time when men think least I will.   [*Exit*]

---

173 sup have supper (the last meal of the day)   **175 uphold** carry on with/support
176 unyoked humour unrestrained behavior, wild whim   **177 sun** common symbol of royalty
178 contagious noxious, infectious; **clouds** were thought to harbor disease   **181 wanted**
missed, lacked   **185 sport** play, entertain oneself   **187 rare accidents** unusual events
191 falsify men's hopes prove expectations of me false   **192 sullen ground** dark background
195 foil contrast, background (technically, setting for a jewel)   **196 so offend** misbehave in
such a way   **skill** art/cunning tactic   **197 Redeeming time** making up for lost time
(**Redeeming** has religious connotations)

Act 1 Scene 3

Enter the King, Northumberland, Worcester, Hotspur, Sir Walter Blunt and others

KING HENRY IV   My blood hath been too cold and temperate,
    Unapt to stir at these indignities,
    And you have found me; for accordingly
    You tread upon my patience. But be sure
5   I will from henceforth rather be myself,
    Mighty and to be feared, than my condition,
    Which hath been smooth as oil, soft as young down,
    And therefore lost that title of respect
    Which the proud soul ne'er pays but to the proud.
10 WORCESTER   Our house, my sovereign liege, little deserves
    The scourge of greatness to be used on it.
    And that same greatness too which our own hands
    Have holp to make so portly.
NORTHUMBERLAND   My lord—   *To the King*
15 KING HENRY IV   Worcester, get thee gone, for I do see
    Danger and disobedience in thine eye.
    O, sir, your presence is too bold and peremptory,
    And majesty might never yet endure
    The moody frontier of a servant brow.
20   You have good leave to leave us. When we need
    Your use and counsel, we shall send for you.—
                                  [*Exit Worcester*]
    You were about to speak.   *To Northumberland*
NORTHUMBERLAND   Yea, my good lord.
    Those prisoners in your highness' name demanded,
25   Which Harry Percy here at Holmedon took,

1.3 *Location: the royal court*   **1 temperate** calm, restrained   **2 Unapt** not inclined or ready to   **3 found me** found me to be so   **4 tread upon** try, take advantage of   **5 myself** my royal self   **6 condition** natural disposition   **8 title of** claim to   **9 proud** fine, splendid, possessed of self-respect   **10 house** family   **11 scourge** punishing whip   **13 holp** helped **portly** prosperous, majestic/overweight, too comfortable   **17 peremptory** determined/imperious   **19 moody frontier** threatening look   **frontier** literally, military fortification   **20 good leave** full permission   **21 use** services

Were, as he says, not with such strength denied
As was delivered to your majesty,
Who either through envy or misprision
Was guilty of this fault and not my son.

30 HOTSPUR   My liege, I did deny no prisoners.   *To the King*
But I remember, when the fight was done,
When I was dry with rage and extreme toil,
Breathless and faint, leaning upon my sword,
Came there a certain lord, neat and trimly dressed,

35 Fresh as a bridegroom, and his chin new reaped
Showed like a stubble-land at harvest-home.
He was perfumèd like a milliner,
And 'twixt his finger and his thumb he held
A pouncet-box, which ever and anon

40 He gave his nose and took't away again,
Who therewith angry, when it next came there,
Took it in snuff. And still he smiled and talked,
And as the soldiers bore dead bodies by,
He called them untaught knaves, unmannerly,

45 To bring a slovenly unhandsome corpse
Betwixt the wind and his nobility.
With many holiday and lady terms
He questioned me, among the rest demanded
My prisoners in your majesty's behalf.

50 I then, all smarting with my wounds being cold,
To be so pestered with a popinjay,

---

26 **with . . . denied** refused so emphatically   27 **delivered** reported   28 **envy or misprision** malice or misunderstanding   32 **dry with rage** thirsty after the fury of battle   34 **neat** elegant   **trimly** finely, immaculately   35 **new reaped** freshly shaven   36 **stubble-land at harvest-home** shorn stalks of crops at the end of the harvest   37 **milliner** seller of fancy goods (originally those from Milan)   39 **pouncet-box** small box with a perforated lid, used for holding perfume or snuff   **ever and anon** time and again   40 **gave** held up to   41 **Who therewith angry** at which (removal of the box) his nose became angry   42 **Took . . . snuff** inhaled/took offense   **still** continually   44 **untaught** ignorant, ill-mannered   45 **slovenly** dirty, untidy   **unhandsome** unattractive, unbecoming   46 **nobility** elegant, aristocratic personage   47 **holiday . . . terms** refined, genteel expressions   48 **questioned** conversed with/asked questions of   50 **cold** untended/congealing   51 **popinjay** parrot (i.e. gaudy prattler)

Out of my grief and my impatience,
Answered neglectingly I know not what,
He should or should not. For he made me mad
To see him shine so brisk and smell so sweet
And talk so like a waiting-gentlewoman
Of guns and drums and wounds — God save the mark! —
And telling me the sovereign'st thing on earth
Was parmaceti for an inward bruise,
And that it was great pity, so it was,
That villainous saltpetre should be digged
Out of the bowels of the harmless earth,
Which many a good tall fellow had destroyed
So cowardly, and but for these vile guns,
He would himself have been a soldier.
This bald unjointed chat of his, my lord,
Made me to answer indirectly, as I said,
And I beseech you let not this report
Come current for an accusation
Betwixt my love and your high majesty.

BLUNT   The circumstance considered, good   *To the King*
my lord,
Whatever Harry Percy then had said
To such a person and in such a place,
At such a time, with all the rest retold,
May reasonably die and never rise
To do him wrong or any way impeach
What then he said, so he unsay it now.

KING HENRY IV   Why, yet he doth deny his prisoners,
But with proviso and exception,

---

52 **grief** pain   53 **neglectingly** unthinkingly, carelessly   55 **brisk** sprucely, smartly
56 **waiting-gentlewoman** woman of good family attending on a great lady   57 **God . . . mark!**
conventional expression of apology   58 **sovereign'st** best, most healing   59 **parmaceti**
corruption of "spermaceti"—fat from the head of a sperm whale, used for treating bruises
61 **saltpetre** potassium nitrate, the chief ingredient of gunpowder, also used medicinally
63 **tall** fine, valiant   66 **bald unjointed chat** empty, incoherent chatter   67 **indirectly**
inattentively   68 **beseech** beg   69 **Come current** be accepted at face value   74 **retold**
related, explained   75 **die** i.e. be forgotten   76 **impeach** discredit, accuse   77 **so** provided
that   78 **yet he** still Hotspur (the king does not reply to him directly)   **deny** refuse (to hand
over)   79 **proviso and exception** terms and conditions

80   That we at our own charge shall ransom straight
      His brother-in-law, the foolish Mortimer,
      Who, in my soul, hath wilfully betrayed
      The lives of those that he did lead to fight
      Against the great magician, damned Glendower,
85   Whose daughter, as we hear, the Earl of March
      Hath lately married. Shall our coffers, then,
      Be emptied to redeem a traitor home?
      Shall we buy treason, and indent with fears
      When they have lost and forfeited themselves?
90   No, on the barren mountain let him starve,
      For I shall never hold that man my friend
      Whose tongue shall ask me for one penny cost
      To ransom home revolted Mortimer.

HOTSPUR   Revolted Mortimer?
95   He never did fall off, my sovereign liege,
      But by the chance of war. To prove that true
      Needs no more but one tongue for all those wounds,
      Those mouthèd wounds, which valiantly he took
      When on the gentle Severn's sedgy bank,
100   In single opposition, hand to hand,
      He did confound the best part of an hour
      In changing hardiment with great Glendower.
      Three times they breathed and three times did they drink,
      Upon agreement, of swift Severn's flood;
105   Who then, affrighted with their bloody looks,
      Ran fearfully among the trembling reeds,
      And hid his crisp head in the hollow bank,

---

80 **charge** expense   **straight** straightaway   85 **Earl of March** i.e. **Mortimer**; in fact,
Shakespeare confuses two Edmund Mortimers: one was indeed the Earl of March, but it was
his uncle of the same name who married Glendower's daughter   86 **coffers** money chests,
treasury   88 **indent** make a contract   **fears** those traitors who give us cause for fear/cowards
93 **revolted** rebellious   95 **fall off** abandon loyalty   98 **mouthèd** open, gaping/famous,
spoken of   99 **Severn's sedgy bank** reed-covered bank of the River Severn, which divided
England and south Wales   101 **confound** spend, consume   102 **changing hardiment**
exchanging valiant blows   103 **breathed** broke off to catch their breath   104 **Upon**
agreement by mutual consent   **flood** water, torrent   105 **affrighted** frightened   107 **crisp**
wavy, rippled (personifies the river as curly-haired)   **hollow** empty, sunken

Bloodstainèd with these valiant combatants.
Never did base and rotten policy
110 Colour her working with such deadly wounds;
Nor never could the noble Mortimer
Receive so many, and all willingly.
Then let him not be slandered with revolt.

KING HENRY IV   Thou dost belie him, Percy, thou dost belie him;
115 He never did encounter with Glendower.
I tell thee, he durst as well have met the devil alone
As Owen Glendower for an enemy.
Art thou not ashamed? But, sirrah, henceforth
Let me not hear you speak of Mortimer.
120 Send me your prisoners with the speediest means,
Or you shall hear in such a kind from me
As will displease ye.— My lord Northumberland,
We license your departure with your son.—
Send us your prisoners, or you'll hear of it.   *To Hotspur*

Exeunt King [Henry, Blunt and train]

125 HOTSPUR   An if the devil come and roar for them
I will not send them. I will after straight
And tell him so, for I will ease my heart,
Although it be with hazard of my head.

NORTHUMBERLAND   What? Drunk with choler? Stay and pause
awhile.
130 Here comes your uncle.

Enter Worcester

HOTSPUR   Speak of Mortimer?
Yes, I will speak of him, and let my soul
Want mercy, if I do not join with him.
In his behalf I'll empty all these veins,
135 And shed my dear blood drop by drop i'th'dust,

---

109 base . . . policy lowly and corrupt plotting   110 Colour disguise/dye   113 slandered
"sland'red" in Folio   revolt i.e. the accusation of being a rebel   114 belie misrepresent,
lie about   115 encounter fight   116 durst (would have) dared   121 kind manner
123 license formally authorize   125 An if if   126 after follow   128 with hazard of at the risk
(of losing)   129 choler anger   133 Want mercy lack God's mercy, i.e. be damned

But I will lift the downfall Mortimer
As high i'th'air as this unthankful king,
As this ingrate and cankered Bullingbrook.

NORTHUMBERLAND   Brother, the king hath made your nephew
    mad.

140   WORCESTER   Who struck this heat up after I was gone?

HOTSPUR   He will, forsooth, have all my prisoners.
    And when I urged the ransom once again
    Of my wife's brother, then his cheek looked pale,
    And on my face he turned an eye of death,
145   Trembling even at the name of Mortimer.

WORCESTER   I cannot blame him: was he not proclaimed
    By Richard, that dead is, the next of blood?

NORTHUMBERLAND   He was. I heard the proclamation.
    And then it was when the unhappy king —
150   Whose wrongs in us God pardon! — did set forth
    Upon his Irish expedition,
    From whence he intercepted did return
    To be deposed and shortly murderèd.

WORCESTER   And for whose death we in the world's wide mouth
155   Live scandalized and foully spoken of.

HOTSPUR   But soft, I pray you; did King Richard then
    Proclaim my brother Mortimer
    Heir to the crown?

NORTHUMBERLAND   He did. Myself did hear it.

160   HOTSPUR   Nay, then I cannot blame his cousin king,
    That wished him on the barren mountains starved.
    But shall it be that you that set the crown

---

136 downfall downfallen   **138 ingrate** ungrateful   **cankered** diseased, corrupted
Bullingbrook Henry's surname before he was king (taken from the castle in which he was
born—Hotspur refuses to acknowledge Henry's royal status)   **140 heat** anger   **141 forsooth**
in truth   **142 urged** pressed, brought forward   **144 eye of death** fearful look, perhaps also
threatening   **146 he** i.e. Mortimer   **147 Richard** Richard II, deposed by Henry   **next of
blood** nearest blood relation, i.e. heir to the throne; confusion between the two Mortimers
continues—it was in fact the younger man who was proclaimed heir, rather than his uncle
(husband of Glendower's daughter and the man who is meant here)   **149 unhappy**
unfortunate   **150 in us** i.e. at our hands—the Percy family had supported Henry against
Richard   **152 intercepted** interrupted (in the middle of his Irish campaign)   **156 soft** wait a
moment   **157 brother** brother-in-law   **160 cousin** may pun on "cozen" (i.e. "cheat")

Upon the head of this forgetful man
And for his sake wore the detested blot
165   Of murderous subornation, shall it be,
That you a world of curses undergo,
Being the agents, or base second means,
The cords, the ladder, or the hangman rather?
O, pardon if that I descend so low,
170   To show the line and the predicament
Wherein you range under this subtle king.
Shall it for shame be spoken in these days,
Or fill up chronicles in time to come,
That men of your nobility and power
175   Did gage them both in an unjust behalf,
As both of you — God pardon it! — have done,
To put down Richard, that sweet lovely rose,
And plant this thorn, this canker, Bullingbrook?
And shall it in more shame be further spoken,
180   That you are fooled, discarded and shook off
By him for whom these shames ye underwent?
No. Yet time serves wherein you may redeem
Your banished honours and restore yourselves
Into the good thoughts of the world again,
185   Revenge the jeering and disdained contempt
Of this proud king, who studies day and night
To answer all the debt he owes unto you
Even with the bloody payment of your deaths:
Therefore, I say—
190 WORCESTER   Peace, cousin, say no more.
And now I will unclasp a secret book,
And to your quick-conceiving discontents
I'll read you matter deep and dangerous,

---

164 blot (moral) stain   **165 subornation** incitement (to Richard's murder)   **167 second means** agents, instruments   **170 line** status (plays on the sense of "rope")   **predicament** category/dangerous situation   **171 range** move/are ranked   **subtle** crafty   **175 gage** pledge   **178 canker** wild rose/worm that destroys plants/ulcer   **180 fooled** made fools of/duped, frustrated   **186 studies** reflects, plans, endeavors   **187 answer** repay   **191 unclasp** i.e. open   **192 quick-conceiving** ready, quick to understand   **193 deep** deep-rooted/grave/cunning

As full of peril and adventurous spirit
195 As to o'er-walk a current roaring loud
On the unsteadfast footing of a spear.
HOTSPUR   If he fall in, goodnight, or sink or swim.
Send danger from the east unto the west,
So honour cross it from the north to south,
200 And let them grapple. The blood more stirs
To rouse a lion than to start a hare!
NORTHUMBERLAND   Imagination of some great exploit   *To Worcester*
Drives him beyond the bounds of patience.
HOTSPUR   By heaven, methinks it were an easy leap,
205 To pluck bright honour from the pale-faced moon,
Or dive into the bottom of the deep,
Where fathom-line could never touch the ground,
And pluck up drownèd honour by the locks,
So he that doth redeem her thence might wear
210 Without corrival, all her dignities:
But out upon this half-faced fellowship!
WORCESTER   He apprehends a world of figures   *To Northumberland*
here,
But not the form of what he should attend.—
Good cousin, give me audience for a while and list to me.
215 HOTSPUR   I cry you mercy.
WORCESTER   Those same noble Scots
That are your prisoners —
HOTSPUR   I'll keep them all.
By heaven, he shall not have a Scot of them.
220 No, if a Scot would save his soul, he shall not.
I'll keep them, by this hand.
WORCESTER   You start away

---

195 o'er-walk cross   196 unsteadfast unsteady   spear i.e. used as a bridge   197 goodnight i.e. he's dead   or . . . swim whether he sinks or swims/he'll either sink or swim   199 So provided   cross meet/thwart, oppose   207 fathom-line weighted line used for measuring the depth of water   209 redeem rescue, restore   thence from there   210 corrival rival, competitor   211 out upon away with   half-faced fellowship partial, unsatisfactory partnership   212 apprehends conceives of, perceives   figures images/forms/figures of speech   213 form essential principle   attend consider   214 list listen   215 cry you mercy beg your pardon   219 Scot puns on the sense of "small payment"

And lend no ear unto my purposes.
Those prisoners you shall keep.

225 HOTSPUR   Nay, I will; that's flat.
He said he would not ransom Mortimer,
Forbade my tongue to speak of Mortimer,
But I will find him when he lies asleep,
And in his ear I'll holla 'Mortimer!'
230 Nay, I'll have a starling shall be taught to speak
Nothing but 'Mortimer', and give it him
To keep his anger still in motion.

WORCESTER   Hear you, cousin, a word.

HOTSPUR   All studies here I solemnly defy,
235 Save how to gall and pinch this Bullingbrook.
And that same sword-and-buckler Prince of Wales,
But that I think his father loves him not
And would be glad he met with some mischance,
I would have poisoned him with a pot of ale.

240 WORCESTER   Farewell, kinsman. I'll talk to you
When you are better tempered to attend.

NORTHUMBERLAND   Why, what a wasp-tongued   *To Hotspur*
and impatient fool
Art thou to break into this woman's mood,
Tying thine ear to no tongue but thine own!

245 HOTSPUR   Why, look you, I am whipped and scourged with
rods,
Nettled and stung with pismires, when I hear
Of this vile politician, Bullingbrook.
In Richard's time — what d'ye call the place? —
A plague upon't, it is in Gloucestershire,
250 'Twas where the madcap duke his uncle kept,
His uncle York, where I first bowed my knee

---

229 **holla** shout   232 **still** constantly   234 **defy** renounce   235 **gall and pinch** irritate and
torment   236 **sword-and-buckler** weapons associated with servants; a gentleman carried
rapier and dagger   **buckler** small shield   237 **But that** were it not for the fact that
238 **mischance** accident   241 **better . . . attend** in the right frame of mind to listen
244 **Tying . . . own** listening to no one but yourself   246 **pismires** ants   247 **politician** crafty
plotter   250 **duke his uncle** i.e. Edmund of Langley, Duke of York   **kept** lived

Unto this king of smiles, this Bullingbrook,
When you and he came back from Ravenspurgh.

NORTHUMBERLAND   At Berkeley Castle.

255 HOTSPUR   You say true.
Why, what a candy deal of courtesy
This fawning greyhound then did proffer me.
'Look when his infant fortune came to age',
And 'gentle Harry Percy' and 'kind cousin'.—

260 O, the devil take such cozeners! — God   *To Worcester*
    forgive me,
Good uncle, tell your tale, for I have done.

WORCESTER   Nay, if you have not, to't again,
We'll stay your leisure.

HOTSPUR   I have done, in sooth.

265 WORCESTER   Then once more to your Scottish prisoners.
Deliver them up without their ransom straight,
And make the Douglas' son your only mean
For powers in Scotland, which, for divers reasons
Which I shall send you written, be assured

270 Will easily be granted.— You, my lord,   *To Northumberland*
Your son in Scotland being thus employed,
Shall secretly into the bosom creep
Of that same noble prelate well beloved,
The archbishop.

275 HOTSPUR   Of York, is't not?

WORCESTER   True, who bears hard
His brother's death at Bristol, the Lord Scroop.
I speak not this in estimation,
As what I think might be, but what I know

280 Is ruminated, plotted and set down,

---

253 **Ravenspurgh** Spurn Head on the Yorkshire coast   254 **Berkeley Castle** a castle in
Gloucestershire, near Bristol   256 **candy deal** sickly sweet (flattering) quantity   258 **Look
when** wait for the time when, as soon as   **infant . . . age** i.e. I come into my inheritance
260 **cozeners** deceivers (puns on "cousin")   263 **stay** await   264 **sooth** truth   267 **the
Douglas' son** i.e. Mordake   **mean For powers** agent or means of raising an army
268 **divers** various   272 **bosom** i.e. confidence, trust   273 **prelate** church dignitary
276 **bears hard** takes badly   277 **Lord Scroop** William Scroop, Earl of Wiltshire, executed by
Bullingbrook in 1399; in fact the archbishop's cousin   278 **estimation** guessing

And only stays but to behold the face
Of that occasion that shall bring it on.

HOTSPUR   I smell it:
Upon my life, it will do wondrous well.

285   NORTHUMBERLAND   Before the game's afoot, thou still let'st slip.

HOTSPUR   Why, it cannot choose but be a noble plot.
And then the power of Scotland and of York,
To join with Mortimer, ha?

WORCESTER   And so they shall.

290   HOTSPUR   In faith, it is exceedingly well aimed.

WORCESTER   And 'tis no little reason bids us speed,
To save our heads by raising of a head.
For, bear ourselves as even as we can,
The king will always think him in our debt,
295   And think we think ourselves unsatisfied,
Till he hath found a time to pay us home.
And see already how he doth begin
To make us strangers to his looks of love.

HOTSPUR   He does, he does. We'll be revenged on him.

300   WORCESTER   Cousin, farewell. No further go in this
Than I by letters shall direct your course.
When time is ripe, which will be suddenly,
I'll steal to Glendower and Lord Mortimer,
Where you and Douglas and our powers at once,
305   As I will fashion it, shall happily meet,
To bear our fortunes in our own strong arms,
Which now we hold at much uncertainty.

NORTHUMBERLAND   Farewell, good brother. We shall thrive, I trust.

HOTSPUR   Uncle, adieu. O, let the hours be short
310   Till fields and blows and groans applaud our sport!

Exeunt

---

281 **stays** waits   **face . . . occasion** i.e. opportunity   283 **smell it** catch the scent, as in
hunting   285 **Before . . . slip** you always release the dogs before the prey has been sighted
287 **power** army   290 **aimed** devised, directed   292 **head** army   293 **even** steadily,
patiently   296 **pay us home** repay us in full/administer a fatal blow   302 **suddenly** soon
303 **steal** go secretly   304 **at once** all at the same time   305 **happily** fortunately   310 **fields**
battlefields

Act 2 Scene 1

running scene 4

Enter a Carrier with a lantern in his hand

FIRST CARRIER   Heigh-ho! An't be not four by the day, I'll be hanged. Charles' wain is over the new chimney, and yet our horse not packed. What, ostler!

OSTLER   Anon, anon.   *Within*

5 FIRST CARRIER   I prithee, Tom, beat Cut's saddle, put a few flocks in the point. The poor jade is wrung in the withers out of all cess.

Enter another Carrier

SECOND CARRIER   Peas and beans are as dank here as a dog, and this is the next way to give poor jades the bots. This house is
10   turned upside down since Robin the ostler died.

FIRST CARRIER   Poor fellow, never joyed since the price of oats rose. It was the death of him.

SECOND CARRIER   I think this is the most villainous house in all London Road for fleas: I am stung like a tench.

15 FIRST CARRIER   Like a tench? There is ne'er a king in Christendom could be better bit than I have been since the first cock.

SECOND CARRIER   Why, you will allow us ne'er a jordan, and then we leak in your chimney, and your chamber-lye breeds
20   fleas like a loach.

FIRST CARRIER   What, ostler! Come away and be hanged! Come away!

2.1 Location: *an innyard on the road between London and Canterbury   Carrier*
delivery-man   **1 by the day** in the morning   **2 Charles' wain** Charlemagne's wagon, old
name for the constellation of the Plow   **3 packed** loaded   **ostler** groom at an inn
4 Anon soon, in a moment   **5 Tom** presumably the Second Carrier, though possibly the Ostler
beat Cut's saddle beating a saddle would soften it; Cut is the horse's name   **flocks** tufts of
wool (for padding)   **6 point** pommel of saddle   **jade** worn-out old horse   **wrung . . . withers**
rubbed sore between the shoulders   **out . . . cess** beyond measure   **8 Peas and beans** i.e.
horses' food   **dank . . . dog** damp   **9 bots** intestinal worms   **house** inn   **11 joyed** was
happy   **14 tench** freshwater fish with spots said to resemble fleabites   **17 first cock** first
cockcrow, midnight   **18 jordan** chamber pot   **19 leak** urinate   **chimney** fireplace
chamber-lye urine   **20 loach** small freshwater fish, thought to harbor **fleas**   **21 Come away**
come along

SECOND CARRIER   I have a gammon of bacon and two razes of
ginger, to be delivered as far as Charing Cross.

25   FIRST CARRIER   The turkeys in my pannier are quite starved.
What, ostler! A plague on thee! Hast thou never an eye in thy
head? Canst not hear? An 'twere not as good a deed as drink
to break the pate of thee, I am a very villain. Come, and be
hanged! Hast no faith in thee?

Enter Gadshill

30   GADSHILL   Good morrow, carriers. What's o'clock?

FIRST CARRIER   I think it be two o'clock.

GADSHILL   I prithee lend me thy lantern to see my gelding in
the stable.

FIRST CARRIER   Nay, soft, I pray ye; I know a trick worth two of

35   that.

GADSHILL   I prithee lend me thine.   *To the Second Carrier*

SECOND CARRIER   Ay, when? Can'st tell? Lend me thy lantern,
quoth a? Marry, I'll see thee hanged first.

GADSHILL   Sirrah carrier, what time do you mean to come to

40   London?

SECOND CARRIER   Time enough to go to bed with a candle, I
warrant thee.— Come, neighbour Mugs, we'll call up the
gentlemen. They will along with company, for they have
great charge.

Exeunt [Carriers]

Enter Chamberlain

45   GADSHILL   What, ho, Chamberlain?

---

23 gammon of bacon ham   razes either "races" (roots) or "rasers" (a measure amounting to
four bushels)   24 Charing Cross village between London and Westminster, site of a market
25 pannier one of a pair of baskets   27 An . . . thee if cracking your skull were not as good a
thing as drinking   29 Hast have you   faith honesty, trustworthiness   31 two o'clock either
an error, since the First Carrier earlier said that he thought it was four o'clock, or a lie to
mislead Gadshill (who may have aroused suspicion)   32 gelding castrated horse
34 I know . . . that i.e. I'm not so stupid as to fall for such an old trick   37 Ay . . . tell? What
time is it? Do you know? (repeating Gadshill's earlier request); or proverbial phrase meaning
"you must be joking"   38 quoth a did you say   41 Time . . . candle i.e. sometime tonight
42 warrant assure   neighbour Mugs i.e. the First Carrier; neighbour is a friendly form of
address   call wake   43 along . . . charge want to travel in a group because they're carrying
valuable goods   *Chamberlain* inn attendant in charge of the bedrooms

CHAMBERLAIN   At hand, quoth pick-purse.

GADSHILL   That's even as fair as — at hand, quoth the chamberlain, for thou variest no more from picking of purses than giving direction doth from labouring. Thou lay'st the plot how.

CHAMBERLAIN   Good morrow, Master Gadshill. It holds current that I told you yesternight: there's a franklin in the wild of Kent hath brought three hundred marks with him in gold. I heard him tell it to one of his company last night at supper, a kind of auditor, one that hath abundance of charge too, God knows what. They are up already, and call for eggs and butter. They will away presently.

GADSHILL   Sirrah, if they meet not with Saint Nicholas' clerks, I'll give thee this neck.

CHAMBERLAIN   No, I'll none of it: I prithee keep that for the hangman, for I know thou worship'st Saint Nicholas as truly as a man of falsehood may.

GADSHILL   What talkest thou to me of the hangman? If I hang, I'll make a fat pair of gallows, for if I hang, old Sir John hangs with me, and thou know'st he's no starveling. Tut, there are other Trojans that thou dream'st not of, the which for sport sake are content to do the profession some grace; that would, if matters should be looked into, for their own credit sake, make all whole. I am joined with no foot-land rakers, no

46 At . . . pick-purse I'm ready, as the pickpocket says   **47 That's . . . fair as** i.e. you might as well have said   **49 giving . . . labouring** giving orders does from working   **50 lay'st . . . how** devise the plan, direct the thief   **51 holds current that** remains true what   **52 franklin** small landowner   **wild of Kent** Kentish weald, wooded country between the North and South Downs of southern England   **53 three . . . gold** i.e. £200, a mark was an accounting unit (rather than a coin) worth two thirds of a pound   **55 auditor** treasury official   **abundance of charge** a lot of baggage   **56 eggs and butter** i.e. breakfast   **57 presently** immediately   **58 Saint Nicholas' clerks** thieves, highwaymen; **Saint Nicholas** was supposedly their patron saint   **59 I'll . . . neck** i.e. you can hang me   **65 starveling** skinny, starving person   **66 Trojans** fine fellows (slang)   **the which** who   **67 profession** i.e. of robbery   **69 make all whole** put everything right, sort things out   **foot-land rakers** thieves who operate on foot (as opposed to on a horse)

70   long-staff sixpenny strikers, none of these mad mustachio
      purple-hued malt-worms, but with nobility and tranquillity,
      burgomasters and great oneyers, such as can hold in, such
      as will strike sooner than speak, and speak sooner than
      drink, and drink sooner than pray. And yet, I lie, for they
75   pray continually unto their saint, the commonwealth; or
      rather not to pray to her, but prey on her, for they ride up and
      down on her and make her their boots.

CHAMBERLAIN   What, the commonwealth their boots? Will she
      hold out water in foul way?

80   GADSHILL   She will, she will; justice hath liquored her. We steal
      as in a castle, cocksure. We have the receipt of fern-seed, we
      walk invisible.

CHAMBERLAIN   Nay, I think rather you are more beholding to the
      night than to fern-seed for your walking invisible.

85   GADSHILL   Give me thy hand. Thou shalt have a share in our
      purpose, as I am a true man.

CHAMBERLAIN   Nay, rather let me have it, as you are a false thief.

GADSHILL   Go to. *Homo* is a common name to all men. Bid the
      ostler bring the gelding out of the stable. Farewell, ye muddy
90   knave.   *Exeunt*

Act 2 Scene 2   *running scene 5*

Enter Prince, Poins and Peto [and Bardolph]

POINS   Come, shelter, shelter. I have removed Falstaff's
      horse, and he frets like a gummed velvet.

---

70 long-staff sixpenny strikers thieves who, merely to steal sixpence, strike their victims with a long stick   **mustachio purple-hued malt-worms** purple-faced drunkards with large mustaches   **71 tranquillity** those living a peaceful life   **72 burgomasters** town officials   **oneyers** exact meaning uncertain, perhaps "ones," i.e. great personages   **hold in** hold firm/keep silent   **75 commonwealth** nation   **76 ride** i.e. like a horse, but also with sexual connotations   **77 boots** booty, plunder (the Chamberlain plays on the sense of "footwear"; there is also a quibble on the sense of "vagina")   **79 hold . . . way** keep you dry on a muddy road/piss herself   **80 liquored** oiled (to make waterproof)/plied with alcohol   **81 as . . . castle** i.e. in complete safety   **cocksure** completely secure   **receipt of fern-seed** recipe for fern seed (supposed to confer invisibility)   **86 true** honest   **88 *Homo*** Latin for "man"   **common name to** general name for   **89 muddy** muddled, dull-witted (plays on the sense of "dirty")   **2.2 *Location: the highway near Gad's Hill*   2 frets . . . velvet** fusses or, literally, frays like cheap velvet stiffened with gum

PRINCE HENRY   Stand close.   *Poins, Peto and Bardolph stand aside*

Enter Falstaff

FALSTAFF   Poins! Poins, and be hanged! Poins!

5   PRINCE HENRY   Peace, ye fat-kidneyed rascal. What a brawling dost thou keep!

FALSTAFF   What, Poins? Hal?

PRINCE HENRY   He is walked up to the top of the hill.   *Stands aside* I'll go seek him.   *with the others*

10   FALSTAFF   I am accursed to rob in that thief's company. That rascal hath removed my horse, and tied him I know not where. If I travel but four foot by the square further afoot, I shall break my wind. Well, I doubt not but to die a fair death for all this, if I scape hanging for killing that rogue. I have

15   forsworn his company hourly any time this two-and-twenty year, and yet I am bewitched with the rogue's company. If the rascal have not given me medicines to make me love him, I'll be hanged; it could not be else: I have drunk medicines. Poins, Hal, a plague upon you both! Bardolph! Peto! I'll starve ere I

20   rob a foot further. An 'twere not as good a deed as to drink, to turn true man and to leave these rogues, I am the veriest varlet that ever chewed with a tooth. Eight yards of uneven ground is threescore and ten miles afoot with me, and the stony-hearted villains know it well enough. A plague upon't

25   when thieves cannot be true one to another!   *They whistle* Whew! A plague light upon you all!   *The Prince, Poins,* Give me my horse, you rogues. Give me   *Peto and Bardolph* my horse, and be hanged!   *come forward*

PRINCE HENRY   Peace, ye fat-guts! Lie down, lay thine ear close to

30   the ground and list if thou can hear the tread of travellers.

FALSTAFF   Have you any levers to lift me up again, being down?

---

3 close concealed   **5 fat-kidneyed** i.e. fat-bellied (**rascal** may play on the sense of "young or inferior deer," a creature Falstaff is frequently compared to)   **6 keep** make, keep up
12 by the square exactly   **square** a measuring instrument   **13 break my wind** lose my breath (plays on the sense of "fart")   **Well . . . rogue** I expect to die well despite everything, as long as I'm not hanged for killing Poins   **17 medicines** potions   **19 ere** before   **20 An** if
21 turn true man reform, become honest/become an informer   **veriest varlet** most complete rogue   **26 Whew!** Expression of alarm or perhaps Falstaff trying to whistle

I'll not bear mine own flesh so far afoot again for all the coin
in thy father's exchequer. What a plague mean ye to colt me
thus?

35   PRINCE HENRY   Thou liest. Thou art not colted, thou art uncolted.

FALSTAFF   I prithee, good Prince Hal, help me to my horse,
good king's son.

PRINCE HENRY   Out, you rogue! Shall I be your ostler?

FALSTAFF   Go, hang thyself in thine own heir-apparent garters!
40   If I be ta'en, I'll peach for this. An I have not ballads made on
all and sung to filthy tunes, let a cup of sack be my poison.
When a jest is so forward, and afoot too! I hate it.

Enter Gadshill

GADSHILL   Stand.

FALSTAFF   So I do, against my will.

45   POINS   O, 'tis our setter. I know his voice.

BARDOLPH   What news?

GADSHILL   Case ye, case ye; on with your vizards. There's money
of the king's coming down the hill, 'tis going to the king's
exchequer.

50   FALSTAFF   You lie, you rogue, 'tis going to the King's Tavern.

GADSHILL   There's enough to make us all.

FALSTAFF   To be hanged.

PRINCE HENRY   You four shall front them in the narrow lane.
Ned and I will walk lower; if they scape from your encounter,
55   then they light on us.

PETO   But how many be of them?

GADSHILL   Some eight or ten.

FALSTAFF   Will they not rob us?

PRINCE HENRY   What, a coward, Sir John Paunch?

---

33 exchequer treasury   **colt** cheat   **35 uncolted** without a horse   **36 to** i.e. to find, but the
prince takes him to mean "to mount"   **39 heir-apparent garters** jokes on the fact that as heir
apparent, the prince belonged to the knightly Order of the Garter   **40 peach** turn informer,
betray (my accomplices)   **ballads . . . all** songs made up about you   **41 filthy** disgraceful,
obscene   **42 forward** far advanced/presumptuous, immodest   **afoot** when the robbery plot is
under way/when I am on foot   **45 setter** one who plans robberies   **47 Case ye** mask
yourselves   **51 make us all** make our fortunes   **53 front** confront   **54 lower** further down
55 light on come upon   **56 be** are there

60 FALSTAFF   Indeed, I am not John of Gaunt, your grandfather; but yet no coward, Hal.

PRINCE HENRY   We'll leave that to the proof.

POINS   Sirrah Jack, thy horse stands behind the hedge. When thou need'st him, there thou shalt find him. Farewell,
65 and stand fast.

FALSTAFF   Now cannot I strike him, if I should be hanged.

PRINCE HENRY   Ned, where are our disguises?   *To Poins*

POINS   Here, hard by. Stand close.   *To Prince Henry*

[*Exeunt Prince Henry and Poins*]

FALSTAFF   Now, my masters, happy man be his dole, say I.
70 Every man to his business.

Enter Travellers

FIRST TRAVELLER   Come, neighbour. The boy shall lead our horses down the hill. We'll walk afoot awhile, and ease our legs.

THIEVES   Stay!

TRAVELLERS   Jesu bless us!

75 FALSTAFF   Strike, down with them! Cut the villains' throats. Ah, whoreson caterpillars, bacon-fed knaves! They hate us youth, down with them, fleece them.

TRAVELLERS   O, we are undone, both we and ours for ever!

FALSTAFF   Hang ye, gorbellied knaves, are you undone? No, ye
80 fat chuffs, I would your store were here! On, bacons, on! What, ye knaves? Young men must live. You are grand-jurors, are ye? We'll jure ye, i'faith.

Here they rob them and bind them   [*Exeunt*]

Enter the Prince and Poins

PRINCE HENRY   The thieves have bound the true men. Now could thou and I rob the thieves and go merrily to London, it would

---

60 **Gaunt** plays on the literal sense of "thin" (though actually the name was a form of "Ghent")
62 **proof** test   68 **hard** near   69 **happy . . . dole** may good fortune be every man's lot
76 **whoreson caterpillars** bastard parasites   **whoreson** son of a whore   **bacon-fed** fat, well-fed   77 **youth** youngsters   78 **undone** ruined   79 **gorbellied** big-bellied   80 **chuffs** clowns/misers   **store** savings, full possessions   **bacons** pigs   81 **grand-jurors** wealthy men, eligible to sit on a jury   82 **jure** judge, see to/make a juror of

85 be argument for a week, laughter for a month and a good jest
for ever.

POINS   Stand close. I hear them coming.

Enter Thieves again

FALSTAFF   Come, my masters, let us share, and then to horse
before day. An the prince and Poins be not two arrant
90 cowards, there's no equity stirring. There's no more valour
in that Poins than in a wild duck.

PRINCE HENRY   Your money!

POINS   Villains!

*As they are sharing, the Prince and Poins set upon them. They all run
away, leaving the booty behind them*

PRINCE HENRY   Got with much ease. Now merrily to horse.
95 The thieves are scattered and possessed with fear
So strongly that they dare not meet each other:
Each takes his fellow for an officer.
Away, good Ned. Falstaff sweats to death,
And lards the lean earth as he walks along.
100 Were't not for laughing, I should pity him.

POINS   How the rogue roared!   *Exeunt*

Act 2 Scene 3   *running scene 6*

Enter Hotspur, solus, reading a letter

HOTSPUR   'But for mine own part, my lord, I could be well
contented to be there, in respect of the love I bear your
house.' He could be contented: why is he not, then? In
respect of the love he bears our house. He shows in this, he
5 loves his own barn better than he loves our house. Let me see
some more. 'The purpose you undertake is dangerous' —
why, that's certain: 'tis dangerous to take a cold, to sleep, to

---

85 **argument** a topic of conversation   88 **my masters** sirs   89 **arrant** absolute   90 **equity
stirring** judgment in the world   91 **wild duck** i.e. easily frightened   99 **lards** drips fat on
2.3 *Location: Hotspur's estate (historically, Warkworth Castle in Northumberland)*
solus alone   3 **house** family (Hotspur goes on to play on the literal meaning, contrasting it
with **barn**)

drink. But I tell you, my lord fool, out of this nettle, danger,
we pluck this flower, safety. 'The purpose you undertake is
10   dangerous, the friends you have named uncertain, the time
itself unsorted and your whole plot too light for the
counterpoise of so great an opposition.' Say you so, say you
so? I say unto you again, you are a shallow cowardly hind,
and you lie. What a lack-brain is this? I protest, our plot is as
15   good a plot as ever was laid; our friends true and constant: a
good plot, good friends, and full of expectation. An excellent
plot, very good friends. What a frosty-spirited rogue is this?
Why, my lord of York commends the plot and the general
course of the action. By this hand if I were now by this
20   rascal, I could brain him with his lady's fan. Is there not my
father, my uncle and myself, Lord Edmund Mortimer, my
lord of York and Owen Glendower? Is there not besides the
Douglas? Have I not all their letters to meet me in arms by the
ninth of the next month? And are they not some of them set
25   forward already? What a pagan rascal is this? An infidel! Ha,
you shall see now in very sincerity of fear and cold heart,
will he to the king and lay open all our proceedings. O, I
could divide myself and go to buffets, for moving such a dish
of skimmed milk with so honourable an action! Hang him.
30   Let him tell the king we are prepared. I will set forwards
tonight.

Enter his Lady

How now, Kate? I must leave you within these two hours.

LADY PERCY   O, my good lord, why are you thus alone?
For what offence have I this fortnight been
35   A banished woman from my Harry's bed?
Tell me, sweet lord, what is't that takes from thee

---

10 **uncertain** unreliable   11 **unsorted** unsuitable   12 **counterpoise** counterbalance
13 **hind** peasant/menial/nervous female deer   14 **lack-brain** idiot   **protest** declare, affirm
16 **expectation** promise   18 **lord of York** the Archbishop of York, Richard Scroop   20 **brain . . .**
fan knock his brains out with a lady's fan—light and suitable for one with little brain   22 **the**
Douglas Archibald, Earl of Douglas; **the** signifies the head of a Scottish clan   26 **in . . . of** i.e.
really motivated by   28 **go to buffets** come to blows (with myself)   **moving** trying to persuade
dish . . . milk i.e. weak, cowardly one   29 **action** course of action/military enterprise/rhetorical
gesture/division in a logical argument   30 **prepared** drawn up for military action

Thy stomach, pleasure and thy golden sleep?
Why dost thou bend thine eyes upon the earth,
And start so often when thou sit'st alone?
40 Why hast thou lost the fresh blood in thy cheeks,
And given my treasures and my rights of thee
To thick-eyed musing and cursed melancholy?
In my faint slumbers I by thee have watched,
And heard thee murmur tales of iron wars,
45 Speak terms of manage to thy bounding steed,
Cry 'Courage! To the field!' And thou hast talked
Of sallies and retires, trenches, tents,
Of palisadoes, frontiers, parapets,
Of basilisks, of cannon, culverin,
50 Of prisoners' ransom and of soldiers slain,
And all the current of a heady fight.
Thy spirit within thee hath been so at war
And thus hath so bestirred thee in thy sleep,
That beads of sweat hath stood upon thy brow
55 Like bubbles in a late-disturbèd stream;
And in thy face strange motions have appeared,
Such as we see when men restrain their breath
On some great sudden haste. O, what portents are these?
Some heavy business hath my lord in hand,
60 And I must know it, else he loves me not.

HOTSPUR   What, ho!

[*Enter a Servant*]

Is Gilliams with the packet gone?

SERVANT   He is, my lord, an hour agone.

---

37 stomach appetite   41 treasures . . . rights treasured intimacy and wifely rights
42 thick-eyed dull-sighted, preoccupied/heavy-lidded (from lack of sleep)   43 faint light,
restless   watched remained awake   45 terms of manage words of control   47 sallies
and retires advances and retreats   48 palisadoes defensive fortifications   49 basilisks
large cannon (named after a mythical reptile)   culverin another type of large cannon
51 current movement, onward flow   heady violent, swiftly moving   56 motions movements,
expressions/emotions   57 restrain hold/catch   59 heavy important, weighty   61 What, ho!
summons to servant   62 Gilliams name of another servant   packet packet of letters,
dispatch

	HOTSPUR	Hath Butler brought those horses from the sheriff?
65	SERVANT	One horse, my lord, he brought even now.
	HOTSPUR	What horse? A roan, a crop-ear, is it not?
	SERVANT	It is, my lord.
	HOTSPUR	That roan shall be my throne.

HOTSPUR   Well, I will back him straight. *Esperance*!

70   Bid Butler lead him forth into the park.   [*Exit Servant*]

LADY PERCY   But hear you, my lord.

HOTSPUR   What say'st thou, my lady?

LADY PERCY   What is it carries you away?

HOTSPUR   Why, my horse, my love, my horse.

75   LADY PERCY   Out, you mad-headed ape!
A weasel hath not such a deal of spleen
As you are tossed with. In sooth,
I'll know your business, Harry, that I will.
I fear my brother Mortimer doth stir
80   About his title, and hath sent for you
To line his enterprise. But if you go—

HOTSPUR   So far afoot, I shall be weary, love.

LADY PERCY   Come, come, you paraquito, answer me
Directly unto this question that I shall ask:
85   Indeed, I'll break thy little finger, Harry,
If thou wilt not tell me true.

HOTSPUR   Away,
Away, you trifler! Love? I love thee not.
I care not for thee, Kate. This is no world
90   To play with mammets and to tilt with lips.
We must have bloody noses and cracked crowns,

---

64 Butler another servant   65 even just   66 roan with a coat of mixed color   crop-ear with the top of the ears cropped   69 back mount   straight straightaway   *Esperance!* Hope! (the Percy family motto was "*Esperance ma comforte*," French for "In hope is my strength/ consolation")   73 carries you away transports you with emotion   76 weasel a notoriously aggressive animal (Hotspur responds literally)   spleen anger, impulsiveness   79 stir become roused, rebellious   80 title claim to the throne   81 line support   83 paraquito little parrot   85 little finger phallic connotations   88 trifler frivolous time-waster   90 mammets dolls, perhaps with play on Latin *mamma* ("breasts")   tilt joust   91 crowns heads (plays on the sense of "coins" as well as having royal connotations)

And pass them current too.— God's me, my horse!

What say'st thou, Kate? What wouldst thou have with me?

LADY PERCY   Do ye not love me? Do ye not, indeed?

95   Well, do not then, for since you love me not,

I will not love myself. Do you not love me?

Nay, tell me if thou speak'st in jest or no.

HOTSPUR   Come, wilt thou see me ride?

And when I am a-horseback, I will swear

100   I love thee infinitely. But hark you, Kate,

I must not have you henceforth question me

Whither I go, nor reason whereabout.

Whither I must, I must. And to conclude,

This evening must I leave thee, gentle Kate.

105   I know you wise, but yet no further wise

Than Harry Percy's wife. Constant you are,

But yet a woman: and for secrecy,

No lady closer, for I well believe

Thou wilt not utter what thou dost not know,

110   And so far will I trust thee, gentle Kate.

LADY PERCY   How? So far?

HOTSPUR   Not an inch further. But hark you, Kate:

Whither I go, thither shall you go too.

Today will I set forth, tomorrow you.

115   Will this content you, Kate?

LADY PERCY   It must of force.   *Exeunt*

Act 2 Scene 4   *running scene 7*

Enter Prince and Poins

PRINCE HENRY   Ned, prithee come out of that fat room, and lend

me thy hand to laugh a little.

POINS   Where hast been, Hal?

---

92 **pass them current** pass them off as good currency   **God's me** God save me
102 **whereabout** speculate why   106 **Constant** faithful, trustworthy   108 **closer** more
tight-lipped   116 **force** necessity   **2.4** *Location: a tavern in Eastcheap, London*
1 **fat** stuffy (possibly "vat")   **lend . . . hand** help me

PRINCE HENRY   With three or four loggerheads amongst three or
5   fourscore hogsheads. I have sounded the very base-string of
humility. Sirrah, I am sworn brother to a leash of drawers,
and can call them by their names, as Tom, Dick and Francis.
They take it already upon their confidence that though I be
but Prince of Wales, yet I am the king of courtesy, telling me
10   flatly I am no proud Jack like Falstaff, but a Corinthian, a lad
of mettle, a good boy, and when I am king of England, I shall
command all the good lads in Eastcheap. They call drinking
deep, dyeing scarlet; and when you breathe in your
watering, then they cry 'Hem!' and bid you play it off. To
15   conclude, I am so good a proficient in one quarter of an hour
that I can drink with any tinker in his own language during
my life. I tell thee, Ned, thou hast lost much honour that
thou wert not with me in this action. But, sweet Ned — to
sweeten which name of Ned, I give thee this pennyworth of
20   sugar, clapped even now into my hand by an under-skinker,
one that never spake other English in his life than 'Eight
shillings and sixpence' and 'You are welcome', with this
shrill addition, 'Anon, anon, sir!— Score a pint of bastard in
the Half-Moon', or so. But, Ned, to drive away time till
25   Falstaff come, I prithee do thou stand in some by-room while
I question my puny drawer to what end he gave me the sugar

---

4 **loggerheads** blockheads, idiots   **three or fourscore** sixty or eighty (a score is twenty)
5 **hogsheads** large wine casks   **sounded . . . humility** played the lowest note of baseness/
humbleness   6 **sworn brother** avowed intimate friend   **leash** set of three (usually animals
tied together)   **drawers** bartenders, waiters   7 **Francis** name of the bartender Hal
subsequently teases   10 **proud** pompous   **Jack** fellow, knave/Jack **Falstaff** (diminutive
version of John)   **Corinthian** fine fellow—Corinth in ancient Greece was notorious for riotous
living   11 **mettle** spirit, worth   13 **dyeing scarlet** probably because heavy drinking reddens
the complexion; perhaps because urine, a product of drinking, was used to fix dye
breathe . . . watering pause for breath while drinking (possibly "fart while urinating")
14 **"Hem!"** sound of disapproval/a clearing of the throat   **play it off** finish it up
16 **drink . . . language** i.e. consort comfortably with a drinker of any social class/drink
heavily (tinkers were reputedly heavy drinkers)   18 **action** encounter (usually military)
19 **pennyworth of sugar** small quantity of sugar used to sweeten wine   20 **under-skinker**
low-ranking waiter (to "skink" is to pour out liquor)   23 **Anon** (I'm) coming, just a moment
Score put on the bill   **bastard** sweet Spanish wine   24 **Half-Moon** one of the rooms in the
tavern   **drive** pass   25 **by-room** side room   26 **puny** inexperienced/young/weedy   **to what
end** why

and do never leave calling 'Francis', that his tale to me may be nothing but 'Anon'. Step aside, and I'll show thee a precedent.

30 POINS   Francis!

PRINCE HENRY   Thou art perfect.

POINS   Francis!   [*Exit Poins*]

Enter Drawer [Francis]

FRANCIS   Anon, anon, sir.— Look down into the Pomgarnet, Ralph.

35 PRINCE HENRY   Come hither, Francis.

FRANCIS   My lord?

PRINCE HENRY   How long hast thou to serve, Francis?

FRANCIS   Forsooth, five years, and as much as to—

POINS   Francis!   *Within*

40 FRANCIS   Anon, anon, sir.

PRINCE HENRY   Five years. By'r lady, a long lease for the clinking of pewter. But Francis, darest thou be so valiant as to play the coward with thy indenture and show it a fair pair of heels and run from it?

45 FRANCIS   O lord, sir, I'll be sworn upon all the books in England, I could find in my heart—

POINS   Francis!   *Within*

FRANCIS   Anon, anon, sir.

PRINCE HENRY   How old art thou, Francis?

50 FRANCIS   Let me see — about Michaelmas next I shall be—

POINS   Francis!   *Within*

FRANCIS   Anon, sir.— Pray you stay a little, my lord.

PRINCE HENRY   Nay, but hark you, Francis, for the sugar thou gavest me, 'twas a pennyworth, was't not?

55 FRANCIS   O lord, sir, I would it had been two!

---

27 leave stop   **29 precedent** example   **31 perfect** word-perfect   **33 Pomgarnet** Pomegranate, the name of another room in the tavern   **37 to serve** left of your apprenticeship (the usual length was seven years; Francis is probably fourteen or sixteen)   **41 By'r lady** by Our Lady (the Virgin Mary)   **long ... pewter** long apprenticeship to learn to be a barman (drinking vessels were made of **pewter**)   **43 indenture** contract by which an apprentice was bound   **45 books** i.e. Bibles   **50 Michaelmas** the feast of Saint Michael, 29 September   **52 stay** wait   **53 for** as for, about

PRINCE HENRY   I will give thee for it a thousand pound. Ask me
when thou wilt, and thou shalt have it.

POINS   Francis!   *Within*

FRANCIS   Anon, anon.

60 PRINCE HENRY   Anon, Francis? No, Francis. But tomorrow,
Francis, or, Francis, on Thursday, or indeed, Francis, when
thou wilt. But, Francis!

FRANCIS   My lord?

PRINCE HENRY   Wilt thou rob this leathern jerkin, crystal-
65 button, not-pated, agate-ring, puke-stocking, caddis-garter,
smooth-tongue, Spanish-pouch—

FRANCIS   O lord, sir, who do you mean?

PRINCE HENRY   Why, then, your brown bastard is your only
drink, for look you, Francis, your white canvas doublet will
70 sully. In Barbary, sir, it cannot come to so much.

FRANCIS   What, sir?

POINS   Francis!   *Within*

PRINCE HENRY   Away, you rogue! Dost thou hear them call?
*Here they both call him. The Drawer stands amazed, not knowing
which way to go*
Enter Vintner

VINTNER   What, stand'st thou still, and hear'st such a calling?
75 Look to the guests within.   [*Exit Francis*]
My lord, old Sir John, with half-a-dozen more, are at the
door: shall I let them in?

PRINCE HENRY   Let them alone awhile, and then open the door.
Poins!   [*Exit Vintner*]
Enter Poins

80 POINS   Anon, anon, sir.

---

64 rob i.e. rob your master of service by running away   leathern jerkin (the master who
wears a) tight-fitting leather jacket   crystal-button fashionable shiny buttons   65 not-pated
short-haired   agate-ring ring set with a carved agate stone   puke-stocking dark-colored
heavy woolen stockings   caddis-garter garter made of woolen tape   66 smooth-tongue
smooth-talker, flatterer   Spanish-pouch wallet of Spanish leather   68 brown bastard
Spanish wine, sweeter than the white variety   your only drink the best of drinks   69 doublet
tight-fitting jacket   70 sully get dirty   Barbary region in northern Africa (from which sugar
was imported)   it i.e. sugar   *amazed* dumbfounded   *Vintner* innkeeper selling wine

PRINCE HENRY   Sirrah, Falstaff and the rest of the thieves are at the door. Shall we be merry?

POINS   As merry as crickets, my lad. But hark ye: what cunning match have you made with this jest of the drawer?
85   Come, what's the issue?

PRINCE HENRY   I am now of all humours that have showed themselves humours since the old days of goodman Adam to the pupil age of this present twelve o'clock at midnight.

[*Enter Francis*]

What's o'clock, Francis?

90   FRANCIS   Anon, anon, sir.   [*Exit*]

PRINCE HENRY   That ever this fellow should have fewer words than a parrot, and yet the son of a woman! His industry is upstairs and downstairs, his eloquence the parcel of a reckoning. I am not yet of Percy's mind, the Hotspur of the north, he that kills
95   me some six or seven dozen of Scots at a breakfast, washes his hands, and says to his wife 'Fie upon this quiet life! I want work'. 'O my sweet Harry', says she, 'how many hast thou killed today?' 'Give my roan horse a drench', says he, and answers 'Some fourteen', an hour after, 'a trifle, a trifle'. I
100   prithee call in Falstaff. I'll play Percy, and that damned brawn shall play Dame Mortimer his wife. 'Rivo!' says the drunkard. Call in ribs, call in tallow.   *Poins calls*

Enter Falstaff, [Gadshill, Bardolph and Peto. Francis follows with wine]

POINS   Welcome, Jack. Where hast thou been?

FALSTAFF   A plague of all cowards, I say, and a vengeance too,
105   marry and amen!— Give me a cup of sack, boy.— Ere I lead

83 **merry as crickets** proverbial presumably because they jump about "singing"   84 **cunning match** clever game, contest of wits   85 **issue** outcome, point   86 **I . . . midnight** I now understand all the moods that have ever existed from the beginning of time until now (i.e. I'm in the mood for anything/I have seen everything)   87 **goodman** title for those below the rank of gentleman (the biblical **Adam** was a gardener)   88 **pupil age** youthful time (i.e. the present)   90 **Anon** puns on "one" (pronounced similarly)   92 **yet** nevertheless (be) **industry** business, labor, diligence   **is** is to run   93 **the . . . reckoning** consists of the items on a bill   94 **mind** opinion, way of thinking   **kills me** kills (**me** is colloquial/emphatic)   98 **drench** drink/draught of medicine   100 **brawn** lump of flesh/fattened boar or pig   101 **"Rivo!"** presumably a drinking cry; of uncertain origin   102 **ribs** fatty meat on bones (i.e. Falstaff)   **tallow** animal fat   104 **of** on

this life long, I'll sew nether stocks and mend them and foot
them too. A plague of all cowards!— Give me   *To Francis*
a cup of sack, rogue. Is there no virtue extant?   *Drinks*

PRINCE HENRY   Didst thou never see Titan kiss a dish of butter —
110   pitiful-hearted Titan — that melted at the sweet tale of the
sun? If thou didst, then behold that compound.

FALSTAFF   You rogue, here's lime in this sack too.—   *To Francis*
There is nothing but roguery to be found in villainous
man; yet a coward is worse than a cup of sack with lime
115   in't. A villainous coward! Go   [*Francis may exit*]
thy ways, old Jack, die when thou wilt, if manhood, good
manhood, be not forgot upon the face of the earth, then am
I a shotten herring. There lives not three good men
unhanged in England, and one of them is fat and grows old.
120   God help the while! A bad world, I say. I would I were a
weaver. I could sing all manner of songs. A plague of all
cowards, I say still.

PRINCE HENRY   How now, wool-sack, what mutter you?

FALSTAFF   A king's son? If I do not beat thee out of thy
125   kingdom with a dagger of lath, and drive all thy subjects
afore thee like a flock of wild geese, I'll never wear hair on my
face more. You Prince of Wales?

PRINCE HENRY   Why, you whoreson round man, what's the
matter?

130   FALSTAFF   Are you not a coward? Answer me to that. And
Poins there?

POINS   Ye fat paunch, an ye call me coward, I'll stab thee.

---

106 **nether stocks** stockings for the lower leg   **foot** darn the sole, repair the foot   108 **virtue
extant** courage still alive   109 **Titan** Roman sun god (large and red-faced like Falstaff as he
"kisses" the cup of sack); there may be sexual innuendo in **butter** (a whore was a "dish of
butter"), **melted** (ejaculated), and **tale** (puns on "tail," i.e. genitals)   110 **pitiful-hearted**
compassionate, tender   111 **compound** mixture (melted butter), i.e. either Falstaff and sack
or Falstaff and sweat   112 **lime** calcium oxide, used to preserve wine   115 **Go thy ways** off
you go   118 **shotten herring** a herring that has spawned its eggs (i.e. thin and weak)
120 **while** present age   121 **weaver** many were Protestant immigrants, known for psalm
singing   123 **wool-sack** large bale of wool; judges traditionally sat on them   125 **dagger of
lath** stage dagger made of soft wood, traditionally used by the comic Vice in morality plays
126 **I'll . . . more** i.e. I'm not a real man   **hair** a beard   128 **round** fat/plain speaking

FALSTAFF   I call thee coward? I'll see thee damned ere I call
thee coward, but I would give a thousand pound I could run
135   as fast as thou canst. You are straight enough in the
shoulders, you care not who sees your back. Call you that
backing of your friends? A plague upon such backing! Give
me them that will face me. Give me a cup of sack. I am a
rogue, if I drunk today.

140   PRINCE HENRY   O, villain, thy lips are scarce wiped since thou
drunk'st last.

FALSTAFF   All's one for that.   *He drinks*
A plague of all cowards, still say I.

PRINCE HENRY   What's the matter?

145   FALSTAFF   What's the matter? Here be four of us have ta'en a
thousand pound this morning.

PRINCE HENRY   Where is it, Jack? Where is it?

FALSTAFF   Where is it? Taken from us it is: a hundred upon
poor four of us.

150   PRINCE HENRY   What, a hundred, man?

FALSTAFF   I am a rogue, if I were not at half-sword with a
dozen of them two hours together. I have scaped by miracle.
I am eight times thrust through the doublet, four through
the hose, my buckler cut through and through, my sword
155   hacked like a hand-saw — *ecce signum!* I never dealt better
since I was a man: all would not do. A plague of all cowards!
Let them speak; if they speak more or less than truth, they
are villains and the sons of darkness.

PRINCE HENRY   Speak, sirs, how was it?

160   GADSHILL   We four set upon some dozen—

---

137 backing supporting/turning one's back, running away   138 face stand face to face/defy,
contradict   139 drunk have had anything to drink   142 All's . . . that so what, it doesn't
matter   145 ta'en taken   149 poor only   151 at half-sword at close quarters/fighting with
short swords   154 hose breeches   buckler small shield—sword and buckler were considered
old-fashioned or lower-class weapons   155 like a hand-saw with the edge so notched from
blows it appears serrated like the blade of a saw   *ecce signum* "behold the sign or proof"
(Latin; echoes words from the Catholic Mass)   dealt fought   156 all . . . do all this was not
enough though   158 sons of darkness biblical phrase (1 Thessalonians 5:5)

FALSTAFF   Sixteen at least, my lord.

GADSHILL   And bound them.

PETO   No, no, they were not bound.

FALSTAFF   You rogue, they were bound, every man of them, or
165   I am a Jew else, an Ebrew Jew.

GADSHILL   As we were sharing, some six or seven fresh men set
upon us—

FALSTAFF   And unbound the rest, and then come in the other.

PRINCE HENRY   What, fought ye with them all?

170   FALSTAFF   All? I know not what ye call all, but if I fought not
with fifty of them, I am a bunch of radish: if there were not
two or three and fifty upon poor old Jack, then am I no two-
legged creature.

POINS   Pray heaven you have not murdered some of them.

175   FALSTAFF   Nay, that's past praying for, I have peppered two of
them: two I am sure I have paid, two rogues in buckram
suits. I tell thee what, Hal, if I tell thee a lie, spit in my face,
call me horse. Thou knowest my old ward. Here I lay and
thus I bore my point. Four rogues in buckram let drive
180   at me—

PRINCE HENRY   What, four? Thou saidst but two even now.

FALSTAFF   Four, Hal, I told thee four.

POINS   Ay, ay, he said four.

FALSTAFF   These four came all a-front, and mainly thrust at
185   me. I made no more ado but took all their seven points in my
target, thus.

PRINCE HENRY   Seven? Why, there were but four even now.

FALSTAFF   In buckram?

POINS   Ay, four, in buckram suits.

---

165 Ebrew Jew a real (Hebrew) Jew, i.e. a knave   168 come . . . other the others came in
175 peppered made it hot for, stabbed repeatedly   176 paid settled with, killed   buckram
coarse linen cloth   178 ward defensive posture (fencing term)   lay positioned myself
179 bore my point pointed my sword   let drive at bore down on, attacked   184 a-front
abreast   mainly violently   185 made . . . ado didn't wait any longer   points sword points
186 target shield

190 FALSTAFF   Seven, by these hilts, or I am a villain else.

PRINCE HENRY   Prithee let him alone. We shall   *Aside to Poins*
have more anon.

FALSTAFF   Dost thou hear me, Hal?

PRINCE HENRY   Ay, and mark thee too, Jack.

195 FALSTAFF   Do so, for it is worth the listening to. These nine in
buckram that I told thee of—

PRINCE HENRY   So, two more already.

FALSTAFF   Their points being broken—

POINS   Down fell his hose.

200 FALSTAFF   Began to give me ground. But I followed me close,
came in foot and hand; and with a thought seven of the
eleven I paid.

PRINCE HENRY   O, monstrous! Eleven buckram men grown out of
two?

205 FALSTAFF   But, as the devil would have it, three misbegotten
knaves in Kendal green came at my back and let drive at me;
for it was so dark, Hal, that thou couldst not see thy hand.

PRINCE HENRY   These lies are like the father that begets them,
gross as a mountain, open, palpable. Why, thou clay-brained

210 guts, thou knotty-pated fool, thou whoreson, obscene,
greasy tallow-catch—

FALSTAFF   What, art thou mad? Art thou mad? Is not the truth
the truth?

PRINCE HENRY   Why, how couldst thou know these men in

215 Kendal green when it was so dark thou couldst not see thy
hand? Come, tell us your reason: what say'st thou to this?

POINS   Come, your reason, Jack, your reason.

FALSTAFF   What, upon compulsion? No. Were I at the

---

190 **these hilts** this sword handle   194 **mark** observe, take note of/keep count   198 **points**
sword points, but Poins takes it to mean the laces attaching the **hose** to the doublet   200 **give
me ground** back away (**me** is emphatic)   201 **foot and hand** at close range   **with a thought**
as quick as thought   205 **misbegotten** wretched, bastard   206 **Kendal green** coarse, green
woolen cloth from Kendal in Cumbria (associated with forest outlaws)   208 **father** i.e.
Falstaff, here compared to the devil—the proverbial "father of lies"   **begets** conceives,
creates   209 **clay-brained** dull-witted   210 **knotty-pated** thickheaded   211 **tallow-catch**
accumulation of animal fat   218 **upon compulsion** under force

strappado, or all the racks in the world, I would not tell you
220 on compulsion. Give you a reason on compulsion? If reasons
were as plentiful as blackberries, I would give no man a
reason upon compulsion, I.

PRINCE HENRY   I'll be no longer guilty of this sin. This sanguine
coward, this bed-presser, this horseback-breaker, this huge
225 hill of flesh—

FALSTAFF   Away, you starveling, you elf-skin, you dried neat's
tongue, bull's pizzle, you stock-fish! O, for breath to utter
what is like thee! You tailor's-yard, you sheath, you bowcase,
you vile standing-tuck—

230 PRINCE HENRY   Well, breathe awhile, and then to't again: and
when thou hast tired thyself in base comparisons, hear me
speak but thus.

POINS   Mark, Jack.

PRINCE HENRY   We two saw you four set on four and bound
235 them, and were masters of their wealth. Mark now, how a
plain tale shall put you down. Then did we two set on you
four, and with a word, out-faced you from your prize, and
have it, yea, and can show it you in the house. And, Falstaff,
you carried your guts away as nimbly, with as quick
240 dexterity, and roared for mercy and still ran and roared, as
ever I heard bull-calf. What a slave art thou, to hack thy
sword as thou hast done, and then say it was in fight! What

219 **strappado** means of torture: the victim was raised by ropes that tied his arms behind his back, then dropped suddenly, which usually dislocated the joints   **racks** instruments of torture: the victim was tied to a frame which was then extended, stretching the arms and legs in opposite directions   220 **reasons** puns on "raisins" (i.e. grapes, less readily available than **blackberries**)   223 **sanguine** red-faced (with **coward**, this creates an oxymoron, as a sanguine temperament was equated with courage)   224 **bed-presser** heavyweight who will strain beds; perhaps also lazy, one who stays in bed   **horseback-breaker** one so fat he breaks horses' backs (pun on "horse"/"whore's")   226 **elf-skin** man of shrunken, fragile form (often emended to "eel-skin")   **neat's** ox's   227 **pizzle** penis; a dried bull's penis was sometimes used as a whip   **stock-fish** dried cod (suggestive of physical weakness and an impotent penis)   228 **tailor's-yard** measuring yardstick/penis (tailors were sometimes imaged as thin or effeminate men)   **sheath** cover for knife or sword, i.e. empty case/vagina   **bowcase** long, thin case for an archer's bow, hence starveling/vagina   229 **standing-tuck** slender sword that is either rigid (i.e. useless because insufficiently resilient) or upright (not engaged in action) or idle, delaying; with phallic connotations   237 **with a word** in a word/with merely a single word   **out-faced** confronted and intimidated   241 **slave** base-minded villain

trick, what device, what starting-hole canst thou now find
out to hide thee from this open and apparent shame?

245 POINS   Come, let's hear, Jack: what trick hast thou now?

FALSTAFF   I knew ye as well as he that made ye. Why, hear ye,
my masters, was it for me to kill the heir-apparent? Should I
turn upon the true prince? Why, thou knowest I am as
valiant as Hercules, but beware instinct. The lion will not
250   touch the true prince. Instinct is a great matter. I was a
coward on instinct. I shall think the better of myself and
thee during my life: I for a valiant lion, and thou for a true
prince. But, lads, I am glad you have the money.— Hostess,
clap to the doors. Watch tonight, pray tomorrow. Gallants,
255   lads, boys, hearts of gold, all the good titles of fellowship
come to you! What, shall we be merry? Shall we have a play
extempore?

PRINCE HENRY   Content, and the argument shall be thy running
away.

260 FALSTAFF   Ah, no more of that, Hal, an thou lovest me!

Enter Hostess [Quickly]

HOSTESS QUICKLY   My lord the prince?

PRINCE HENRY   How now, my lady the hostess? What say'st thou
to me?

HOSTESS QUICKLY   Marry, my lord, there is a nobleman of the
265   court at door would speak with you: he says he comes from
your father.

PRINCE HENRY   Give him as much as will make him a royal man,
and send him back again to my mother.

FALSTAFF   What manner of man is he?

270 HOSTESS QUICKLY   An old man.

---

243 **starting-hole** bolt-hole, hiding place   244 **apparent** evident   246 **knew** recognized
249 **Hercules** Greek hero renowned for strength   **instinct** impulse/innate tendency/intuition
lion . . . prince lions were popularly thought to recognize and refuse to harm royalty
254 **clap to** shut   **Watch** remain awake (for revelry)/be on guard   **Gallants** fine, fashionable
young men   255 **hearts** fine companions   257 **extempore** immediately, improvised without
rehearsal   258 **argument** plot, theme   260 **an** if   267 **royal** plays on the sense of "coin of
greater value than the 'noble' [another type of coin]"

FALSTAFF   What doth gravity out of his bed at midnight? Shall I give him his answer?

PRINCE HENRY   Prithee do, Jack.

FALSTAFF   'Faith, and I'll send him packing.   *Exit*

275 PRINCE HENRY   Now, sirs: you fought fair; so did you, Peto, so did you, Bardolph. You are lions too, you ran away upon instinct. You will not touch the true prince; no, fie!

BARDOLPH   'Faith, I ran when I saw others run.

PRINCE HENRY   Tell me now in earnest, how came Falstaff's
280   sword so hacked?

PETO   Why, he hacked it with his dagger, and said he would swear truth out of England but he would make you believe it was done in fight, and persuaded us to do the like.

BARDOLPH   Yea, and to tickle our noses with spear-grass to
285   make them bleed, and then to beslubber our garments with it and swear it was the blood of true men. I did that I did not this seven years before, I blushed to hear his monstrous devices.

PRINCE HENRY   O, villain, thou stolest a cup of sack eighteen
290   years ago, and wert taken with the manner, and ever since thou hast blushed extempore. Thou hadst fire and sword on thy side, and yet thou ran'st away; what instinct hadst thou for it?

BARDOLPH   My lord, do you see these meteors? Do you behold
295   these exhalations?

PRINCE HENRY   I do.

BARDOLPH   What think you they portend?

PRINCE HENRY   Hot livers and cold purses.

---

271 **gravity** aged respectability   277 **fie** expression of reproach or disgust   282 **swear . . .
England** swear (falsely) with such conviction that truth fled the country   284 **spear-grass**
tough, coarse grass   285 **beslubber** daub, smear   286 **true** valiant/honest   **that** something
287 **monstrous devices** outrageous tricks   290 **taken . . . manner** caught red-handed with
the evidence/got into the habit   291 **extempore** spontaneously (i.e. Bardolph has a
permanently red face from drinking)   **fire** i.e. a fiery face   294 **meteors . . . exhalations** i.e.
red blotches on Bardolph's face; meteors were considered bad omens and thought to result
from the sun sucking up poisonous vapors from the earth   297 **portend** foretell
298 **Hot . . . purses** drunkenness and poverty

BARDOLPH   Choler, my lord, if rightly taken.

300   PRINCE HENRY   No, if rightly taken, halter.

Enter Falstaff

Here comes lean Jack, here comes bare-bone.— How now, my sweet creature of bombast? How long is't ago, Jack, since thou saw'st thine own knee?

FALSTAFF   My own knee? When I was about thy years, Hal, I
305   was not an eagle's talon in the waist. I could have crept into any alderman's thumb-ring. A plague of sighing and grief! It blows a man up like a bladder. There's villainous news abroad: here was Sir John Braby from your father; you must go to the court in the morning. That same mad fellow of the
310   north, Percy, and he of Wales that gave Amamon the bastinado and made Lucifer cuckold and swore the devil his true liegeman upon the cross of a Welsh hook — what a plague call you him?

POINS   O, Glendower.

315   FALSTAFF   Owen, Owen the same, and his son-in-law Mortimer, and old Northumberland, and that sprightly Scot of Scots, Douglas, that runs o'horseback up a hill perpendicular—

PRINCE HENRY   He that rides at high speed and with a pistol kills a sparrow flying.

320   FALSTAFF   You have hit it.

PRINCE HENRY   So did he never the sparrow.

FALSTAFF   Well, that rascal hath good mettle in him. He will not run.

---

299 **Choler** anger (choler was one of the four bodily "humors" governing the disposition)
rightly taken correctly understood (the prince shifts the sense to "justly arrested")   300 **halter**
a noose (Hal puns on **choler**/collar)   302 **bombast** padding/high-flown language
305 **an . . . in** the width of an eagle's claw around   306 **alderman's thumb-ring** seal ring
often worn by wealthy citizens on the thumb   310 **Percy** i.e. Hotspur   **he of Wales** i.e.
Glendower   **Amamon** name of a demon   311 **bastinado** beating with a stick   **Lucifer** the
devil   **cuckold** man with an unfaithful wife   **swore . . . liegeman** made the devil swear to be
his true servant   312 **Welsh hook** hooked staff used as a weapon and lacking the cross shape
of a sword (on which oaths were customarily sworn)   **what a plague** intensified form of
"what"   320 **hit it** got it right (the prince plays on the literal sense)   322 **mettle** spirit (plays
on the sense of "metal," i.e. not fluid and liable to **run**)   323 **run** flee (plays on sense of "melt")

PRINCE HENRY   Why, what a rascal art thou then, to praise him
325   so for running?

FALSTAFF   A-horseback, ye cuckoo, but afoot he will not budge
a foot.

PRINCE HENRY   Yes, Jack, upon instinct.

FALSTAFF   I grant ye, upon instinct. Well, he is there too, and
330   one Mordake, and a thousand blue-caps more. Worcester is
stolen away by night. Thy father's beard is turned white with
the news; you may buy land now as cheap as stinking
mackerel.

PRINCE HENRY   Then 'tis like, if there come a hot sun and this
335   civil buffeting hold, we shall buy maidenheads as they buy
hob-nails, by the hundreds.

FALSTAFF   By the mass, lad, thou say'st true. It is like we shall
have good trading that way. But tell me, Hal, art not thou
horrible afeard? Thou being heir apparent, could the world
340   pick thee out three such enemies again as that fiend
Douglas, that spirit Percy, and that devil Glendower? Art not
thou horrible afraid? Doth not thy blood thrill at it?

PRINCE HENRY   Not a whit, I lack some of thy instinct.

FALSTAFF   Well, thou wilt be horrible chid tomorrow when
345   thou comest to thy father: if thou do love me, practise an
answer.

PRINCE HENRY   Do thou stand for my father, and examine me
upon the particulars of my life.

FALSTAFF   Shall I? Content. This chair shall be my state, this
350   dagger my sceptre and this cushion my crown.

---

325 **running** i.e. speeding   326 **cuckoo** i.e. mindless repeater of words   330 **blue-caps**
Scottish soldiers, who wore blue hats   332 **you . . . mackerel** i.e. for very little indeed—
mackerel was a cheap fish even when fresh; perhaps land was being sold off to raise money for
war or because of general economic anxiety about conflict (**mackerel** plays on the sense of
"pimp/whore")   334 **like** likely   **hot** plays on angry/lecherous   335 **buffeting hold** strife
continues   **maidenheads** virginities   **as . . . hundreds** i.e. as cheaply as nails for boots,
suggesting that in troubled times women will be raped or forced to sell themselves
338 **trading** commerce/prostitution/sex   341 **spirit** devil (though the word also has
connotations of "courage")   342 **thrill** tremble/go cold   344 **chid** scolded   347 **stand for**
stand in for, play the part of   348 **particulars** details   349 **Content** I'm content, very well

PRINCE HENRY   Thy state is taken for a joint-stool, thy golden sceptre for a leaden dagger, and thy precious rich crown for a pitiful bald crown.

FALSTAFF   Well, an the fire of grace be not quite out of thee,
355   now shalt thou be moved. Give me a cup of sack to make mine eyes look red, that it may be thought I have wept, for I must speak in passion, and I will do it in King Cambyses' vein.

PRINCE HENRY   Well, here is my leg.   *He bows or kneels*

360   FALSTAFF   And here is my speech. Stand aside, nobility.

HOSTESS QUICKLY   This is excellent sport, i'faith!

FALSTAFF   Weep not, sweet queen, for trickling tears are vain.

HOSTESS QUICKLY   O, the father, how he holds his countenance!

FALSTAFF   For God's sake, lords, convey my tristful queen,
365   For tears do stop the flood-gates of her eyes.

HOSTESS QUICKLY   O, rare, he doth it as like one of these harlotry players as ever I see!

FALSTAFF   Peace, good pint-pot, peace, good   *↓Quickly may exit,*
tickle-brain.— Harry, I do not only marvel   *perhaps escorted*
370   where thou spendest thy time, but also how   *by Bardolph↓*
thou art accompanied, for though the camomile, the more it is trodden the faster it grows, yet youth, the more it is wasted the sooner it wears. Thou art my son, I have partly thy mother's word, partly my opinion, but chiefly a villainous
375   trick of thine eye and a foolish hanging of thy nether lip that

351 **state** throne   **joint-stool** low stool made by a joiner ("I took you for a joint stool" was a way of mockingly apologizing for ignoring someone)   353 **crown** head   354 **fire of grace** effects of divine grace   355 **moved** affected emotionally, stirred   357 **King Cambyses' vein** ranting style; Cambyses was the tyrant in Thomas Preston's *Life of Cambyses, King of Persia* (1569)   360 **Stand aside, nobility** presumably those in the tavern are being asked to clear a space   362 **Weep . . . vain** Falstaff addresses Mistress Quickly, who is presumably weeping from merriment (puns on "quean," i.e. harlot, whore)   363 **O, the father** i.e. in God's name; or refers to Falstaff acting the part of the prince's father   **holds his countenance** keeps a straight face, remains in character   364 **convey** take away/escort (to a seat)   **tristful** sorrowful   365 **stop** fill up   366 **rare** marvelous   **harlotry players** knavish actors 368 **pint-pot** Falstaff addresses Mistress Quickly with a nickname for one who sells beer 369 **tickle-brain** potent liquor (here, one who sells it)   371 **camomile** daisy-like plant with medicinal qualities; it grows rapidly, proverbially more so when trodden on   375 **trick** habit, feature   **foolish . . . lip** way of hanging your lower lip, regarded as a sign of loose living **foolish** affected/idiotic/lecherous

doth warrant me. If then thou be son to me, here lieth the
point: why, being son to me, art thou so pointed at? Shall the
blessed sun of heaven prove a micher and eat blackberries?
A question not to be asked. Shall the son of England prove a
380 thief and take purses? A question to be asked. There is a
thing, Harry, which thou hast often heard of and it is known
to many in our land by the name of pitch: this pitch, as
ancient writers do report, doth defile; so doth the company
thou keepest. For, Harry, now I do not speak to thee in drink
385 but in tears: not in pleasure but in passion: not in words only,
but in woes also. And yet there is a virtuous man whom I
have often noted in thy company, but I know not his name.

PRINCE HENRY   What manner of man, an it like your majesty?

FALSTAFF   A goodly portly man, i'faith, and a corpulent: of a
390 cheerful look, a pleasing eye and a most noble carriage, and
as I think, his age some fifty, or, by'r lady, inclining to
threescore; and now I remember me, his name is Falstaff. If
that man should be lewdly given, he deceives me; for, Harry,
I see virtue in his looks. If then the tree may be known by the
395 fruit, as the fruit by the tree, then peremptorily I speak it,
there is virtue in that Falstaff: him keep with, the rest banish.
And tell me now, thou naughty varlet, tell me, where hast
thou been this month?

PRINCE HENRY   Dost thou speak like a king? Do thou stand for
400 me, and I'll play my father.

FALSTAFF   Depose me? If thou dost it half so gravely, so
majestically, both in word and matter, hang me up by the
heels for a rabbit-sucker or a poulter's hare.

PRINCE HENRY   Well, here I am set.

376 warrant assure   377 pointed at i.e. gossiped about/mocked   378 sun puns on "son"
micher truant/loiterer/petty thief   382 pitch black tar-like substance   383 defile stain,
corrupt; Falstaff paraphrases Ecclesiastes 13:1: "Whoso toucheth pitch shall be defiled"
385 passion sincere emotion, distress   388 an it like if it please   389 portly dignified/fat
corpulent solid, well-built/fat   390 noble carriage dignified bearing   392 threescore sixty
393 lewdly given wickedly, lasciviously inclined   395 peremptorily determinedly
397 naughty wicked   403 rabbit-sucker unweaned baby rabbit   poulter's hare hare
hanging up in a poulterer's shop (which sold fowl and game)   404 set seated (on the mock
throne)

405 FALSTAFF   And here I stand. Judge, my masters.

PRINCE HENRY   Now, Harry, whence come you?

FALSTAFF   My noble lord, from Eastcheap.

PRINCE HENRY   The complaints I hear of thee are grievous.

FALSTAFF   I'faith, my lord, they are false. — Nay, I'll tickle ye
410   for a young prince.

PRINCE HENRY   Swearest thou, ungracious boy? Henceforth ne'er
look on me. Thou art violently carried away from grace: there
is a devil haunts thee in the likeness of a fat old man; a
tun of man is thy companion. Why dost thou converse with
415   that trunk of humours, that bolting-hutch of beastliness, that
swollen parcel of dropsies, that huge bombard of sack, that
stuffed cloak-bag of guts, that roasted Manningtree ox with
the pudding in his belly, that reverend Vice, that grey Iniquity,
that father Ruffian, that Vanity in years? Wherein is he good,
420   but to taste sack and drink it? Wherein neat and cleanly, but
to carve a capon and eat it? Wherein cunning, but in craft?
Wherein crafty, but in villainy? Wherein villainous, but in all
things? Wherein worthy, but in nothing?

FALSTAFF   I would your grace would take me with you: whom
425   means your grace?

PRINCE HENRY   That villainous abominable misleader of youth,
Falstaff, that old white-bearded Satan.

FALSTAFF   My lord, the man I know.

PRINCE HENRY   I know thou dost.

---

405 Judge, my masters the tavern audience must decide who is the more kingly   409 tickle
ye amuse you in the role of   411 ungracious without grace, blasphemous   414 tun large
barrel especially for wine or beer/ton weight   converse associate   415 trunk container/body
humours diseases/fluids that determine the disposition: blood, bile, choler, phlegm   bolting-
hutch large bin used for sifting grain   416 dropsies diseases which made the body swell with
an accumulation of fluid   bombard a leather wine jug   417 cloak-bag large bag for
carrying clothes   Manningtree Essex town with a well-known fair and cattle market   418
pudding stuffing/sausage   reverend worthy of respect   Vice comic character in medieval
morality plays who tempted the youthful hero   grey gray-haired   Iniquity
sinfulness/allegorical name for morality play character   419 father i.e. elderly   Vanity vain,
proud, foolish, worthless character   in years i.e. advanced in years, aged   Wherein . . . good
what is he good for   420 neat and cleanly refined and skillful   421 cunning knowledgeable,
skillful   craft deceit   422 crafty skillful   424 take . . . you enable me to follow you, help me
to understand   428 the . . . know i.e. I recognize the man but not the description

HENRY IV PART I • 2.4 55

430 FALSTAFF   But to say I know more harm in him than in myself, were to say more than I know. That he is old, the more the pity, his white hairs do witness it. But that he is, saving your reverence, a whoremaster, that I utterly deny. If sack and sugar be a fault, heaven help the wicked: if to be old and

435 merry be a sin, then many an old host that I know is damned: if to be fat be to be hated, then Pharaoh's lean kine are to be loved. No, my good lord, banish Peto, banish Bardolph, banish Poins, but for sweet Jack Falstaff, kind Jack Falstaff, true Jack Falstaff, valiant Jack Falstaff, and therefore

440 more valiant, being, as he is old Jack Falstaff, banish not him thy Harry's company, banish not him thy Harry's company: banish plump Jack, and banish all the world.

PRINCE HENRY   I do, I will.   *Knocking*

Enter Bardolph, running

BARDOLPH   O, my lord, my lord! The sheriff with a most

445 monstrous watch is at the door.

FALSTAFF   Out, you rogue!— Play out the play: I have much to say in the behalf of that Falstaff.

Enter the Hostess [Quickly]

HOSTESS QUICKLY   O, my lord, my lord!

PRINCE HENRY   Heigh, heigh! The devil rides upon a fiddlestick.

450 What's the matter?

HOSTESS QUICKLY   The sheriff and all the watch are at the door: they are come to search the house. Shall I let them in?

FALSTAFF   Dost thou hear, Hal? Never call a true piece of gold a counterfeit: thou art essentially made, without seeming so.

---

432 **saving your reverence** begging your pardon/if you will excuse my language
433 **whoremaster** user of whores, i.e. a wicked man   435 **host** innkeeper, pub landlord
436 **Pharaoh's lean kine** biblical reference to Pharaoh's dream in which the seven lean **kine** (cattle) devour the seven fat kine, foretelling famine to come (Genesis 41:1–31)
445 **monstrous** unnaturally large   **watch** group of citizens responsible for keeping order in the streets at night   449 **The . . . fiddlestick** i.e. here's a fine commotion (proverbial)
453 **Never . . . counterfeit** a much debated line; Falstaff seems to be referring to himself as genuine gold (i.e. loyal, worthy), despite the prince's earlier accusations of cowardice and hypocrisy   454 **thou . . . so** another obscure line; probably either "you are basically true (**essentially made**) to your friends, even if some of your recent declarations seem to contradict this" or "you are fundamentally a deceptive playactor (**made**), despite seeming to be loyal"; some editors adopt a later reading, and substitute "mad" for "made"

455 PRINCE HENRY   And thou a natural coward, without instinct.

FALSTAFF   I deny your major. If you will deny the sheriff, so: if
not, let him enter: if I become not a cart as well as another
man, a plague on my bringing up! I hope I shall as soon be
strangled with a halter as another.

460 PRINCE HENRY   Go, hide thee behind the arras. The rest walk up
above. Now, my masters, for a true face and good conscience.

FALSTAFF   Both which I have had: but their date   *Falstaff hides*
is out, and therefore I'll hide me.   *behind the arras*

PRINCE HENRY   Call in the sheriff.

Exeunt [all except Prince Henry and Peto]

Enter Sheriff and the Carrier

465 Now, master sheriff, what is your will with me?

SHERIFF   First, pardon me, my lord. A hue and cry
Hath followed certain men unto this house.

PRINCE HENRY   What men?

SHERIFF   One of them is well known, my gracious lord,
470 A gross fat man.

CARRIER   As fat as butter.

PRINCE HENRY   The man, I do assure you, is not here,
For I myself at this time have employed him.
And, sheriff, I will engage my word to thee
475 That I will, by tomorrow dinnertime,
Send him to answer thee, or any man,
For anything he shall be charged withal:
And so let me entreat you leave the house.

SHERIFF   I will, my lord. There are two gentlemen
480 Have in this robbery lost three hundred marks.

---

456 deny your major reject your main premise   **deny the** refuse entrance to the   **so** so be it
457 become suit, befit   **cart** wagon used to transport the condemned man to the gallows
458 bringing up upbringing, breeding (which entitled him, as a knight, to death by
beheading)/being brought before the authorities/being hanged   **soon** willingly/quickly
460 arras large tapestry wall hanging (hung so that there was space behind it to hide)   **walk
up above** go upstairs   **461 true** honest   **462 date is out** lease has expired, i.e. it's too late for
that   **466 hue and cry** the noise and shouting of citizens in pursuit of a felon   **474 engage**
pledge   **475 dinnertime** i.e. midday   **476 answer thee** respond to your charges, account for
himself to you   **477 withal** with

PRINCE HENRY   It may be so: if he have robbed these men,
He shall be answerable, and so farewell.

SHERIFF   Goodnight, my noble lord.

PRINCE HENRY   I think it is good morrow, is it not?

485 SHERIFF   Indeed, my lord, I think it be two o'clock.

Exeunt [Sheriff and Carrier]

PRINCE HENRY   This oily rascal is known as well as Paul's. Go,
call him forth.   *To Peto*

PETO   Falstaff! Fast asleep behind the arras, and snorting
like a horse.

490 PRINCE HENRY   Hark, how hard he fetches breath. Search his
pockets.

He searcheth his pockets, and findeth certain papers
What hast thou found?

PETO   Nothing but papers, my lord.

PRINCE HENRY   Let's see, what be they? Read them.

495 PETO   'Item, A capon, 2s 2d. *Item*, Sauce, 4d.   *Reads*
Item, Sack, two gallons, 5s 8d. *Item*, Anchovies and sack
after supper, 2s 6d. *Item*, Bread, ob.'

PRINCE HENRY   O, monstrous! But one halfpenny-worth of bread
to this intolerable deal of sack? What there is else, keep close,
500 we'll read it at more advantage. There let him sleep till day.
I'll to the court in the morning. We must all to the wars, and
thy place shall be honourable. I'll procure this fat rogue a
charge of foot, and I know his death will be a march of
twelvescore. The money shall be paid back again with
505 advantage. Be with me betimes in the morning, and so, good
morrow, Peto.

PETO   Good morrow, good my lord.   *Exeunt*

482 answerable held responsible   484 morrow morning   486 oily greasy/cunning, slippery
Paul's St. Paul's Cathedral, the tallest landmark in London at this time   495 2s 2d two
shillings and two pence   497 ob abbreviation of "obolus," i.e. halfpenny   498 But merely
499 intolerable deal excessive quantity   close hidden, safe   500 advantage a better
opportunity   503 charge of foot command of an infantry company   504 twelvescore i.e.
240 yards   money i.e. that was stolen   505 advantage interest   betimes early

Act 3 Scene 1

running scene 8

Enter Hotspur, Worcester, Lord Mortimer and Owen Glendower

MORTIMER   These promises are fair, the parties sure,

And our induction full of prosperous hope.

HOTSPUR   Lord Mortimer, and cousin Glendower,

Will you sit down?

5   And uncle Worcester — a plague upon it,

I have forgot the map!

GLENDOWER   No, here it is.   *Shows a map*

Sit, cousin Percy, sit, good cousin Hotspur —

For by that name as oft as Lancaster

10   Doth speak of you, his cheeks look pale and with

A rising sigh he wisheth you in heaven.

HOTSPUR   And you in hell, as oft as he hears Owen Glendower

spoke of.

GLENDOWER   I cannot blame him: at my nativity

15   The front of heaven was full of fiery shapes,

Of burning cressets, and at my birth

The frame and foundation of the earth

Shaked like a coward.

HOTSPUR   Why, so it would have done at the same season, if

20   your mother's cat had but kittened, though yourself had

never been born.

GLENDOWER   I say the earth did shake when I was born.

HOTSPUR   And I say the earth was not of my mind,

If you suppose as fearing you it shook.

25   GLENDOWER   The heavens were all on fire, the earth did tremble.

HOTSPUR   O, then the earth shook to see the heavens on fire,

And not in fear of your nativity.

Diseasèd nature oftentimes breaks forth

3.1 *Location: unspecified; probably in Glendower's house*   **1 promises** i.e. of support
sure secure, reliable   **2 induction** beginning   **prosperous hope** hope of prospering
9 Lancaster i.e. King Henry; Glendower deliberately refers to him by his former title (Duke of
Lancaster)   **15 front** forehead, face   **16 cressets** torches (literally fires burning in iron
baskets), hence meteors (signs of ill omen)   **24 as fearing you** because it feared you

In strange eruptions; and the teeming earth
30 Is with a kind of colic pinched and vexed
By the imprisoning of unruly wind
Within her womb, which, for enlargement striving,
Shakes the old beldam earth and tumbles down
Steeples and moss-grown towers. At your birth
35 Our grandam earth, having this distemperature,
In passion shook.

GLENDOWER   Cousin, of many men
I do not bear these crossings. Give me leave
To tell you once again that at my birth
40 The front of heaven was full of fiery shapes,
The goats ran from the mountains, and the herds
Were strangely clamorous to the frighted fields.
These signs have marked me extraordinary,
And all the courses of my life do show
45 I am not in the roll of common men.
Where is the living, clipped in with the sea
That chides the banks of England, Scotland and Wales,
Which calls me pupil, or hath read to me?
And bring him out that is but woman's son
50 Can trace me in the tedious ways of art
And hold me pace in deep experiments.

HOTSPUR   I think there's no man speaks better Welsh.
I'll to dinner.

MORTIMER   Peace, cousin Percy, you will make him mad.
55 GLENDOWER   I can call spirits from the vasty deep.

---

29 **eruptions** outbreaks of disease/natural or meteorological disturbances   **teeming** fertile, breeding   30 **colic** severe stomach pains   32 **womb** bowels/stomach   **enlargement** release   33 **beldam** old woman, grandmother   34 **moss-grown** overgrown with moss, old   35 **grandam** grandmother   **distemperature** bodily disturbance   36 **passion** suffering, bodily affliction   38 **crossings** contradictions   42 **clamorous** noisy   **frighted fields** fields full of fear   43 **marked me** marked me out as   44 **courses** events   45 **roll** list   46 **the living** any person living   **clipped in with** surrounded by   47 **chides** beats, contends with   48 **read to** i.e. instructed, educated   50 **trace** follow   **tedious** time-consuming, lengthy, complex   **art** scholarship/magic, occult arts   51 **hold me pace** keep up with me   **deep experiments** profound, learned investigations   52 **Welsh** i.e. nonsense, gibberish   55 **call** summon, invoke (Hotspur shifts the sense to "call out to")   **vasty deep** immense abyss

HOTSPUR   Why, so can I, or so can any man.
But will they come when you do call for them?

GLENDOWER   Why, I can teach thee, cousin, to command the
devil.

HOTSPUR   And I can teach thee, cousin, to shame the devil
60   By telling truth: tell truth and shame the devil.
If thou have power to raise him, bring him hither,
And I'll be sworn I have power to shame him hence.
O, while you live, tell truth and shame the devil!

MORTIMER   Come, come, no more of this unprofitable chat.

65   GLENDOWER   Three times hath Henry Bullingbrook made head
Against my power: thrice from the banks of Wye
And sandy-bottomed Severn have I sent him
Bootless home and weather-beaten back.

HOTSPUR   Home without boots, and in foul weather too!
70   How scapes he agues, in the devil's name?

GLENDOWER   Come, here's the map: shall we divide our right
According to our threefold order ta'en?

MORTIMER   The archdeacon hath divided it
Into three limits very equally:
75   England, from Trent and Severn hitherto,
By south and east is to my part assigned:
All westward, Wales beyond the Severn shore,
And all the fertile land within that bound,
To Owen Glendower: and, dear coz, to you
80   The remnant northward, lying off from Trent.
And our indentures tripartite are drawn,
Which being sealèd interchangeably —
A business that this night may execute—

---

60 tell . . . devil proverbial   65 made head advanced   66 power army   Wye river on the
Welsh-English border   68 Bootless unsuccessful, without gain (Hotspur plays on the literal
sense)   70 agues violent fevers characterized by shaking   71 right just claim (to land)
72 threefold order ta'en three-way agreement   73 archdeacon not identified; chronicle
sources suggest Archdeacon of Bangor   74 limits regions   75 Trent . . . hitherto the rivers
Trent and Severn up to this point (presumably Mortimer indicates the map)   81 indentures
tripartite contracts drawn up in triplicate   drawn drawn up   82 sealèd interchangeably
each party has a copy signed and sealed by all   83 this . . . execute can be done tonight

Tomorrow, cousin Percy, you and I
85   And my good lord of Worcester will set forth
To meet your father and the Scottish power,
As is appointed us, at Shrewsbury.
My father Glendower is not ready yet,
Nor shall we need his help these fourteen days.—
90   Within that space you may have drawn together   *To Glendower*
Your tenants, friends and neighbouring gentlemen.
GLENDOWER   A shorter time shall send me to you, lords.
And in my conduct shall your ladies come,
From whom you now must steal and take no leave,
95   For there will be a world of water shed
Upon the parting of your wives and you.
HOTSPUR   Methinks my moiety, north from   *Looks at map*
        Burton here,
In quantity equals not one of yours:
See how this river comes me cranking in,
100   And cuts me from the best of all my land
A huge half-moon, a monstrous cantle out.
I'll have the current in this place dammed up,
And here the smug and silver Trent shall run
In a new channel, fair and evenly.
105   It shall not wind with such a deep indent,
To rob me of so rich a bottom here.
GLENDOWER   Not wind? It shall, it must. You see it doth.
MORTIMER   Yea, but
Mark how he bears his course, and runs me up
110   With like advantage on the other side,

87 appointed agreed by   Shrewsbury town on the Welsh-English border   88 father father-
in-law   90 space period of time   93 in my conduct escorted by me   94 steal slip away
95 a . . . water i.e. many tears   97 moiety share, portion   Burton Derbyshire town of
Burton-upon-Trent   99 comes . . . in twists sharply into my section; Hotspur objects that the
river turns north from Burton and deprives him of the fertile lands of Lincolnshire and part of
Nottinghamshire   101 cantle out corner or portion cut off   103 smug smooth   105 deep
indent sharp angled section, indentation   106 bottom river valley   109 he it (the river Trent)
runs me runs   110 like advantage the same effect

Gelding the opposèd continent as much
As on the other side it takes from you.

WORCESTER   Yea, but a little charge will trench him here
And on this north side win this cape of land,

115   And then he runs straight and even.

HOTSPUR   I'll have it so. A little charge will do it.

GLENDOWER   I'll not have it altered.

HOTSPUR   Will not you?

GLENDOWER   No, nor you shall not.

120   HOTSPUR   Who shall say me nay?

GLENDOWER   Why, that will I.

HOTSPUR   Let me not understand you, then. Speak it in Welsh.

GLENDOWER   I can speak English, lord, as well as you,
For I was trained up in the English court;

125   Where, being but young, I framed to the harp
Many an English ditty lovely well
And gave the tongue a helpful ornament;
A virtue that was never seen in you.

HOTSPUR   Marry,

130   And I am glad of it with all my heart.
I had rather be a kitten and cry mew
Than one of these same metre ballad-mongers.
I had rather hear a brazen candlestick turned,
Or a dry wheel grate on the axle-tree,

135   And that would set my teeth nothing on edge,
Nothing so much as mincing poetry:
'Tis like the forced gait of a shuffling nag.

---

111 Gelding depriving, cutting (land) off from   **opposèd continent** land on the opposite side
113 charge cost/gunpowder used in blasting   **trench** create a trench or channel
114 cape spur, projecting piece   **122 Let . . . Welsh** i.e. say it in Welsh (which I don't
understand) so that I won't understand (and take offense)   **125 being but young** since I was
young at the time   **framed to** composed for   **126 ditty** poem, ballad   **lovely** beautifully
127 gave . . . ornament adorned the English language with music and poetry/decorated the
words with the music/improved the sound of the language with my Welsh accent   **128 virtue**
accomplishment, skill   **132 metre ballad-mongers** sellers of predictably rhymed popular
ballads   **133 brazen** brass   **turned** i.e. on a lathe (which made an unpleasant grating noise)
134 dry unoiled   **axle-tree** axle   **136 Nothing . . . as** nothing like as much as   **mincing**
affectedly dainty   **137 nag** feeble old horse

GLENDOWER   Come, you shall have Trent turned.

HOTSPUR   I do not care: I'll give thrice so much land
140   To any well-deserving friend;
But in the way of bargain, mark ye me,
I'll cavil on the ninth part of a hair.
Are the indentures drawn? Shall we be gone?

GLENDOWER   The moon shines fair, you may away by night.
145   I'll haste the writer and withal
Break with your wives of your departure hence.
I am afraid my daughter will run mad,
So much she doteth on her Mortimer.   *Exit*

MORTIMER   Fie, cousin Percy, how you cross my father!
150   HOTSPUR   I cannot choose: sometime he angers me
With telling me of the mouldwarp and the ant,
Of the dreamer Merlin and his prophecies,
And of a dragon and a finless fish,
A clip-winged griffin and a moulten raven,
155   A couching lion and a ramping cat,
And such a deal of skimble-skamble stuff
As puts me from my faith. I tell you what,
He held me last night at least nine hours
In reck'ning up the several devils' names
160   That were his lackeys: I cried 'Hum', and 'Well, go to',
But marked him not a word. O, he is as tedious
As a tired horse, a railing wife,

141 **in . . . bargain** when it comes to bargaining   142 **cavil on** dispute insistently over
143 **drawn** drawn up   145 **haste the writer** hurry the writer of the indentures   **withal** at the
same time   146 **Break with** speak to, inform   148 **doteth on** loves very dearly, is infatuated
with   149 **cross** antagonize   150 **choose** help it   151 **mouldwarp** mole; according to
Holinshed's *Chronicles* the division of the map was arranged in accordance with a prophecy
that imaged Henry IV as a mole and the others as dragon, lion, and wolf   152 **dreamer**
visionary   **Merlin** wizard and prophet at the legendary court of King Arthur   154 **clip-
winged** with its wings clipped, i.e. prevented from flying   **griffin** mythical beast, half lion,
half eagle   **moulten** having moulted, lost its feathers   155 **couching** lying down (form of
"couchant," a heraldic term)   **ramping** rearing, standing on its hind legs (form of "rampant,"
a heraldic term)   156 **skimble-skamble** incoherent, nonsensical   157 **puts . . . faith** makes
me forget or disbelieve my religion   159 **reck'ning up** listing, recounting   **several** various
160 **lackeys** servants, followers   **'Hum'** noncommittal sound expressing agreement
'Well, go to' i.e. you don't say, well I never   161 **marked him** took no notice of   162 **railing**
complaining, scolding

Worse than a smoky house. I had rather live
With cheese and garlic in a windmill far,
165 Than feed on cates and have him talk to me
In any summer-house in Christendom.

MORTIMER   In faith, he was a worthy gentleman,
Exceeding well read, and profited
In strange concealments, valiant as a lion
170 And wondrous affable and as bountiful
As mines of India. Shall I tell you, cousin?
He holds your temper in a high respect
And curbs himself even of his natural scope
When you do cross his humour — 'faith, he does.
175 I warrant you, that man is not alive
Might so have tempted him as you have done,
Without the taste of danger and reproof:
But do not use it oft, let me entreat you.

WORCESTER   In faith, my lord, you are too wilful-blame,   *To Hotspur*
180 And since your coming hither have done enough
To put him quite besides his patience.
You must needs learn, lord, to amend this fault:
Though sometimes it show greatness, courage, blood —
And that's the dearest grace it renders you —
185 Yet oftentimes it doth present harsh rage,
Defect of manners, want of government,
Pride, haughtiness, opinion and disdain,
The least of which haunting a nobleman
Loseth men's hearts and leaves behind a stain

---

164 cheese . . . windmill i.e. poor food in uncomfortable, noisy accommodation
165 cates delicacies   166 summer-house rich man's country house   167 In faith truly
168 profited . . . concealments proficient in secret arts   171 India i.e. the West Indies
172 temper temperament, character   173 scope freedom of expression   174 do . . . humour
antagonize him   176 tempted provoked   177 taste . . . reproof experiencing harm and
rebuke   178 use it oft do it often   179 wilful-blame blameworthy for being obstinately self-
willed   181 besides out of   182 must needs must   183 show is evidence of   blood spirit
184 dearest grace most valuable advantage   renders offers   185 present represent,
demonstrate   186 want of government lack of self-control   187 opinion arrogance, conceit
188 haunting being associated with   189 Loseth causes him to lose

190   Upon the beauty of all parts besides,
        Beguiling them of commendation.
    HOTSPUR   Well, I am schooled. Good manners be your speed!
        Here come our wives, and let us take our leave.
    Enter Glendower with the Ladies
    MORTIMER   This is the deadly spite that angers me:
195   My wife can speak no English, I no Welsh.
    GLENDOWER   My daughter weeps. She'll not part with you,
        She'll be a soldier too, she'll to the wars.
    MORTIMER   Good father, tell her that she and my aunt Percy
        Shall follow in your conduct speedily.
    Glendower speaks to her in Welsh, and she answers him in the same
200   GLENDOWER   She is desperate here: a peevish self-willed harlotry,
        One that no persuasion can do good upon.
                                    The Lady speaks in Welsh
    MORTIMER   I understand thy looks: that pretty Welsh
        Which thou pour'st down from these swelling heavens
        I am too perfect in, and, but for shame,
205   In such a parley should I answer thee.
                              The Lady [speaks] again in Welsh
        I understand thy kisses and thou mine,
        And that's a feeling disputation.
        But I will never be a truant, love,
        Till I have learned thy language, for thy tongue
210   Makes Welsh as sweet as ditties highly penned,

190 **parts besides** other qualities   191 **Beguiling** depriving   192 **schooled**
instructed/admonished   **be your speed** bring you good fortune   194 **spite** vexation, regret
198 **aunt Percy** more confusion between the two Edmund Mortimers: Lady Percy (Hotspur's
wife) was in fact the sister of the Mortimer married to Glendower's daughter and aunt of the
younger man   199 **in your conduct** under your escort   200 **desperate here** recklessly
determined on this point (her decision not to leave Mortimer)   **peevish self-willed harlotry**
obstinate headstrong hussy   202 **pretty Welsh** i.e. her eloquent tears   203 **swelling heavens**
i.e. her eyes filled with tears   204 **too perfect** only too accomplished, fluent   205 **parley**
language, conversation (perhaps, picking up on **soldier**, with a sense of "military negotiation")
207 **feeling disputation** moving, heartfelt discussion/conversation conducted through touch
208 **truant** negligent student   210 **highly penned** elaborately composed

Sung by a fair queen in a summer's bow'r,
With ravishing division, to her lute.

GLENDOWER   Nay, if thou melt, then will she run mad.

The Lady speaks again in Welsh

MORTIMER   O, I am ignorance itself in this!

215   GLENDOWER   She bids you on the wanton rushes lay you down
And rest your gentle head upon her lap,
And she will sing the song that pleaseth you
And on your eyelids crown the god of sleep,
Charming your blood with pleasing heaviness,

220   Making such difference 'twixt wake and sleep
As is the difference betwixt day and night
The hour before the heavenly-harnessed team
Begins his golden progress in the east.

MORTIMER   With all my heart I'll sit and hear her sing:

225   By that time will our book, I think, be drawn.

GLENDOWER   Do so,
And those musicians that shall play to you
Hang in the air a thousand leagues from hence,
And straight they shall be here: sit, and attend.

230   HOTSPUR   Come, Kate, thou art perfect in lying down: come,
quick, quick, that I may lay my head in thy lap.

LADY PERCY   Go, ye giddy goose.   *The music plays*

HOTSPUR   Now I perceive the devil understands Welsh, and 'tis
no marvel he is so humorous. By'r lady, he's a good musician.

235   LADY PERCY   Then would you be nothing but musical, for you are
altogether governed by humours. Lie still, ye thief, and hear
the lady sing in Welsh.

---

212 **division** ornamentation, variation (specifically, passage in which a series of short notes
elaborates on a longer passage)   213 **melt** give way to your feelings, weep   214 **this** i.e. Welsh
215 **wanton rushes** luxuriant floor covering of reeds   218 **crown** give power to
219 **heaviness** drowsiness   222 **heavenly-harnessed team** horses that drew the sun god's
chariot   223 **progress** course/royal journey   225 **book** indentures, legal contracts   **drawn**
drawn up   228 **Hang . . . air** i.e. they're spirits   **thousand leagues** three thousand miles
229 **straight** straightaway   230 **perfect in** expert at, practiced at   **lying down** with sexual
connotations (continued in **lap**)   233 **devil understands Welsh** i.e. because the supposed
spirits have answered Glendower's call and music is playing   234 **humorous** capricious,
whimsical   236 **humours** moods, whims (thought to be generated by bodily fluids or
"humors")

HOTSPUR   I had rather hear Lady, my brach, howl in Irish.

LADY PERCY   Wouldst have thy head broken?

240   HOTSPUR   No.

LADY PERCY   Then be still.

HOTSPUR   Neither, 'tis a woman's fault.

LADY PERCY   Now God help thee!

HOTSPUR   To the Welsh lady's bed.

245   LADY PERCY   What's that?

HOTSPUR   Peace, she sings.

Here the Lady sings a Welsh song

HOTSPUR   Come, I'll have your song too.   *To Lady Percy*

LADY PERCY   Not mine, in good sooth.

HOTSPUR   Not yours, in good sooth?

250   You swear like a comfit-maker's wife.
               'Not you, in good sooth', and 'As true as I live',
               And 'As God shall mend me' and 'As sure as day!'
               And givest such sarcenet surety for thy oaths,
               As if thou never walk'st further than Finsbury.

255   Swear me, Kate, like a lady as thou art,
               A good mouth-filling oath, and leave 'in sooth',
               And such protest of pepper-gingerbread,
               To velvet-guards and Sunday-citizens.
               Come, sing.

260   LADY PERCY   I will not sing.

HOTSPUR   'Tis the next way to turn tailor, or be red-breast
           teacher. An the indentures be drawn, I'll away within these
           two hours, and so, come in when ye will.   *Exit*

---

238 brach bitch, female dog (called **Lady**)   **Irish** designed as insult here; may possibly suggest
his bitch's breed   **239 broken** beaten, grazed   **241 still** quiet, calm   **242 Neither** i.e. I won't
do that either   **woman's fault** i.e. being silent (or sexually passive) is a woman's trait; may
play on "broken head" as "broken maidenhead" (lost virginity), perhaps with **fault** quibbling
on its sense of "vagina/sinful sexual yielding"   **248 sooth** truth   **250 comfit-maker's**
confectioner's; Hotspur makes fun of a genteel oath and offers several more   **253 sarcenet
surety** flimsy assurance   **sarcenet** fine silken cloth   **254 Finsbury** Finsbury Fields, popular
place of recreation just outside the city of London   **255 Swear me** swear/swear for me
257 protest of pepper-gingerbread i.e. mild oaths   **pepper-gingerbread** in which pepper was
partly substituted for ginger, making the gingerbread less spicy and pungent   **258 velvet-
guards** velvet trimmings on clothes, or those who wore them   **Sunday-citizens** those keeping
their best clothes for Sunday   **261 tailor** tailors were supposed to be enthusiastic singers
be red-breast teacher teach singing to robins (small red-breasted birds)

GLENDOWER   Come, come, Lord Mortimer, you are as slow

265   As hot Lord Percy is on fire to go.

By this our book is drawn, we'll but seal,

And then to horse immediately.

MORTIMER   With all my heart.   *Exeunt*

Act 3 Scene 2   *running scene 9*

Enter the King, Prince of Wales and others

KING HENRY IV   Lords, give us leave. The Prince of Wales and I

Must have some private conference. But be near at hand,

For we shall presently have need of you.   *Exeunt Lords*

I know not whether heaven will have it so,

5   For some displeasing service I have done,

That in his secret doom, out of my blood

He'll breed revengement and a scourge for me.

But thou dost in thy passages of life

Make me believe that thou art only marked

10   For the hot vengeance and the rod of heaven

To punish my mistreadings. Tell me else,

Could such inordinate and low desires,

Such poor, such bare, such lewd, such mean attempts,

Such barren pleasures, rude society,

15   As thou art matched withal and grafted to,

Accompany the greatness of thy blood

And hold their level with thy princely heart?

PRINCE HENRY   So please your majesty, I would I could

Quit all offences with as clear excuse

---

266 **this** this time   **but seal** just put our seals on the documents   **3.2** *Location: the royal
court*   1 **give us leave** please leave us alone   6 **doom** judgment   **blood** family, offspring
7 **scourge** punishment of divine origin/punishing whip   8 **passages** course through, way of
9 **only marked For** solely designated to be   10 **rod** i.e. of punishment   11 **mistreadings**
wrongful steps, sins   **else** how else   12 **inordinate** immoderate, disorderly   13 **bare**
wretched, paltry/undisguised   **lewd** vulgar, low   **attempts** undertakings   14 **rude society**
vulgar, uncivilized companionship   15 **withal** with   **grafted** united   17 **hold their level**
think themselves equal to   19 **Quit** acquit myself of   **clear** honest

20   As well as I am doubtless I can purge
      Myself of many I am charged withal:
      Yet such extenuation let me beg,
      As, in reproof of many tales devised,
      Which oft the ear of greatness needs must hear
25   By smiling pick-thanks and base news-mongers,
      I may, for some things true, wherein my youth
      Hath faulty wand'red and irregular,
      Find pardon on my true submission.

      KING HENRY IV   Heaven pardon thee! Yet let me wonder, Harry,
30   At thy affections, which do hold a wing
      Quite from the flight of all thy ancestors.
      Thy place in council thou hast rudely lost,
      Which by thy younger brother is supplied,
      And art almost an alien to the hearts
35   Of all the court and princes of my blood.
      The hope and expectation of thy time
      Is ruined, and the soul of every man
      Prophetically do forethink thy fall.
      Had I so lavish of my presence been,
40   So common-hackneyed in the eyes of men,
      So stale and cheap to vulgar company,
      Opinion, that did help me to the crown,
      Had still kept loyal to possession
      And left me in reputeless banishment,
45   A fellow of no mark nor likelihood.
      By being seldom seen, I could not stir

20 doubtless sure   23 reproof refutation, disproof   24 greatness the great, the high-ranking   25 pick-thanks flatterers and informers   news-mongers tellers of tales, gossips   26 things true genuine misdemeanors   27 faulty . . . irregular gone astray off the proper path   28 true submission honest admission   29 wonder express surprise   30 affections tastes, inclinations   hold a wing fly   32 rudely violently, in an uncivilized manner (according to an apocryphal tale, the prince was expelled from the King's Privy Council for hitting the Lord Chief Justice)   33 supplied filled   34 alien stranger   36 time youth, life   38 forethink expect/prophesy   40 common-hackneyed cheapened by habitual exposure (from "hackney," a horse for hire)   42 Opinion public opinion   43 Had . . . possession would have remained loyal to the holder of the crown (Richard II, deposed by Henry)   44 reputeless inglorious, shameful/anonymous, unacknowledged   45 mark significance   likelihood prospect of success

But like a comet I was wondered at,
That men would tell their children, 'This is he'.
Others would say, 'Where? Which is Bullingbrook?'
50   And then I stole all courtesy from heaven,
And dressed myself in such humility
That I did pluck allegiance from men's hearts,
Loud shouts and salutations from their mouths,
Even in the presence of the crownèd king.
55   Thus I did keep my person fresh and new;
My presence, like a robe pontifical,
Ne'er seen but wondered at: and so my state,
Seldom but sumptuous, showed like a feast
And won by rareness such solemnity.
60   The skipping king, he ambled up and down
With shallow jesters and rash bavin wits,
Soon kindled and soon burnt, carded his state,
Mingled his royalty with carping fools,
Had his great name profanèd with their scorns
65   And gave his countenance, against his name,
To laugh at gibing boys and stand the push
Of every beardless vain comparative;
Grew a companion to the common streets,
Enfeoffed himself to popularity,
70   That, being daily swallowed by men's eyes,
They surfeited with honey and began
To loathe the taste of sweetness, whereof a little

---

50 stole . . . heaven adopted a manner of heavenly graciousness   56 pontifical belonging to a
bishop   57 state magnificence, kingship   58 Seldom infrequently seen   feast special
occasion, celebration   59 solemnity ceremonious dignity   60 skipping frivolous   up and
down i.e. aimlessly   61 rash bavin quickly burned up   bavin brushwood or kindling soon
ignited and burned   62 carded his state destroyed his dignity, kingly status (to "card" is
either to mix or to comb impurities from wool)   63 carping chattering (Quarto has "capring,"
so most editors print "capering")   64 scorns foolishness, mockeries/contemptuous way of
speaking   65 against his name to the detriment of his royal reputation   66 gibing mocking,
taunting   stand the push expose himself to the proximity/mockery of   67 beardless vain
comparative immature, worthless maker of mocking comparisons   69 Enfeoffed committed,
bound (literally, to vow loyalty to a lord in return for land)   71 surfeited grew overindulged
and sick   72 loathe . . . sweetness i.e. they got sick of the sight of him

More than a little is by much too much.
So when he had occasion to be seen,
75   He was but as the cuckoo is in June,
Heard, not regarded, seen, but with such eyes
As, sick and blunted with community,
Afford no extraordinary gaze,
Such as is bent on sun-like majesty
80   When it shines seldom in admiring eyes.
But rather drowsed and hung their eyelids down,
Slept in his face and rendered such aspect
As cloudy men use to do to their adversaries,
Being with his presence glutted, gorged and full.
85   And in that very line, Harry, standest thou,
For thou hast lost thy princely privilege
With vile participation. Not an eye
But is a-weary of thy common sight,
Save mine, which hath desired to see thee more,
90   Which now doth that I would not have it do,
Make blind itself with foolish tenderness.

PRINCE HENRY   I shall hereafter, my thrice-gracious lord,
Be more myself.

KING HENRY IV   For all the world
95   As thou art to this hour was Richard then,
When I from France set foot at Ravenspurgh,
And even as I was then is Percy now.
Now, by my sceptre and my soul to boot,
He hath more worthy interest to the state
100   Than thou, the shadow of succession;
For of no right, nor colour like to right,

---

75 cuckoo . . . June i.e. commonplace by midsummer, not noticed any longer   77 community
familiarity   78 extraordinary gaze special notice   82 face i.e. presence   rendered such
aspect with such an expression   83 cloudy sullen, gloomy   use to habitually   85 line
category   87 vile participation associating with commoners and base, vulgar people
88 common widespread, public/cheap, vulgar   91 tenderness i.e. tears of affection
93 Be more myself act in a manner more befitting my position   94 For . . . world i.e. in every
way   99 He . . . state He (Percy) has a more honorable claim to the crown   100 shadow
of succession mere shadow of a proper heir   101 of having   colour like to semblance,
pretext of

He doth fill fields with harness in the realm,
Turns head against the lion's armèd jaws,
And, being no more in debt to years than thou,
105 Leads ancient lords and reverend bishops on
To bloody battles and to bruising arms.
What never-dying honour hath he got
Against renownèd Douglas, whose high deeds,
Whose hot incursions and great name in arms
110 Holds from all soldiers chief majority
And military title capital
Through all the kingdoms that acknowledge Christ!
Thrice hath the Hotspur, Mars in swaddling clothes,
This infant warrior, in his enterprises
115 Discomfited great Douglas, ta'en him once,
Enlargèd him and made a friend of him,
To fill the mouth of deep defiance up
And shake the peace and safety of our throne.
And what say you to this? Percy, Northumberland,
120 The archbishop's grace of York, Douglas, Mortimer,
Capitulate against us and are up.
But wherefore do I tell these news to thee?
Why, Harry, do I tell thee of my foes,
Which art my near'st and dearest enemy?
125 Thou that art like enough, through vassal fear,
Base inclination and the start of spleen,

---

102 **harness** armor, i.e. armed men   103 **Turns head** directs his attention/leads his army
lion's i.e. the king's (the lion is a traditional symbol of royalty)   104 **in . . . years** older
(historically Hotspur was actually twenty-three years older than the prince)   105 **ancient**
long-established   106 **bruising** damaging, crushing   108 **whose** i.e. Hotspur's   **high**
illustrious, noble   109 **hot incursions** fierce attacks   110 **chief . . . capital** military fame and
preeminence   113 **Mars** Roman god of war   **swaddling clothes** wrappings for babies (refers
to Hotspur's youth)   114 **enterprises** military undertakings   115 **Discomfited** defeated
ta'en him once captured him on one occasion   116 **Enlargèd** released   117 **fill . . . up**
complete the number of opponents/add to the roar of opposition   121 **Capitulate** have
formed a league, draw up agreements   **up** i.e. in arms   124 **dearest** most precious,
loved/worst, most bitter   125 **like** likely   **vassal** base, servile   126 **Base inclination** taste for
the inferior/acceding to base motives   **start of spleen** rush of anger

To fight against me under Percy's pay,
To dog his heels and curtsy at his frowns,
To show how much thou art degenerate.

130   PRINCE HENRY   Do not think so. You shall not find it so.
And heaven forgive them that so much have swayed
Your majesty's good thoughts away from me!
I will redeem all this on Percy's head
And in the closing of some glorious day

135   Be bold to tell you that I am your son,
When I will wear a garment all of blood
And stain my favours in a bloody mask,
Which, washed away, shall scour my shame with it.
And that shall be the day, whene'er it lights,

140   That this same child of honour and renown,
This gallant Hotspur, this all-praisèd knight,
And your unthought-of Harry chance to meet.
For every honour sitting on his helm,
Would they were multitudes, and on my head

145   My shames redoubled! For the time will come,
That I shall make this northern youth exchange
His glorious deeds for my indignities.
Percy is but my factor, good my lord,
To engross up glorious deeds on my behalf,

150   And I will call him to so strict account,
That he shall render every glory up,
Yea, even the slightest worship of his time,
Or I will tear the reckoning from his heart.
This, in the name of heaven, I promise here:

---

128 **curtsy** bow, show respect   133 **redeem . . . head** atone for my sins with Percy's head/make Percy pay for all this   134 **in . . . day** at the end of some victorious battle   137 **favours** facial features/chivalric tokens worn to symbolize pledges or great feats   **bloody mask** face made unrecognizable because covered in blood/mass, covering of blood   138 **scour** cleanse, get rid of   139 **lights** arrives/dawns   142 **unthought-of** ignored, associated with no great expectations   143 **helm** helmet   148 **factor** agent, commercial broker   149 **engross up** accumulate, buy up   152 **worship . . . time** honor gained in his lifetime   153 **reckoning** account, bill

155 The which if I perform and do survive
I do beseech your majesty may salve
The long-grown wounds of my intemperature.
If not, the end of life cancels all bonds,
And I will die a hundred thousand deaths
160 Ere break the smallest parcel of this vow.

KING HENRY IV   A hundred thousand rebels die in this:
Thou shalt have charge and sovereign trust herein.

Enter Blunt

How now, good Blunt? Thy looks are full of speed.

BLUNT   So hath the business that I come to speak of.
165 Lord Mortimer of Scotland hath sent word
That Douglas and the English rebels met
The eleventh of this month at Shrewsbury.
A mighty and a fearful head they are,
If promises be kept on every hand,
170 As ever offered foul play in a state.

KING HENRY IV   The Earl of Westmorland set forth today,
With him my son, Lord John of Lancaster,
For this advertisement is five days old.
On Wednesday next, Harry, thou shalt set forward:
175 On Thursday we ourselves will march.
Our meeting is Bridgnorth, and, Harry, you shall march
Through Gloucestershire, by which account,
Our business valuèd, some twelve days hence
Our general forces at Bridgnorth shall meet.
180 Our hands are full of business: let's away.
Advantage feeds him fat while men delay.   *Exeunt*

---

156 salve apply healing ointment to   **157 intemperature** intemperance, lack of restraint/diseased body, disordered health   **160 parcel** part   **162 charge** command (of troops)   **sovereign** supreme, royal (perhaps continuing the disease imagery with play on the sense of "healing")   **163 speed** urgency   **168 head** military force   **169 If . . . hand** if all who have promised to join them do so   **173 advertisement** announcement, news   **176 Bridgnorth** small Shropshire town on the River Severn, south of Shrewsbury   **178 Our business valuèd** according to this reckoning   **181 Advantage . . . fat** opportunity (for rebellion) increases

Act 3 Scene 3

running scene 10

Enter Falstaff and Bardolph

FALSTAFF   Bardolph, am I not fallen away vilely since this last action? Do I not bate? Do I not dwindle? Why my skin hangs about me like an old lady's loose gown. I am withered like an old apple-john. Well, I'll repent, and that suddenly, while I

5   am in some liking. I shall be out of heart shortly, and then I shall have no strength to repent. An I have not forgotten what the inside of a church is made of, I am a peppercorn, a brewer's horse. The inside of a church! Company, villainous company, hath been the spoil of me.

10   BARDOLPH   Sir John, you are so fretful, you cannot live long.

FALSTAFF   Why, there is it: come sing me a bawdy song, make me merry. I was as virtuously given as a gentleman need to be; virtuous enough: swore little, diced not — above seven times a week, went to a bawdy-house not above once in a

15   quarter — of an hour, paid money that I borrowed — three of four times, lived well and in good compass: and now I live out of all order, out of compass.

BARDOLPH   Why, you are so fat, Sir John, that you must needs be out of all compass, out of all reasonable compass, Sir John.

20   FALSTAFF   Do thou amend thy face, and I'll amend my life: thou art our admiral, thou bearest the lantern in the poop, but 'tis in the nose of thee; thou art the Knight of the Burning Lamp.

BARDOLPH   Why, Sir John, my face does you no harm.

3.3 *Location: the tavern in Eastcheap*   1 fallen away vilely horribly shrunken   **2 action** engagement, battle (i.e. the robbery on Gad's Hill)   **bate** decrease   **4 apple-john** type of apple said to be in best eating condition when shriveled   **suddenly** immediately   **5 in some liking** in the mood/in good physical condition   **out of heart** disheartened/out of condition   **6 strength** i.e. physical or spiritual   **7 peppercorn** i.e. small and shriveled   **8 brewer's horse** i.e. old and worn out   **10 fretful** restless, anxious/frayed, worn   **11 there is it** i.e. exactly, that's the situation   **12 given** inclined   **14 bawdy-house** brothel   **16 compass** measure, moderation/circumference (referring to his wide girth), belt   **21 admiral** flagship with a **lantern** to guide the rest of the fleet   **poop** stern or rear of a ship   **22 nose** i.e. because it is red from drinking   **Knight . . . Lamp** mock-chivalric title parodying heroic names in tales of romance

25 FALSTAFF   No, I'll be sworn, I make as good use of it as many a
man doth of a death's-head or a *memento mori*: I never see thy
face but I think upon hellfire and Dives that lived in purple, for
there he is in his robes, burning, burning. If thou wert any
way given to virtue, I would swear by thy face; my oath
30 should be 'By this fire', but thou art altogether given over; and
wert indeed, but for the light in thy face, the son of utter
darkness. When thou ran'st up Gad's Hill in the night to
catch my horse, if I did not think that thou hadst been an
ignis fatuus or a ball of wildfire, there's no purchase in money.
35 O, thou art a perpetual triumph, an everlasting bonfire-light!
Thou hast saved me a thousand marks in links and torches,
walking with thee in the night betwixt tavern and tavern. But
the sack that thou hast drunk me would have bought me
lights as good cheap as the dearest chandler's in Europe. I
40 have maintained that salamander of yours with fire any time
this two and thirty years. Heaven reward me for it!

BARDOLPH   I would my face were in your belly!

FALSTAFF   So should I be sure to be heart-burned.

Enter Hostess [Quickly]

How now, Dame Partlet the hen! Have you inquired yet who
45 picked my pocket?

HOSTESS QUICKLY   Why, Sir John, what do you think, Sir John?
Do you think I keep thieves in my house? I have searched, I
have inquired, so has my husband, man by man, boy by boy,

---

26 **death's-head** skull (i.e. emblem of mortality, often carved into a stone set in a ring)
memento mori object used to symbolize death (Latin: "reminder of death")   27 **Dives . . .
purple** refers to Christ's parable of Dives, the rich man clothed in purple who goes to hell for
allowing the pauper, Lazarus, to starve (Luke 16:19–31)   30 **given over** lost to virtue,
committed to sin   34 *ignis fatuus* will-o'-the-wisp, marsh gas which gives off phosphorescent
light and misleads night wanderers   **ball of wildfire** will-o'-the-wisp/ball of lightning/skin
disease characterized by vivid eruptions   **purchase** value   35 **bonfire-light** Folio spells
"Bone-fire-Light," suggesting both etymology and original pronunciation   36 **links** torches
38 **drunk me** drunk (**me** is emphatic)   39 **good cheap** cheap   **chandler's** candlemaker's
40 **salamander** lizard-like creature supposed to live in fire   42 **I . . . belly!** proverbial retort
(compares to modern "Get stuffed!")   43 **be heart-burned** have indigestion/my heart would
be literally on fire   44 **Dame Partlet** traditional name for a hen

servant by servant. The tithe of a hair was never lost in my
house before.

FALSTAFF   Ye lie, hostess: Bardolph was shaved and lost many
a hair; and I'll be sworn my pocket was picked. Go to, you are
a woman, go.

HOSTESS QUICKLY   Who, I? I defy thee. I was never called so in
mine own house before.

FALSTAFF   Go to, I know you well enough.

HOSTESS QUICKLY   No, Sir John, you do not know me, Sir John. I
know you, Sir John: you owe me money, Sir John, and now
you pick a quarrel to beguile me of it. I bought you a dozen
of shirts to your back.

FALSTAFF   Dowlas, filthy dowlas: I have given them away to
bakers' wives, and they have made bolters of them.

HOSTESS QUICKLY   Now, as I am a true woman, holland of eight
shillings an ell. You owe money here besides, Sir John, for
your diet and by-drinkings, and money lent you, four and
twenty pounds.

FALSTAFF   He had his part of it, let him pay.   *Points to Bardolph*

HOSTESS QUICKLY   He? Alas, he is poor, he hath nothing.

FALSTAFF   How? Poor? Look upon his face. What call you rich?
Let them coin his nose, let them coin his cheeks. I'll not pay
a denier. What, will you make a younker of me? Shall I not
take mine ease in mine inn but I shall have my pocket picked?
I have lost a seal-ring of my grandfather's worth forty mark.

HOSTESS QUICKLY   I have heard the prince tell him, I know not
how oft, that that ring was copper!

---

49 **tithe** tenth part   51 **was shaved** had his beard cut/went bald through syphilis/had his
head shaved to get rid of lice/was robbed; **hair** may play on "whore"   53 **woman** i.e.
inadequate/deceitful/promiscuous   56 **know** am acquainted with/have sexual knowledge of
59 **beguile** cheat   60 **to your back** for you to wear   61 **Dowlas** coarse linen (from Doulas in
Brittany)   62 **bolters** cloths used for sifting flour   63 **holland** fine linen (originally from
Holland)   64 **ell** a measure of length (forty-five inches)   65 **diet and by-drinkings** meals and
drinks in between meals   71 **denier** small coin worth one tenth of a penny   **younker**
fashionable and gullible young man, easily duped   72 **take mine ease** relax   73 **seal-ring**
engraved ring used for sealing documents with wax, frequently an heirloom   **forty mark** a
substantial sum of money; a **mark** was worth two thirds of a pound

FALSTAFF   How? The prince is a jack, a sneak-cup. An if he were here, I would cudgel him like a dog, if he would say so.

Enter the Prince marching [with Peto], and Falstaff meets him playing on his truncheon like a fife

How now, lad? Is the wind in that door? Must we all march?

BARDOLPH   Yea, two and two, Newgate fashion.

80   HOSTESS QUICKLY   My lord, I pray you hear me.

PRINCE HENRY   What say'st thou, Mistress Quickly? How does thy husband? I love him well. He is an honest man.

HOSTESS QUICKLY   Good my lord, hear me.

FALSTAFF   Prithee let her alone, and list to me.

85   PRINCE HENRY   What say'st thou, Jack?

FALSTAFF   The other night I fell asleep here behind the arras and had my pocket picked. This house is turned bawdy-house: they pick pockets.

PRINCE HENRY   What didst thou lose, Jack?

90   FALSTAFF   Wilt thou believe me, Hal, three or four bonds of forty pound apiece, and a seal-ring of my grandfather's?

PRINCE HENRY   A trifle, some eight-penny matter.

HOSTESS QUICKLY   So I told him, my lord; and I said I heard your grace say so. And, my lord, he speaks most vilely of you, like

95   a foul-mouthed man as he is, and said he would cudgel you.

PRINCE HENRY   What? He did not?

HOSTESS QUICKLY   There's neither faith, truth, nor womanhood in me else.

FALSTAFF   There's no more faith in thee than a stewed prune,

100   nor no more truth in thee than in a drawn fox. And for womanhood, Maid Marian may be the deputy's wife of the ward to thee. Go, you nothing, go.

---

76 jack knave, rascal   **sneak-cup** sneaky person, knave/one who sneaks drinks from others' cups   **truncheon** cudgel (symbol of his new military office)   **78 Is . . . door?** i.e. is that the situation   **door** direction   **79 two . . . fashion** prisoners were shackled together and led in pairs to Newgate, the City prison   **88 pick pockets** plays on the sense of "plunder vaginas"   **90 bonds** deeds promising the bearer payment   **99 stewed prune** commonly available in brothels, hence "whore/pimp"   **100 drawn fox** hunted fox (**drawn** from cover and dependent on its cunning for safety)   **101 Maid Marian** a disreputable character in morris dances and May games, played by a boy in female clothing   **deputy's . . . ward** wife of the deputy of the ward (an administrative district), i.e. a respectable woman   **102 to** compared to   **nothing** thing of no significance/vagina ("no thing")

HOSTESS QUICKLY   Say, what thing? What thing?

FALSTAFF   What thing? Why, a thing to thank heaven on.

105   HOSTESS QUICKLY   I am no thing to thank heaven on, I would thou shouldst know it. I am an honest man's wife, and, setting thy knighthood aside, thou art a knave to call me so.

FALSTAFF   Setting thy womanhood aside, thou art a beast to say otherwise.

110   HOSTESS QUICKLY   Say, what beast, thou knave, thou?

FALSTAFF   What beast? Why, an otter.

PRINCE HENRY   An otter, Sir John? Why an otter?

FALSTAFF   Why? She's neither fish nor flesh; a man knows not where to have her.

115   HOSTESS QUICKLY   Thou art an unjust man in saying so; thou or any man knows where to have me, thou knave, thou!

PRINCE HENRY   Thou say'st true, hostess, and he slanders thee most grossly.

HOSTESS QUICKLY   So he doth you, my lord, and said this other

120   day you owed him a thousand pound.

PRINCE HENRY   Sirrah, do I owe you a thousand pound?

FALSTAFF   A thousand pound, Hal? A million. Thy love is worth a million: thou ow'st me thy love.

HOSTESS QUICKLY   Nay, my lord, he called you Jack, and said he

125   would cudgel you.

FALSTAFF   Did I, Bardolph?

BARDOLPH   Indeed, Sir John, you said so.

FALSTAFF   Yea, if he said my ring was copper.

PRINCE HENRY   I say 'tis copper. Dar'st thou be as good as thy

130   word now?

FALSTAFF   Why, Hal, thou know'st, as thou art but a man, I dare, but as thou art a prince, I fear thee as I fear the roaring of the lion's whelp.

PRINCE HENRY   And why not as the lion?

135   FALSTAFF   The king himself is to be feared as the lion: dost

---

104 thing whore/vagina   **on** for   **107 thy knighthood** the respect usually due to one who is a knight   **111 otter** an aquatic mammal whose exact nature and type was a subject of debate   **114 have** place, categorize/have sex with   **133 whelp** cub, offspring

thou think I'll fear thee as I fear thy father? Nay, if I do, let my
girdle break.

PRINCE HENRY   O, if it should, how would thy guts fall about thy
knees! But, sirrah, there's no room for faith, truth, nor
140   honesty in this bosom of thine: it is all filled up with guts and
midriff. Charge an honest woman with picking thy pocket?
Why, thou whoreson, impudent, embossed rascal, if there
were anything in thy pocket but tavern-reck'nings,
memorandums of bawdy-houses, and one poor penny-
145   worth of sugar-candy to make thee long-winded: if thy
pocket were enriched with any other injuries but these, I am
a villain. And yet you will stand to it, you will not pocket up
wrong. Art thou not ashamed?

FALSTAFF   Dost thou hear, Hal? Thou know'st in the state of
150   innocency Adam fell, and what should poor Jack Falstaff do
in the days of villainy? Thou seest I have more flesh than
another man, and therefore more frailty. You confess then,
you picked my pocket?

PRINCE HENRY   It appears so by the story.

155   FALSTAFF   Hostess, I forgive thee. Go, make ready breakfast,
love thy husband, look to thy servants and cherish thy guests.
Thou shalt find me tractable to any honest reason: thou seest
I am pacified still. Nay, prithee be gone.—   *Exit Hostess*
Now Hal, to the news at court: for the robbery, lad, how is
160   that answered?

PRINCE HENRY   O, my sweet beef, I must still be good angel to
thee. The money is paid back again.

FALSTAFF   O, I do not like that paying back, 'tis a double labour.

---

136 **let . . . break** the breaking of one's belt (**girdle**) proverbially signified bad luck
142 **embossed** swollen/foaming at the mouth with exhaustion like a hunted animal   **rascal**
rogue/young, inferior deer   144 **memorandums** bills, invoices   145 **sugar-candy . . . long-
winded** sugar was used to improve stamina   146 **injuries** items whose loss you claim has
caused you injury   147 **stand to it** insist, maintain your grievance   **pocket up** accept (plays
on literal sense of "pocket")   151 **flesh . . . frailty** Falstaff plays with the biblical saying "the
flesh is frail" (Matthew 26:41 and elsewhere)   158 **still** always   160 **answered** accounted for
161 **sweet beef** plump, fresh, unsalted beef   **good angel** guardian angel   163 **double labour**
i.e. first taking it, then returning it

PRINCE HENRY   I am good friends with my father and may do
165   anything.

FALSTAFF   Rob me the exchequer the first thing thou dost, and
do it with unwashed hands too.

BARDOLPH   Do, my lord.

PRINCE HENRY   I have procured thee, Jack, a charge of foot.

170   FALSTAFF   I would it had been of horse. Where shall I find one
that can steal well? O, for a fine thief, of two-and-twenty or
thereabout! I am heinously unprovided. Well, God be
thanked for these rebels, they offend none but the virtuous. I
laud them, I praise them.

175   PRINCE HENRY   Bardolph.

BARDOLPH   My lord?

PRINCE HENRY   Go bear this letter to Lord John of   *Gives letters*
Lancaster,
To my brother John. This to my lord of Westmorland.—
                                                    [*Exit Bardolph*]
Go, Peto, to horse, for thou and I
180   Have thirty miles to ride yet ere dinner time.—
                                                    [*Exit Peto*]
Jack, meet me tomorrow in the Temple hall
At two o'clock in the afternoon.
There shalt thou know thy charge and there receive
Money and order for their furniture.
185   The land is burning, Percy stands on high,
And either they or we must lower lie.
                                                    [*Exit Prince Henry*]

FALSTAFF   Rare words! Brave world! Hostess, my breakfast,
come!
O, I could wish this tavern were my drum!   *Exit*

---

166 **exchequer** royal treasury   167 **with unwashed hands** straightaway/without scruple
169 **charge of foot** command of an infantry company   172 **unprovided** ill-equipped (for
villainous exploits)   173 **they . . . virtuous** i.e. by causing war, which provides opportunities
for theft and profiteering   174 **laud** celebrate, praise   181 **Temple hall** the Inner Temple at
one of the London Inns of Court (where young men studied law)   183 **charge** company,
regiment   184 **furniture** equipment   187 **Rare** marvelous   **Brave** splendid
188 **tavern . . . drum** Falstaff wishes he might remain at the inn; a **drum** summoned
soldiers to battle (possible pun on **tavern**/"taborin," a type of drum)

Act 4 Scene 1   *running scene 11*

Enter Harry Hotspur, Worcester and Douglas

HOTSPUR   Well said, my noble Scot. If speaking truth
    In this fine age were not thought flattery,
    Such attribution should the Douglas have,
    As not a soldier of this season's stamp
5   Should go so general current through the world.
    By heaven, I cannot flatter: I defy
    The tongues of soothers. But a braver place
    In my heart's love hath no man than yourself.
    Nay, task me to my word, approve me, lord.
10 DOUGLAS   Thou art the king of honour:
    No man so potent breathes upon the ground
    But I will beard him.

Enter a Messenger   *With letters*

HOTSPUR   Do so, and 'tis well.—
    What letters hast there? — I can but thank you.
15 MESSENGER   These letters come from your father.
HOTSPUR   Letters from him? Why comes he not himself?
MESSENGER   He cannot come, my lord, he is grievous sick.
HOTSPUR   How? Has he the leisure to be sick now
    In such a jostling time? Who leads his power?
20   Under whose government come they along?
MESSENGER   His letters bears his mind, not I his mind.
WORCESTER   I prithee tell me, doth he keep his bed?
MESSENGER   He did, my lord, four days ere I set forth,
    And at the time of my departure thence
25   He was much feared by his physician.

4.1 *Location: the rebel camp near Shrewsbury*   **2 fine** overrefined   **3 attribution** honor,
praise   **4 As not a** that no other   **season's stamp** year's design or mint (coinage term)
5 general current generally accepted (continues coining imagery)   **6 defy** reject, challenge
7 soothers flatterers   **braver** more honorable   **9 task** hold   **approve me** prove, test
11 breathes . . . ground lives   **12 beard** i.e. challenge, defy (literally, pull insultingly by the
beard)   **14 but** only   **19 jostling** clashing, contentious   **power** army   **20 government**
leadership   **21 bears** contain/reveal   **I his mind** this Folio reading makes sense, though it is
cheeky for the messenger to answer back in this way; most modern editors emend to "not I, my
lord."   **22 keep** keep to   **25 He . . . by** his health was much feared for

WORCESTER   I would the state of time had first been whole
          Ere he by sickness had been visited:
          His health was never better worth than now.
HOTSPUR   Sick now? Droop now? This sickness doth infect
30   The very life-blood of our enterprise,
          'Tis catching hither, even to our camp.
          He writes me here that inward sickness —
          And that his friends by deputation could not
          So soon be drawn, nor did he think it meet
35   To lay so dangerous and dear a trust
          On any soul removed but on his own.
          Yet doth he give us bold advertisement,
          That with our small conjunction we should on,
          To see how fortune is disposed to us,
40   For, as he writes, there is no quailing now,
          Because the king is certainly possessed
          Of all our purposes. What say you to it?
WORCESTER   Your father's sickness is a maim to us.
HOTSPUR   A perilous gash, a very limb lopped off:
45   And yet, in faith, it is not. His present want
          Seems more than we shall find it. Were it good
          To set the exact wealth of all our states
          All at one cast? To set so rich a main
          On the nice hazard of one doubtful hour?
50   It were not good, for therein should we read
          The very bottom and the soul of hope,
          The very list, the very utmost bound
          Of all our fortunes.

---

26 would wish   **state of time** present situation   **whole** sound, healthy   **28 better worth**
more important   **31 catching hither** contagious even here   **32 He . . . sickness**   possibly
an incomplete line, or one that expresses Hotspur's hasty manner of speaking   **33 by**
deputation through those acting on his behalf   **34 drawn** drawn together, assembled   **meet**
fitting, appropriate   **35 dear** important   **37 bold advertisement** resolute advice/advice to be
resolute   **38 conjunction** combined forces   **on** proceed   **41 possessed** informed   **43 maim**
serious injury   **45 present want** absence now   **46 more . . . it** worse than it will actually
prove to be   **47 set** hazard, stake   **48 cast** throw of the dice   **main** army/gambling stake
49 nice hazard delicate risk/precarious game of dice   **doubtful** uncertain   **50 read** discern
51 very bottom full extent   **52 list** limit   **bound** extent, boundary

DOUGLAS   'Faith, and so we should,
55   Where now remains a sweet reversion,
        We may boldly spend upon the hope of what
        Is to come in.
        A comfort of retirement lives in this.
HOTSPUR   A rendezvous, a home to fly unto,
60   If that the devil and mischance look big
        Upon the maidenhead of our affairs.
WORCESTER   But yet I would your father had been here.
        The quality and hair of our attempt
        Brooks no division: it will be thought
65   By some, that know not why he is away,
        That wisdom, loyalty and mere dislike
        Of our proceedings kept the earl from hence.
        And think how such an apprehension
        May turn the tide of fearful faction
70   And breed a kind of question in our cause,
        For well you know, we of the off'ring side
        Must keep aloof from strict arbitrement,
        And stop all sight-holes, every loop from whence
        The eye of reason may pry in upon us:
75   This absence of your father draws a curtain,
        That shows the ignorant a kind of fear
        Before not dreamt of.
HOTSPUR   You strain too far.
        I rather of his absence make this use:
80   It lends a lustre and more great opinion,
        A larger dare to our great enterprise,
        Than if the earl were here, for men must think,

---

55 **reversion** backup, something to be relied on (literally, future inheritance)   58 **retirement**
something to fall back on/peace, seclusion   59 **rendezvous** retreat, refuge   60 **big**
threateningly, menacingly   61 **maidenhead** beginning, first trial (literally, virginity)
63 **hair** nature   64 **Brooks** tolerates   66 **loyalty** i.e. to the king   **mere** absolute
68 **apprehension** thought, perception   69 **fearful faction** (rebel) alliances that generate
fear/frightened groups (of rebel sympathizers)   70 **question** doubt, mistrust   71 **off'ring**
challenging, aggressing   72 **strict arbitrement** close scrutiny, rigorous judgment   73 **loop**
loophole, aperture   75 **draws** opens   78 **strain too far** exaggerate   79 **make this use** find
this advantage   80 **opinion** renown, prestige   81 **dare** boldness

If we without his help can make a head
To push against the kingdom, with his help

85   We shall o'erturn it topsy-turvy down.
Yet all goes well, yet all our joints are whole.

DOUGLAS   As heart can think. There is not such a word
Spoke of in Scotland as this dream of fear.

Enter Sir Richard Vernon

HOTSPUR   My cousin Vernon, welcome, by my soul.

90   VERNON   Pray God my news be worth a welcome, lord.
The Earl of Westmorland, seven thousand strong,
Is marching hitherwards, with him Prince John.

HOTSPUR   No harm: what more?

VERNON   And further, I have learned,

95   The king himself in person hath set forth,
Or hitherwards intended speedily,
With strong and mighty preparation.

HOTSPUR   He shall be welcome too. Where is his son,
The nimble-footed madcap Prince of Wales,

100   And his comrades that daffed the world aside
And bid it pass?

VERNON   All furnished, all in arms,
All plumed like estriches that with the wind
Bated like eagles having lately bathed,

105   Glittering in golden coats like images,
As full of spirit as the month of May,
And gorgeous as the sun at midsummer,
Wanton as youthful goats, wild as young bulls.
I saw young Harry with his beaver on,

110   His cuisses on his thighs, gallantly armed,

---

83 **make a head** raise an army   86 **Yet** still   **joints** limbs   87 **As . . . think** i.e. as can
possibly be wished   93 **No harm** i.e. that doesn't matter   96 **intended** is about to leave
97 **preparation** equipped military force   100 **daffed** tossed carelessly   102 **furnished**
equipped   103 **estriches** ostriches (presumably the men's helmets are adorned with feathers)
104 **Bated** fluttered   105 **golden coats** sleeveless outer garments richly adorned with
heraldic arms, worn over armor   **images** gilded statues/emblems   107 **gorgeous** brightly
colored, magnificent   108 **Wanton** wild, frolicsome, carefree   109 **beaver** helmet
(technically, the visor)   110 **cuisses** thigh armor

Rise from the ground like feathered Mercury,
And vaulted with such ease into his seat,
As if an angel dropped down from the clouds,
To turn and wind a fiery Pegasus
115   And witch the world with noble horsemanship.

HOTSPUR   No more, no more. Worse than the sun in March,
This praise doth nourish agues. Let them come.
They come like sacrifices in their trim,
And to the fire-eyed maid of smoky war
120   All hot and bleeding will we offer them:
The mailèd Mars shall on his altar sit
Up to the ears in blood. I am on fire
To hear this rich reprisal is so nigh
And yet not ours. Come, let me take my horse,
125   Who is to bear me like a thunderbolt
Against the bosom of the Prince of Wales.
Harry to Harry, shall hot horse to horse
Meet and ne'er part till one drop down a corpse!
O, that Glendower were come!

130   VERNON   There is more news:
I learned in Worcester, as I rode along,
He cannot draw his power this fourteen days.

DOUGLAS   That's the worst tidings that I hear of yet.

WORCESTER   Ay, by my faith, that bears a frosty sound.

135   HOTSPUR   What may the king's whole battle reach unto?

VERNON   To thirty thousand.

HOTSPUR   Forty let it be.
My father and Glendower being both away,
The powers of us may serve so great a day.

---

111 **feathered Mercury** Roman messenger of the gods, usually depicted with wings on cap and
sandals   112 **seat** i.e. saddle   114 **wind** wheel about, turn   **Pegasus** winged horse in Greek
mythology   115 **witch** bewitch   117 **agues** violent fevers thought to be bred or worsened by
the early spring **sun**   118 **trim** finery, adornment (like animals garlanded for sacrifice)
119 **maid . . . war** Bellona, the Roman goddess of war   121 **mailèd Mars** Roman god of war,
clad in armor   123 **reprisal** prize   131 **Worcester** English town on the River Severn
132 **draw . . . days** gather his forces for a fortnight   135 **What . . . unto?** What is the total
number of the king's troops?   139 **powers of us** forces we have   **serve** suffice for

140   Come, let us take a muster speedily:

      Doomsday is near; die all, die merrily.

    DOUGLAS   Talk not of dying. I am out of fear

      Of death or death's hand for this one-half year.   *Exeunt*

Act 4 Scene 2   *running scene 12*

Enter Falstaff and Bardolph

    FALSTAFF   Bardolph, get thee before to Coventry. Fill me a bottle of sack. Our soldiers shall march through, we'll to Sutton Coldfield tonight.

    BARDOLPH   Will you give me money, captain?

5   FALSTAFF   Lay out, lay out.

    BARDOLPH   This bottle makes an angel.

    FALSTAFF   An if it do, take it for thy labour. And if it make twenty, take them all, I'll answer the coinage. Bid my lieutenant Peto meet me at the town's end.

10   BARDOLPH   I will, captain. Farewell.   *Exit*

    FALSTAFF   If I be not ashamed of my soldiers, I am a soused gurnet. I have misused the king's press damnably. I have got, in exchange of a hundred and fifty soldiers, three hundred and odd pounds. I press me none but good householders,

15   yeoman's sons, inquire me out contracted bachelors, such as had been asked twice on the banns, such a commodity

---

140 **muster** roll call   141 **Doomsday** Judgment Day   142 **out of** free from   143 **this one-half year** six months; Douglas does not expect to die within this period   **4.2 *Location: the road (they are traveling, probably along the Roman road Watling Street from London to Shrewsbury via Coventry, a Midlands town near Stratford-upon-Avon)***   1 **get thee before** you go on ahead   3 **Sutton Coldfield** Warwickshire town twenty miles northwest of Coventry   5 **Lay out** pay for it yourself   6 **makes** brings the amount you owe me to (Falstaff responds to the sense of "creates")   **angel** a gold coin variously worth between 6s 8d and 10s   8 **answer the coinage** be responsible for the validity of the coins   11 **soused gurnet** type of pickled fish/drunkard   12 **press** power of conscription   **I . . . pounds** Falstaff has allowed those who can afford it to buy their way out of being soldiers   13 **of** for   14 **good** substantial, wealthy   15 **yeoman's sons** the sons of freeholders of small landed estates **inquire me out** ask for, seek   **contracted** engaged (to be married)   16 **banns** public notice of the intention to marry, announced in church on three successive Sundays; the **bachelors** here are to be married soon   **commodity** portion, quantity

of warm slaves as had as lieve hear the devil as a drum;
such as fear the report of a caliver worse than a struck fowl
or a hurt wild duck. I pressed me none but such toasts-
20   and-butter, with hearts in their bellies no bigger than pins'
heads, and they have bought out their services. And now my
whole charge consists of ancients, corporals, lieutenants,
gentlemen of companies, slaves as ragged as Lazarus in the
painted cloth, where the glutton's dogs licked his sores; and
25   such as indeed were never soldiers, but discarded unjust
servingmen, younger sons to younger brothers, revolted
tapsters and ostlers trade-fallen, the cankers of a calm world
and long peace, ten times more dishonourable ragged than
an old-faced ancient; and such have I, to fill up the rooms of
30   them that have bought out their services, that you would
think that I had a hundred and fifty tattered prodigals lately
come from swine-keeping, from eating draff and husks. A
mad fellow met me on the way and told me I had unloaded
all the gibbets and pressed the dead bodies. No eye hath seen
35   such scarecrows. I'll not march through Coventry with
them, that's flat. Nay, and the villains march wide betwixt
the legs, as if they had gyves on; for indeed, I had the most of
them out of prison. There's not a shirt and a half in all my
company, and the half shirt is two napkins tacked together
40   and thrown over the shoulders like a herald's coat without
sleeves, and the shirt, to say the truth, stolen from my host of

17 **warm** comfortably off/sexually eager   **lieve** soon   **drum** i.e. customarily sounded to enlist
recruits or call men to battle   18 **caliver** musket, lightweight firearm   19 **toasts-and-butter**
milksops, pampered fellows   20 **hearts . . . heads** i.e. those with little appetite for fighting
21 **bought . . . services** bribed Falstaff to be exempted from military service   22 **charge**
command, unit   **ancients** ensigns, i.e. soldiers who carried military banners (plays on the sense
of "elderly people")   23 **gentlemen of companies** gentlemen soldiers without formal rank
Lazarus . . . sores refers to the biblical story of the beggar Lazarus and the contemptuous
rich man (Luke 16:19–21)   24 **painted cloth** cheap wall hanging depicting the biblical tale
25 **discarded unjust servingmen** dismissed dishonest servants   26 **younger . . . brothers** i.e.
those with no hope of a substantial inheritance   **revolted tapsters** apprentice barmen who
have run away from their masters   27 **ostlers trade-fallen** out-of-work stablemen   **cankers**
ulcers/parasites   29 **ancient** military banner   **rooms** places   31 **prodigals** in the biblical
parable, the prodigal (extravagant) son wasted his inheritance and was reduced to feeding with
the pigs   32 **draff and husks** pigswill and corn husks   34 **gibbets** gallows   37 **gyves** leg-irons,
shackles   40 **herald's . . . sleeves** the tabard was a sleeveless outer garment open down the sides

Saint Albans, or the red-nose innkeeper of Daventry. But that's all one, they'll find linen enough on every hedge.

Enter the Prince and the Lord of Westmorland

PRINCE HENRY   How now, blown Jack? How now, quilt?

45 FALSTAFF   What, Hal? How now, mad wag? What a devil dost thou in Warwickshire? — My good lord of Westmorland, I cry you mercy: I thought your honour had already been at Shrewsbury.

WESTMORLAND   'Faith, Sir John, 'tis more than time that I were
50 there, and you too, but my powers are there already. The king, I can tell you, looks for us all: we must away all tonight.

FALSTAFF   Tut, never fear me. I am as vigilant as a cat to steal cream.

PRINCE HENRY   I think to steal cream indeed, for thy theft hath
55 already made thee butter. But tell me, Jack, whose fellows are these that come after?

FALSTAFF   Mine, Hal, mine.

PRINCE HENRY   I did never see such pitiful rascals.

FALSTAFF   Tut, tut, good enough to toss: food for powder, food
60 for powder. They'll fill a pit as well as better. Tush, man, mortal men, mortal men.

WESTMORLAND   Ay, but, Sir John, methinks they are exceeding poor and bare, too beggarly.

FALSTAFF   Faith, for their poverty, I know not where they had
65 that; and for their bareness, I am sure they never learned that of me.

PRINCE HENRY   No, I'll be sworn, unless you call three fingers on the ribs bare. But, sirrah, make haste. Percy is already in the field.

---

42 **Saint Albans** town along Watling Street about twenty-five miles north of London
Daventry Northamptonshire town southeast of Coventry   43 **find . . . hedge** i.e. they'll steal
clothes left to dry on hedgerows   44 **blown** swollen/short of breath   **quilt** padded
covering/fat man (plays on Falstaff's name, Jack, which could also mean a padded tunic worn
instead of armor)   47 **cry you mercy** beg your pardon   51 **looks for** expects   52 **fear** doubt
55 **butter** i.e. fat   59 **toss** throw away/impale on a pike   **food for powder** cannon fodder
60 **pit** mass grave   **as well as better** just as well as better men would   **Tush** exclamation of
contempt   63 **bare** poorly clothed/inadequately equipped (Falstaff shifts the sense to "bare-
boned, thin")   67 **three . . . ribs** three fingers' depth of fat covering his ribs; a "finger"
measured three quarters of an inch   69 **field** battlefield

70   FALSTAFF   What, is the king encamped?

WESTMORLAND   He is, Sir John. I fear we shall stay too long.

FALSTAFF   Well,
To the latter end of a fray and the beginning of a feast
Fits a dull fighter and a keen guest.   *Exeunt*

Act 4 Scene 3   *running scene 13*

Enter Hotspur, Worcester, Douglas and Vernon

HOTSPUR   We'll fight with him tonight.

WORCESTER   It may not be.

DOUGLAS   You give him then advantage.

VERNON   Not a whit.

5   HOTSPUR   Why say you so? Looks he not for supply?

VERNON   So do we.

HOTSPUR   His is certain, ours is doubtful.

WORCESTER   Good cousin, be advised, stir not tonight.

VERNON   Do not, my lord.

10   DOUGLAS   You do not counsel well:
You speak it out of fear and cold heart.

VERNON   Do me no slander, Douglas: by my life,
And I dare well maintain it with my life,
If well-respected honour bid me on,
15   I hold as little counsel with weak fear
As you, my lord, or any Scot that this day lives.
Let it be seen tomorrow in the battle
Which of us fears.

DOUGLAS   Yea, or tonight.

20   VERNON   Content.

HOTSPUR   Tonight, say I.

71 stay delay   73 To . . . guest i.e. the end of a fight and the beginning of a feast is the best time to arrive for one keener on eating than fighting (proverbial)   4.3 *Location: the rebel camp near Shrewsbury*   1 him i.e. the king   3 then in that case, if you wait 5 Looks . . . supply? Is he not expecting reinforcements?   13 maintain justify, support, prove 14 well-respected well-considered   bid me on urges me forward   15 counsel conference

VERNON   Come, come it may not be. I wonder much,
Being men of such great leading as you are,
That you foresee not what impediments

25   Drag back our expedition: certain horse
Of my cousin Vernon's are not yet come up,
Your uncle Worcester's horse came but today,
And now their pride and mettle is asleep,
Their courage with hard labour tame and dull,

30   That not a horse is half the half of himself.

HOTSPUR   So are the horses of the enemy
In general, journey-bated and brought low.
The better part of ours are full of rest.

WORCESTER   The number of the king exceedeth ours:

35   For God's sake, cousin, stay till all come in.

The trumpet sounds a parley

Enter Sir Walter Blunt

BLUNT   I come with gracious offers from the king,
If you vouchsafe me hearing and respect.

HOTSPUR   Welcome, Sir Walter Blunt, and would to God
You were of our determination.

40   Some of us love you well, and even those some
Envy your great deservings and good name,
Because you are not of our quality,
But stand against us like an enemy.

BLUNT   And heaven defend but still I should stand so,

45   So long as out of limit and true rule
You stand against anointed majesty.
But to my charge: the king hath sent to know
The nature of your griefs, and whereupon

---

23 leading leadership   **25 Drag** hold   **expedition** speedy action   **horse** horses, cavalry
28 pride and mettle spirit and liveliness   **30 That . . . himself** so that none of the horses is
even a quarter of its normal strength   **32 journey-bated** exhausted by traveling   *parley*
trumpet summons to negotiation between enemy forces   **37 vouchsafe** permit   **respect**
consideration   **39 determination** mind, conviction   **40 even those some** those very people
42 quality party   **44 defend** forbid   **45 out of limit** past the bounds of natural order and
allegiance   **46 anointed** i.e. rightful, legitimate (having been marked with holy oil as part of
the coronation ceremony)   **47 charge** duty, task   **48 griefs** grievances, complaints
whereupon on what grounds

You conjure from the breast of civil peace
50 Such bold hostility, teaching his duteous land
Audacious cruelty. If that the king
Have any way your good deserts forgot,
Which he confesseth to be manifold,
He bids you name your griefs, and with all speed
55 You shall have your desires with interest,
And pardon absolute for yourself and these
Herein misled by your suggestion.
HOTSPUR   The king is kind, and well we know the king
Knows at what time to promise, when to pay.
60 My father, my uncle and myself
Did give him that same royalty he wears,
And when he was not six and twenty strong,
Sick in the world's regard, wretched and low,
A poor unminded outlaw sneaking home,
65 My father gave him welcome to the shore.
And when he heard him swear and vow to God
He came but to be Duke of Lancaster,
To sue his livery and beg his peace,
With tears of innocency and terms of zeal,
70 My father, in kind heart and pity moved,
Swore him assistance and performed it too.
Now when the lords and barons of the realm
Perceived Northumberland did lean to him,
The more and less came in with cap and knee,
75 Met him in boroughs, cities, villages,
Attended him on bridges, stood in lanes,

---

49 conjure call forth (with connotations of magical invocation and bewitchment)   51 If that
if   52 deserts deservings, merits   55 with interest and more in addition   57 suggestion
prompting, incitement   62 was . . . strong had fewer than twenty-six followers
63 Sick . . . regard suffering poor public reputation   64 unminded disregarded   outlaw
Richard II had banished Henry Bullingbrook; he returned following his father's death and
Richard's seizure of his land and titles   68 sue his livery legally claim his right to inherit his
father's lands and title   beg his peace seek reconciliation with King Richard   69 terms of
zeal i.e. eager assurances of loyalty   74 more . . . knee those of higher and lower social status
offered him allegiance—with cap in hand and knees bent in a bow/kneeling   76 Attended
awaited/accompanied   lanes paths/rows

Laid gifts before him, proffered him their oaths,
Gave him their heirs, as pages followed him
Even at the heels in golden multitudes.
80   He presently, as greatness knows itself,
Steps me a little higher than his vow
Made to my father, while his blood was poor,
Upon the naked shore at Ravenspurgh,
And now, forsooth, takes on him to reform
85   Some certain edicts and some strait decrees
That lay too heavy on the commonwealth,
Cries out upon abuses, seems to weep
Over his country's wrongs, and by this face,
This seeming brow of justice, did he win
90   The hearts of all that he did angle for.
Proceeded further — cut me off the heads
Of all the favourites that the absent king
In deputation left behind him here,
When he was personal in the Irish war.
95   BLUNT   Tut, I came not to hear this.
    HOTSPUR   Then to the point.
In short time after, he deposed the king.
Soon after that, deprived him of his life,
And in the neck of that, tasked the whole state.
100   To make that worse, suffered his kinsman March —
Who is, if every owner were placed,
Indeed his king — to be engaged in Wales,
There without ransom to lie forfeited,

---

78 **heirs . . . followed** punctuated thus in Folio, but most editors emend to "heirs as pages, followed," thus altering the sense   79 **golden** splendidly or brightly dressed/celebratory, joyous/rich, abundant   80 **presently** soon   **greatness knows itself** those in power come to understand their situation   81 **Steps . . . higher** becomes more ambitious   82 **his . . . poor** he was still humble/before he was king   84 **forsooth** in truth, perhaps used ironically here   85 **strait** harsh, strict   87 **Cries . . . abuses** condemns corruption, draws attention to wrongs   91 **cut . . . favourites** Richard's favorite courtiers were beheaded   **cut me** cut (**me** is emphatic)   93 **In deputation** as his deputies   94 **was personal in** went in person to   99 **in . . . of** on the strength of/immediately after   **tasked** taxed   100 **March** the Earl of March, Edmund Mortimer   101 **if . . . placed** if every claimant were entitled to occupy their rightful position   102 **engaged** held hostage   103 **forfeited** abandoned

Disgraced me in my happy victories,
105 Sought to entrap me by intelligence,
Rated my uncle from the council board,
In rage dismissed my father from the court,
Broke oath on oath, committed wrong on wrong,
And in conclusion drove us to seek out
110 This head of safety; and withal to pry
Into his title, the which we find
Too indirect for long continuance.

BLUNT   Shall I return this answer to the king?

HOTSPUR Not so, Sir Walter. We'll withdraw awhile.
115 Go to the king, and let there be impawned
Some surety for a safe return again,
And in the morning early shall my uncle
Bring him our purpose. And so farewell.

BLUNT   I would you would accept of grace and love.

120 HOTSPUR And't may be so we shall.

BLUNT   Pray heaven you do.   *Exeunt*

Act 4 Scene 4   *running scene 14*

Enter the Archbishop of York and Sir Michael

ARCHBISHOP OF YORK Hie, good Sir Michael; bear   *Gives a letter*
this sealèd brief
With wingèd haste to the Lord Marshal,
This to my cousin Scroop, and all the rest
To whom they are directed. If you knew
5   How much they do import, you would make haste.

---

104 Disgraced . . . victories i.e. by demanding my prisoners, the King turned my triumphs into
disgrace   105 intelligence spying   106 Rated chided angrily, dismissed   110 head of safety
defensive army   withal furthermore   pry . . . title examine his claim (to the throne)
112 indirect insufficiently direct in the line of succession/devious, irregular   for long
continuance to last long   115 impawned pledged, held in pawn   116 surety guarantee
119 accept . . . love i.e. be reconciled   **4.4** *Location: unspecified; presumably in the
Archbishop of York's palace*   Sir Michael presumably a priest or a knight; "sir" can be a
courtesy title for clergymen   1 Hie go quickly   brief letter, dispatch   4 directed addressed
5 much . . . import much information they contain/important they are

SIR MICHAEL   My good lord,
I guess their tenor.
ARCHBISHOP OF YORK   Like enough you do.
Tomorrow, good Sir Michael, is a day
10   Wherein the fortune of ten thousand men
Must bide the touch, for, sir, at Shrewsbury,
As I am truly given to understand,
The king with mighty and quick-raisèd power
Meets with Lord Harry. And I fear, Sir Michael,
15   What with the sickness of Northumberland,
Whose power was in the first proportion,
And what with Owen Glendower's absence thence,
Who with them was rated firmly too
And comes not in, o'er-ruled by prophecies,
20   I fear the power of Percy is too weak
To wage an instant trial with the king.
SIR MICHAEL   Why, my good lord, you need not fear.
There is Douglas and Lord Mortimer.
ARCHBISHOP OF YORK   No, Mortimer is not there.
25   SIR MICHAEL   But there is Mordake, Vernon, Lord Harry Percy,
And there is my lord of Worcester and a head
Of gallant warriors, noble gentlemen.
ARCHBISHOP OF YORK   And so there is. But yet the king hath
drawn
The special head of all the land together:
30   The Prince of Wales, Lord John of Lancaster,
The noble Westmorland and warlike Blunt;
And many more corrivals and dear men
Of estimation and command in arms.
SIR MICHAEL   Doubt not, my lord, he shall be well opposed.

---

7 **tenor** substance, drift   8 **Like** likely   11 **bide the touch** be put to the test (as gold is tested with a touchstone)   14 **Lord Harry** i.e. Hotspur   16 **power . . . proportion** army was of the greatest size/importance   18 **rated firmly** considered to be strong, a powerful source of support   19 **comes not in** does not participate   **o'er-ruled by prophecies** i.e. he is staying away due to unfavorable predictions of events   21 **instant trial** immediate test of strength   26 **head** force, army   29 **special head** exceptional military leadership   32 **corrivals** partners **dear** honorable/valuable   33 **estimation** worth, reputation

35   ARCHBISHOP OF YORK   I hope no less, yet needful 'tis to fear.
      And, to prevent the worst, Sir Michael, speed;
      For if Lord Percy thrive not, ere the king
      Dismiss his power, he means to visit us,
      For he hath heard of our confederacy,
40   And 'tis but wisdom to make strong against him:
      Therefore make haste. I must go write again
      To other friends, and so farewell, Sir Michael.   *Exeunt*

Act 5 Scene 1   *running scene 15*

*Enter the King, Prince of Wales, Lord John of Lancaster, Earl of
Westmorland, Sir Walter Blunt and Falstaff*

KING HENRY IV   How bloodily the sun begins to peer
      Above yon busky hill! The day looks pale
      At his distemperature.

PRINCE HENRY   The southern wind
5   Doth play the trumpet to his purposes,
      And by his hollow whistling in the leaves
      Foretells a tempest and a blust'ring day.

KING HENRY IV   Then with the losers let it sympathize,
      For nothing can seem foul to those that win.
                                          The trumpet sounds
Enter Worcester [and Vernon]
10   How now, my lord of Worcester? 'Tis not well
      That you and I should meet upon such terms
      As now we meet. You have deceived our trust,
      And made us doff our easy robes of peace,
      To crush our old limbs in ungentle steel:
15   This is not well, my lord, this is not well.
      What say you to it? Will you again unknit

---

37 **thrive** flourish, succeed   39 **confederacy** league, conspiracy (with the rebels)   40 **make
strong** strengthen our defenses   **5.1** *Location: the king's camp near Shrewsbury*
2 **busky** bush-covered   3 **distemperature** unhealthy, unnatural appearance   5 **the trumpet**
part of trumpeter or herald   9 **foul** gloomy, bad (weather)   13 **doff** take off   **easy**
comfortable   14 **ungentle steel** hard, uncomfortable steel armor   16 **unknit** undo

This churlish knot of all-abhorrèd war?
And move in that obedient orb again
Where you did give a fair and natural light,
20   And be no more an exhaled meteor,
A prodigy of fear and a portent
Of broachèd mischief to the unborn times?

WORCESTER   Hear me, my liege:
For mine own part, I could be well content
25   To entertain the lag-end of my life
With quiet hours, for I do protest,
I have not sought the day of this dislike.

KING HENRY IV   You have not sought it? How comes it, then?

FALSTAFF   Rebellion lay in his way, and he found it.

30   PRINCE HENRY   Peace, chewet, peace!

WORCESTER   It pleased your majesty to turn your looks
Of favour from myself and all our house;
And yet I must remember you, my lord,
We were the first and dearest of your friends.
35   For you my staff of office did I break
In Richard's time, and posted day and night
To meet you on the way, and kiss your hand,
When yet you were in place and in account
Nothing so strong and fortunate as I.
40   It was myself, my brother and his son,
That brought you home and boldly did outdare
The danger of the time. You swore to us,
And you did swear that oath at Doncaster,
That you did nothing of purpose gainst the state,
45   Nor claim no further than your new-fall'n right,

17 churlish rude, ungracious, base   18 orb orbit, sphere   20 exhaled meteor meteors were
believed to be formed of vapors drawn from the earth ("exhaled") by the sun; they were
considered bad omens   21 prodigy omen/unnatural thing   22 broachèd already begun
mischief evil, calamity   unborn times future   25 entertain occupy   lag-end latter part
27 dislike animosity, discord   30 chewet chough, jackdaw, i.e. chatterer/minced meat or
fish pie   33 remember remind   35 staff of office Worcester had been steward of the king's
household   36 posted rode speedily   39 Nothing nowhere near   41 brought escorted,
accompanied   outdare defy   43 Doncaster town in the northeast of England
44 did . . . state had no intention of threatening the realm   45 new-fall'n right recently
inherited title (after his father's death)

The seat of Gaunt, dukedom of Lancaster.
To this we swore our aid. But in short space
It rained down fortune show'ring on your head,
And such a flood of greatness fell on you —
50   What with our help, what with the absent king,
What with the injuries of wanton time,
The seeming sufferances that you had borne,
And the contrarious winds that held the king
So long in the unlucky Irish wars
55   That all in England did repute him dead —
And from this swarm of fair advantages
You took occasion to be quickly wooed
To gripe the general sway into your hand,
Forgot your oath to us at Doncaster,
60   And being fed by us, you used us so
As that ungentle gull, the cuckoo's bird,
Useth the sparrow, did oppress our nest,
Grew by our feeding to so great a bulk
That even our love durst not come near your sight
65   For fear of swallowing. But with nimble wing
We were enforced, for safety sake, to fly
Out of your sight and raise this present head,
Whereby we stand opposèd by such means
As you yourself have forged against yourself
70   By unkind usage, dangerous countenance,
And violation of all faith and troth
Sworn to us in your younger enterprise.

---

46 seat estate   **Gaunt** John of Gaunt, Henry's father   **51 injuries** abuses, wrongdoing
wanton ungoverned, poorly managed   **52 seeming sufferances** apparent wrongs
53 contrarious opposing, unfavorable   **54 unlucky** ill-fated   **55 repute** believe him to be
57 occasion the opportunity   **wooed** persuaded   **58 gripe** grip, grasp   **general sway**
overall power   **61 ungentle gull** cruel/dishonorable young bird   **cuckoo's . . . sparrow** the
cuckoo lays its eggs in other birds' nests to be hatched and fed; cuckoo chicks are much bigger
and eventually take over the nest   **64 our love** those of us who loved you   **durst not** did not
dare   **65 swallowing** being eaten   **68 opposèd . . . means** in opposition to you as a result of
such factors   **70 unkind** cruel/unnatural   **71 troth** honesty, integrity   **72 younger** earlier,
original

KING HENRY IV   These things indeed you have articulated,
Proclaimed at market-crosses, read in churches,

75   To face the garment of rebellion
With some fine colour that may please the eye
Of fickle changelings and poor discontents,
Which gape and rub the elbow at the news
Of hurly-burly innovation:

80   And never yet did insurrection want
Such water-colours to impaint his cause,
Nor moody beggars, starving for a time
Of pell-mell havoc and confusion.

PRINCE HENRY   In both our armies there is many a soul

85   Shall pay full dearly for this encounter,
If once they join in trial. Tell your nephew,
The Prince of Wales doth join with all the world
In praise of Henry Percy: by my hopes —
This present enterprise set off his head —

90   I do not think a braver gentleman,
More active-valiant or more valiant-young,
More daring or more bold, is now alive
To grace this latter age with noble deeds.
For my part, I may speak it to my shame,

95   I have a truant been to chivalry,
And so I hear he doth account me too.
Yet this before my father's majesty:
I am content that he shall take the odds
Of his great name and estimation,

100 And will, to save the blood on either side,
Try fortune with him in a single fight.

75 **face** adorn, cover   76 **colour** hue/pretexts, pretense   77 **changelings** turncoats,
changeable people   **discontents** discontented persons   78 **rub the elbow** hug themselves in
pleasure   79 **hurly-burly** chaotic   **innovation** novelty, change, revolution   80 **want** need,
lack   81 **water-colours** watery deceptions   **impaint** paint, color   82 **moody** sullen, angry
83 **havoc** plundering, violent disorder   84 **both our** i.e. the king's and the rebels'   86 **trial**
battle   88 **by my hopes** i.e. of salvation   89 **set . . . head** not counted against him
90 **braver** finer/more courageous   93 **latter** recent, present   97 **this** I say this   98 **odds**
advantages   99 **estimation** reputation

KING HENRY IV   And, Prince of Wales, so dare we venture thee,
    Albeit considerations infinite
    Do make against it. No, good Worcester, no,
105   We love our people well; even those we love
    That are misled upon your cousin's part.
    And, will they take the offer of our grace,
    Both he and they and you, yea, every man
    Shall be my friend again and I'll be his.
110   So tell your cousin, and bring me word
    What he will do. But if he will not yield,
    Rebuke and dread correction wait on us
    And they shall do their office. So, be gone,
    We will not now be troubled with reply.
115   We offer fair, take it advisedly.

Exeunt Worcester [and Vernon]

PRINCE HENRY   It will not be accepted, on my life.
    The Douglas and the Hotspur both together
    Are confident against the world in arms.

KING HENRY IV   Hence, therefore, every leader to his charge,
120   For on their answer will we set on them;
    And God befriend us as our cause is just!

Exeunt all but Prince and Falstaff

FALSTAFF   Hal, if thou see me down in the battle and bestride
me, so; 'tis a point of friendship.

PRINCE HENRY   Nothing but a colossus can do thee that
125   friendship. Say thy prayers, and farewell.

FALSTAFF   I would it were bedtime, Hal, and all well.

PRINCE HENRY   Why, thou ow'st heaven a death.

[Exit Prince Henry]

---

102 **venture** hazard, risk   103 **Albeit** despite the fact that   104 **make** weigh, argue
106 **cousin's** relative's (i.e. nephew's)   107 **grace** pardon   112 **Rebuke** shame, disgrace
dread correction terrible punishment   **wait on us** are at my command   113 **office** duty, task
115 **fair** fairly, fair terms   **take it advisedly** consider it carefully   119 **charge** command/
company, unit/responsibility   120 **on their answer** once we've had their answer, i.e. refusal of
the terms   122 **bestride** stand astride a fallen man in order to defend him   123 **so** thus—
presumably Falstaff demonstrates the gesture   124 **colossus** giant; the Colossus of Rhodes, a
gigantic statue of Apollo, supposedly stood astride the entrance to the harbor   127 **death**
proverbial; puns on "debt"

FALSTAFF   'Tis not due yet. I would be loath to pay him before
his day. What need I be so forward with him that calls not on
130   me? Well, 'tis no matter, honour pricks me on. But how if
honour prick me off when I come on? How then? Can
honour set to a leg? No. Or an arm? No. Or take away the
grief of a wound? No. Honour hath no skill in surgery, then?
No. What is honour? A word. What is that word 'honour'?
135   Air. A trim reckoning! Who hath it? He that died
o'Wednesday. Doth he feel it? No. Doth he hear it? No. Is it
insensible, then? Yea, to the dead. But will it not live with the
living? No. Why? Detraction will not suffer it. Therefore I'll
none of it. Honour is a mere scutcheon: and so ends my
140   catechism.   *Exit*

Act 5 Scene 2   *running scene 16*

Enter Worcester and Sir Richard Vernon
WORCESTER   O, no, my nephew must not know, Sir Richard,
The liberal kind offer of the king.
VERNON   'Twere best he did.
WORCESTER   Then we are all undone.
5   It is not possible, it cannot be,
The king would keep his word in loving us.
He will suspect us still and find a time
To punish this offence in other faults.
Supposition all our lives shall be stuck full of eyes;
10   For treason is but trusted like the fox,
Who, ne'er so tame, so cherished and locked up,
Will have a wild trick of his ancestors.

---

129 forward eager   130 pricks spurs   131 prick me off marks me down (for a dead man)
132 set . . . leg join together, set a broken leg   133 grief pain   135 trim fine, neat
137 insensible cannot be felt by the senses   138 Detraction slander   139 scutcheon heraldic
shield, decorated with coats of arms and often used at funerals   140 catechism set series of
questions and answers (used as a form of instruction by the Church)   5.2 *Location: the
rebel camp near Shrewsbury, then the battlefield*   4 undone ruined   7 still always
9 Supposition notions, uncertainty, speculation   stuck . . . eyes always watching, suspicious
11 ne'er so tame however tame he appears   12 trick trait

Look how he can, or sad or merrily,
Interpretation will misquote our looks,
15   And we shall feed like oxen at a stall,
The better cherished, still the nearer death.
My nephew's trespass may be well forgot,
It hath the excuse of youth and heat of blood,
And an adopted name of privilege,
20   A hare-brained Hotspur, governed by a spleen:
All his offences live upon my head
And on his father's. We did train him on,
And, his corruption being ta'en from us,
We as the spring of all, shall pay for all.
25   Therefore, good cousin, let not Harry know,
In any case, the offer of the king.

VERNON   Deliver what you will, I'll say 'tis so.
Here comes your cousin.

Enter Hotspur [and Douglas]

HOTSPUR   My uncle is returned.
30   Deliver up my lord of Westmorland.—
Uncle, what news?

WORCESTER   The king will bid you battle presently.

DOUGLAS   Defy him by the lord of Westmorland.

HOTSPUR   Lord Douglas, go you and tell him so.

35   DOUGLAS   Marry, and shall, and very willingly.

Exit Douglas

WORCESTER   There is no seeming mercy in the king.

HOTSPUR   Did you beg any? God forbid!

---

13 **Look . . . can** however one appears   **or sad** either sad   14 **misquote** falsely report,
misinterpret   16 **The . . . death** refers to the fact that **oxen** are fattened up before being killed
17 **trespass** wrongdoing, transgression   19 **adopted . . . privilege** nickname which gives him
license (i.e. **Hotspur**, signifying rash impulsiveness)   20 **hare-brained** reckless, rash   **spleen**
violent bad temper (from the abdominal organ regarded as the location of strong emotion)
21 **live upon** shall be blamed on   22 **train** lead   23 **ta'en** derived, caught (like an infectious
disease)   24 **spring** source   26 **In any case** whatever happens   27 **Deliver . . . so** say
what you like, I'll agree   30 **Deliver up** release—Westmorland has been held as surety for
Worcester's safe return   32 **battle** to engage in battle   33 **Defy him by** send our defiant
response through   36 **seeming** apparent

WORCESTER   I told him gently of our grievances,
Of his oath-breaking, which he mended thus,
40   By now forswearing that he is forsworn.
He calls us rebels, traitors, and will scourge
With haughty arms this hateful name in us.

Enter Douglas

DOUGLAS   Arm, gentlemen, to arms! For I have thrown
A brave defiance in King Henry's teeth,
45   And Westmorland that was engaged did bear it,
Which cannot choose but bring him quickly on.

WORCESTER   The Prince of Wales stepped forth before the king,
And, nephew, challenged you to single fight.

HOTSPUR   O, would the quarrel lay upon our heads,
50   And that no man might draw short breath today
But I and Harry Monmouth! Tell me, tell me,
How showed his talking? Seemed it in contempt?

VERNON   No, by my soul. I never in my life
Did hear a challenge urged more modestly,
55   Unless a brother should a brother dare
To gentle exercise and proof of arms.
He gave you all the duties of a man,
Trimmed up your praises with a princely tongue,
Spoke your deservings like a chronicle,
60   Making you ever better than his praise
By still dispraising praise valued with you.
And, which became him like a prince indeed,
He made a blushing cital of himself,

---

38 gently with dignity, like a gentleman   **39 mended** improved on, contributed to
40 forswearing . . . forsworn falsely swearing that he had not broken his word   **41 scourge**
punish   **43 Arm** prepare, put on your armor   **45 engaged** held as hostage   **bear** convey
49 would . . . heads if only the quarrel was just between the two of us   **50 draw short breath**
become out of breath (from fighting)/die   **51 Monmouth** nickname for the prince; the name
of the town on the Welsh-English border where he was born   **54 urged** proposed   **56 gentle**
honorable/not excessively violent   **proof of arms** trial of fighting skills   **57 duties of** respect
due to   **58 Trimmed . . . praises** adorned his praise of you   **59 chronicle** factual historical
account   **60 Making . . . you** increasing your worth since no praise of his could do justice to
your merits   **63 blushing cital** modest account

And chid his truant youth with such a grace
65 As if he mastered there a double spirit
Of teaching and of learning instantly.
There did he pause. But let me tell the world,
If he outlive the envy of this day,
England did never owe so sweet a hope,
70 So much misconstrued in his wantonness.
HOTSPUR   Cousin, I think thou art enamourèd
On his follies: never did I hear
Of any prince so wild a liberty.
But be he as he will, yet once ere night
75 I will embrace him with a soldier's arm,
That he shall shrink under my courtesy.
Arm, arm with speed. And, fellows, soldiers, friends,
Better consider what you have to do
Than I, that have not well the gift of tongue,
80 Can lift your blood up with persuasion.

Enter a Messenger

MESSENGER   My lord, here are letters for you.
HOTSPUR   I cannot read them now.
O, gentlemen, the time of life is short!
To spend that shortness basely were too long,
85 If life did ride upon a dial's point,
Still ending at the arrival of an hour.
And if we live, we live to tread on kings,
If die, brave death, when princes die with us!
Now, for our consciences, the arms are fair,
90 When the intent for bearing them is just.

Enter another Messenger

---

64 chid rebuked, condemned   truant neglectful, misspent   65 double . . . instantly two sides
of himself, both teacher and pupil, at the same time   68 envy malice, hostility   69 owe own
70 wantonness wild, dissolute behavior   72 On of   73 so . . . liberty who indulged in so
much lawless freedom, wild behavior   76 shrink . . . courtesy be overwhelmed by my degree
of courtesy/collapse, be wounded by me   78 Better . . . persuasion you are better off
thinking for yourselves about what you have to do than expecting me, who lacks the gift of
eloquence, to try to rouse your spirits   84 To . . . hour a life spent basely goes on for too long
even if it only lasts an hour   85 If even if   dial's point hand of a clock   88 brave glorious
89 fair justifiable

MESSENGER   My lord, prepare, the king comes on apace.

HOTSPUR   I thank him, that he cuts me from my tale,
For I profess not talking. Only this:
Let each man do his best. And here I draw a sword
95   Whose worthy temper I intend to stain
With the best blood that I can meet withal
In the adventure of this perilous day.
Now, *Esperance!* Percy! And set on.
Sound all the lofty instruments of war,
100   And by that music let us all embrace,
For, heaven to earth, some of us never shall
A second time do such a courtesy.

*They embrace [and exeunt]. The trumpets sound. The King entereth
with his power. Alarum unto the battle. Then enter Douglas and Sir
Walter Blunt [dressed like the King]*

BLUNT   What is thy name, that in battle thus
Thou crossest me? What honour dost thou seek
105   Upon my head?

DOUGLAS   Know then, my name is Douglas,
And I do haunt thee in the battle thus
Because some tell me that thou art a king.

BLUNT   They tell thee true.

110   DOUGLAS   The Lord of Stafford dear today hath bought
Thy likeness, for instead of thee, King Harry,
This sword hath ended him. So shall it thee,
Unless thou yield thee as a prisoner.

---

91 **apace** swiftly   92 **cuts me** forces me to break off   93 **profess** not don't claim to be expert
at   95 **temper** character/degree of hardness   97 **adventure** risky venture   98 *Esperance!*
hope (French; part of the Percy family motto)   99 **instruments** i.e. trumpets, drums
101 **heaven to earth** I'll wager heaven against earth (i.e. something eternal and valuable
against something transitory and unimportant)   **[and exeunt]** most editions introduce a
scene break here, but Folio does not have one and the action continues, with the imaginary
location shifting seamlessly from rebel camp to battlefield   *Alarum* call to battle (played on a
trumpet)   **[dressed like the King]** wearing the king's colors, Blunt is acting as a decoy. Most
editors introduce a scene break at this stage direction, since the stage is momentarily bare and
the imaginary location shifts from the rebel camp to the battlefield, but in the early texts and
onstage the action is continuous   107 **haunt** follow   110 **dear** at great cost   **bought Thy
likeness** paid for appearing like you (i.e. Stafford was also dressed like the king)

BLUNT   I was not born to yield, thou haughty Scot,
115   And thou shalt find a king that will revenge
Lord Stafford's death.   *Fight. Blunt is slain*

Then enters Hotspur

HOTSPUR   O Douglas, had'st thou fought at Holmedon thus,
I never had triumphed o'er a Scot.

DOUGLAS   All's done, all's won, here breathless lies the king.

120   HOTSPUR   Where?

DOUGLAS   Here.

HOTSPUR   This, Douglas? No. I know this face full well:
A gallant knight he was, his name was Blunt,
Semblably furnished like the king himself.

125   DOUGLAS   Ah, fool, go with thy soul, whither it goes!
A borrowed title hast thou bought too dear.
Why didst thou tell me that thou wert a king?

HOTSPUR   The king hath many marching in his coats.

DOUGLAS   Now, by my sword, I will kill all his coats.

130   I'll murder all his wardrobe, piece by piece,
Until I meet the king.

HOTSPUR   Up, and away!
Our soldiers stand full fairly for the day.   *Exeunt*

Alarum, and enter Falstaff, solus

FALSTAFF   Though I could scape shot-free at London, I fear the
135   shot here: here's no scoring but upon the pate. Soft! Who are
you? Sir Walter Blunt. There's honour for you! Here's no
vanity! I am as hot as molten lead, and as heavy too; heaven
keep lead out of me! I need no more weight than mine own
bowels. I have led my ragamuffins where they are peppered:

---

117 **Holmedon** town in Northumberland   122 **full** extremely   124 **Semblably furnished**
similarly dressed and armed   128 **marching . . . coats** wearing the same clothing as him
coats sleeveless outer garments adorned with heraldic arms, worn over armor
133 **stand . . . day** seem likely to win the battle   *solus* alone   134 **shot-free** without paying
the tavern bill/without getting shot   135 **scoring** adding to tavern bill/being wounded
pate head   136 **Here's no vanity!** There's no self-conceit or concern for frivolity in death!
137 **molten** melted   138 **keep lead** i.e. bullets   139 **bowels** guts, stomach   **ragamuffins** i.e.
his ragged company of soldiers   **peppered** shot and killed; this would enable Falstaff to
pocket his soldiers' pay

140   there's not three of my hundred and fifty left alive, and they
        for the town's end, to beg during life. But who comes here?

Enter the Prince

PRINCE HENRY   What, stand'st thou idle here? Lend me thy
        sword.
        Many a nobleman lies stark and stiff
        Under the hoofs of vaunting enemies,
145   Whose deaths are unrevenged. Prithee
        Lend me thy sword.

FALSTAFF   O Hal, I prithee give me leave to breathe awhile.
        Turk Gregory never did such deeds in arms as I have done
        this day. I have paid Percy, I have made him sure.

150 PRINCE HENRY   He is, indeed, and living to kill thee. I prithee lend
        me thy sword.

FALSTAFF   Nay, Hal, if Percy be alive, thou get'st not my sword;
        but take my pistol, if thou wilt.

PRINCE HENRY   Give it me. What, is it in the case?

155 FALSTAFF   Ay, Hal, 'tis hot. There's that will sack a city.

                          The Prince draws out a bottle of sack

PRINCE HENRY   What, is it a time to jest and dally now?

                          Exit. [He] throws it at him [as he leaves]

FALSTAFF   If Percy be alive, I'll pierce him. If he do come in my
        way, so: if he do not, if I come in his willingly, let him make a
        carbonado of me. I like not such grinning honour as Sir
160   Walter hath. Give me life, which if I can save, so: if not,
        honour comes unlooked for, and there's an end.   *Exit*

---

141 **town's end** outskirts of the town where beggars congregate   144 **vaunting** bragging,
vainglorious   148 **Turk Gregory** Pope Gregory VII or XIII; both had violent reputations
Turk violent barbarian   149 **paid** repaid, settled with (i.e. killed)   **sure** i.e. dead, but the
prince shifts the sense to "out of danger"   154 **case** holster   155 **hot** Falstaff claims it has
recently been fired frequently   **sack** destroy   *out* i.e. from Falstaff's holster   157 **pierce**
pronounced "perse"—the word puns on "Percy"   158 **so** so be it/thus—presumably miming
his action   159 **carbonado** dish of scored, grilled meat   **grinning honour** i.e. the sort of
honor Blunt has earned, whose expression is now fixed as death stiffens his facial muscles
160 **so** all well and good   161 **unlooked for** without being sought, unexpectedly   **an end**
death/of my speech

Act 5 Scene 3   *running scene 16 continues*

Alarum. Excursions. Enter the King, the Prince, Lord John of Lan-
caster and Earl of Westmorland   The Prince has been wounded

KING HENRY IV   I prithee,

    Harry, withdraw thyself, thou bleed'st too much.

    Lord John of Lancaster, go you with him.

PRINCE JOHN   Not I, my lord, unless I did bleed too.

5   PRINCE HENRY   I beseech your majesty, make up,

    Lest your retirement do amaze your friends.

KING HENRY IV   I will do so.

    My lord of Westmorland, lead him to his tent.

WESTMORLAND   Come, my lord, I'll lead you to your tent.

10   PRINCE HENRY   Lead me, my lord? I do not need your help;

    And heaven forbid a shallow scratch should drive

    The Prince of Wales from such a field as this,

    Where stained nobility lies trodden on,

    And rebels' arms triumph in massacres!

15   PRINCE JOHN   We breathe too long: come, cousin Westmorland,

    Our duty this way lies. For heaven's sake, come.

                   [*Exeunt Lancaster and Westmorland*]

PRINCE HENRY   By heaven, thou hast deceived me, Lancaster.

    I did not think thee lord of such a spirit:

    Before, I loved thee as a brother, John;

20   But now, I do respect thee as my soul.

KING HENRY IV   I saw him hold Lord Percy at the point

    With lustier maintenance than I did look for

    Of such an ungrown warrior.

PRINCE HENRY   O, this boy lends mettle to us all!   *Exit*

Enter Douglas

5.3 *Location: the battlefield at Shrewsbury*   **Excursions** outbursts of fighting moving
across the stage   **5 make up** advance, bring up your forces   **6 retirement** retreat,
insufficiently aggressive strategy   **amaze** alarm, bewilder   **13 stained** bloodstained (may
play on sense of "dishonored")   **15 breathe** rest, pause   **21 point** i.e. of his sword
22 lustier maintenance more vigorous bearing   **23 ungrown** immature; historically, John
was thirteen at the time of the battle   **24 mettle** courage, spirit

25   DOUGLAS   Another king? They grow like Hydra's heads.
         I am the Douglas, fatal to all those
         That wear those colours on them. What art thou,
         That counterfeit'st the person of a king?
         KING HENRY IV   The king himself, who, Douglas, grieves at heart
30   So many of his shadows thou hast met
         And not the very king. I have two boys
         Seek Percy and thyself about the field:
         But, seeing thou fall'st on me so luckily,
         I will assay thee, so defend thyself.
35   DOUGLAS   I fear thou art another counterfeit,
         And yet, in faith, thou bear'st thee like a king.
         But mine I am sure thou art, whoe'er thou be,
         And thus I win thee.

They fight, the King being in danger

Enter Prince

         PRINCE HENRY   Hold up thy head, vile Scot, or thou art like
40   Never to hold it up again! The spirits
         Of valiant Shirley, Stafford, Blunt, are in my arms;
         It is the Prince of Wales that threatens thee,
         Who never promiseth but he means to pay.

They fight. Douglas flieth

         Cheerly, my lord. How fares your grace?
45   Sir Nicholas Gawsey hath for succour sent,
         And so hath Clifton: I'll to Clifton straight.
         KING HENRY IV   Stay, and breathe awhile.
         Thou hast redeemed thy lost opinion,
         And showed thou mak'st some tender of my life,
50   In this fair rescue thou hast brought to me.
         PRINCE HENRY   O heaven! They did me too much injury
         That ever said I hearkened to your death.

---

25 Hydra's heads in Greek mythology, the Hydra was a monster that grew two heads for
every one that was cut off   **27 colours** i.e. the king's   **28 counterfeit'st** impersonates
30 shadows reflections/those in disguise, actors   **31 very** real, true   **32 Seek** who seek
34 assay test   **37 mine** my victim, conquest   **39 like** likely   **41 are . . . arms** lend strength
to my arms   **43 pay** settle the debt/kill   *flieth* runs away   **44 Cheerly** expression of
encouragement   **48 opinion** reputation   **49 mak'st . . . life** have some care for my life
52 hearkened waited eagerly for, sought

If it were so, I might have let alone
The insulting hand of Douglas over you,
55   Which would have been as speedy in your end
As all the poisonous potions in the world
And saved the treacherous labour of your son.

KING HENRY IV   Make up to Clifton, I'll to Sir Nicholas Gawsey.

Exit

Enter Hotspur

HOTSPUR   If I mistake not, thou art Harry Monmouth.

60   PRINCE HENRY   Thou speak'st as if I would deny my name.

HOTSPUR   My name is Harry Percy.

PRINCE HENRY   Why, then I see
A very valiant rebel of that name.
I am the Prince of Wales; and think not, Percy,
65   To share with me in glory any more:
Two stars keep not their motion in one sphere,
Nor can one England brook a double reign,
Of Harry Percy and the Prince of Wales.

HOTSPUR   Nor shall it, Harry, for the hour is come
70   To end the one of us; and would to heaven
Thy name in arms were now as great as mine!

PRINCE HENRY   I'll make it greater ere I part from thee,
And all the budding honours on thy crest
I'll crop, to make a garland for my head.

75   HOTSPUR   I can no longer brook thy vanities.   *Fight*

Enter Falstaff

FALSTAFF   Well said, Hal! To it Hal! Nay, you shall find no boy's
play here, I can tell you.

Enter Douglas, he fights with Falstaff, who falls down as if he were dead

[*Exit Douglas*]

---

54 insulting threatening, harmful/boastful, contemptuous   **58 Make up to** move your forces
forward   **66 motion** course, trajectory, orbit   **sphere** orbit; stars and planets were thought
to be contained within crystalline spheres   **67 brook** endure   **71 name in arms** military
reputation   **73 budding . . . crest** literally, chivalric favors decorating his helmet; figuratively,
his glorious reputation   **75 vanities** vain boasts   **76 said** done

The Prince killeth Percy [Hotspur]

HOTSPUR   O, Harry, thou hast robbed me of my youth!
    I better brook the loss of brittle life
80   Than those proud titles thou hast won of me.
    They wound my thoughts worse than the sword my flesh:
    But thought's the slave of life, and life, time's fool;
    And time that takes survey of all the world
    Must have a stop. O, I could prophesy,
85   But that the earth and the cold hand of death
    Lies on my tongue. No, Percy, thou art dust
    And food for—   *Dies*
PRINCE HENRY   For worms, brave Percy. Farewell, great heart!
    Ill-weaved ambition, how much art thou shrunk?
90   When that this body did contain a spirit,
    A kingdom for it was too small a bound,
    But now two paces of the vilest earth
    Is room enough. This earth that bears thee dead
    Bears not alive so stout a gentleman.
95   If thou wert sensible of courtesy,
    I should not make so great a show of zeal,
    But let my favours hide thy mangled face,   *Covers Hotspur's face*
    And, even in thy behalf, I'll thank myself
    For doing these fair rites of tenderness.
100   Adieu, and take thy praise with thee to heaven!
    Thy ignominy sleep with thee in the grave,
    But not remembered in thy epitaph!—
    What? Old acquaintance? Could not all this flesh   *He sees*
    Keep in a little life? Poor Jack, farewell!   *Falstaff on the ground*
105   I could have better spared a better man.
    O, I should have a heavy miss of thee,

---

killeth i.e. fatally wounds   **79 brittle** fragile   **80 titles** claims to honor   **84 prophesy**
conventional belief held that the dying were able to foretell the future   **89 Ill-weaved** devious,
tangled   **91 too ... bound** insufficient to contain it   **94 stout** strong, valiant   **95 sensible**
aware   **96 show of zeal** expression of feeling   **97 favours** chivalric tokens worn on his
helmet   **101 ignominy** shame   **106 heavy ... thee** miss you greatly (**heavy** plays on the
sense of "weighty, fat")

If I were much in love with vanity!
Death hath not struck so fat a deer today,
Though many dearer, in this bloody fray.
110   Embowelled will I see thee by and by:
Till then in blood by noble Percy lie.   *Exit*

Falstaff riseth up

FALSTAFF   Embowelled! If thou embowel me today, I'll give you
leave to powder me and eat me too tomorrow. 'Twas time to
counterfeit, or that hot termagant Scot had paid me scot and
115   lot too. Counterfeit? I am no counterfeit; to die, is to be a
counterfeit, for he is but the counterfeit of a man who hath
not the life of a man. But to counterfeit dying, when a man
thereby liveth, is to be no counterfeit, but the true and
perfect image of life indeed. The better part of valour is
120   discretion, in the which better part I have saved my life. I am
afraid of this gunpowder Percy, though he be dead. How, if
he should counterfeit too and rise? I am afraid he would
prove the better counterfeit: therefore I'll make him sure,
yea, and I'll swear I killed him. Why may not he rise as well
125   as I? Nothing confutes me but eyes, and nobody sees me.
Therefore, sirrah, with a new wound in your   *Stabs him*
thigh, come you along with me.   *Takes Hotspur on his back*

Enter Prince and John of Lancaster

PRINCE HENRY   Come, brother John, full bravely hast thou
fleshed
Thy maiden sword.

130   PRINCE JOHN   But, soft! Who have we here?
Did you not tell me this fat man was dead?

---

109 dearer more noble/more valuable   **110 Embowelled** disemboweled (in preparation for
embalming)   **111 in blood** in his own blood (plays on hunting term; a **deer** that was **in blood**
was vigorous and full of life)   **113 powder** embalm/preserve in salt (like venison)
114 termagant savage, violent   **scot and lot** in full   **120 discretion** good judgment
121 gunpowder i.e. fiery, explosive   **125 confutes** refutes, contradicts   **128 fleshed** initiated
into fighting (plays on sense "sexually initiated"; from the practice of feeding hunting dogs
raw meat to excite them)   **129 maiden** virgin, previously unused   **sword** with phallic
connotations

PRINCE HENRY   I did. I saw him dead,
Breathless and bleeding on the ground.—
Art thou alive? Or is it fantasy   *To Falstaff*
135 That plays upon our eyesight? I prithee speak.
We will not trust our eyes without our ears.
Thou art not what thou seem'st.

FALSTAFF   No, that's certain: I am not a double man. But if I be
not Jack Falstaff, then am I a jack. There is   *Throws the*
140 Percy. If your father will do me any honour,   *body down*
so: if not, let him kill the next Percy himself. I look to be
either earl or duke, I can assure you.

PRINCE HENRY   Why, Percy I killed myself and saw thee dead.

FALSTAFF   Didst thou? Lord, Lord, how the world is given to
145 lying! I grant you I was down and out of breath, and so was
he. But we rose both at an instant and fought a long hour by
Shrewsbury clock. If I may be believed, so: if not, let them
that should reward valour bear the sin upon their own
heads. I'll take't on my death, I gave him this wound in the
150 thigh: if the man were alive and would deny it, I would make
him eat a piece of my sword.

PRINCE JOHN This is the strangest tale that e'er I heard.

PRINCE HENRY   This is the strangest fellow, brother John.—
Come, bring your luggage nobly on your back.   *To Falstaff*
155 For my part, if a lie may do thee grace,
I'll gild it with the happiest terms I have.—

A retreat is sounded

The trumpets sound retreat, the day is ours.—
Come, brother, let's to the highest of the field,
To see what friends are living, who are dead.

Exeunt [Prince Henry and Lancaster]

---

134 **fantasy** illusion, imagination   138 **double man** ghost/two men (referring to the fact
he carries Hotspur on his back)   139 **jack** knave   146 **at an instant** simultaneously
147 **Shrewsbury clock** perhaps referring to an actual clock (e.g. the church clock), or a
metaphorical phrase   149 **take't . . . death** swear as though I were about to die and my soul
depended upon it   154 **luggage** i.e. Hotspur   155 **do thee grace** bring you honor
156 **gild** embellish   **happiest** most favorable   *retreat* specific trumpet call signaling retreat
157 **the . . . ours** we have won   158 **highest** highest vantage point

160 FALSTAFF   I'll follow, as they say, for reward. He that rewards me, heaven reward him! If I do grow great again, I'll grow less, for I'll purge, and leave sack, and live cleanly as a nobleman should do.   *Exit*

Act 5 Scene 4   *running scene 16 continues*

The trumpets sound. Enter the King, Prince of Wales, Lord John of Lancaster, Earl of Westmorland [and others], with Worcester and Vernon prisoners

KING HENRY IV   Thus ever did rebellion find rebuke.
Ill-spirited Worcester, did we not send grace,
Pardon and terms of love to all of you?
And wouldst thou turn our offers contrary?
5   Misuse the tenor of thy kinsman's trust?
Three knights upon our party slain today,
A noble earl and many a creature else
Had been alive this hour,
If like a Christian thou hadst truly borne
10   Betwixt our armies true intelligence.
WORCESTER   What I have done my safety urged me to,
And I embrace this fortune patiently,
Since not to be avoided it falls on me.
KING HENRY IV   Bear Worcester to death and Vernon too:
15   Other offenders we will pause upon.
                            Exeunt Worcester and Vernon, [guarded]
How goes the field?
PRINCE HENRY   The noble Scot, Lord Douglas, when he saw
The fortune of the day quite turned from him,
The noble Percy slain, and all his men

---

161 do . . . less become a powerful nobleman/I'll slim down   162 purge repent, purify myself/take laxatives or emetics to cause weight loss   leave give up   **5.4** 1 rebuke punishment   2 Ill-spirited wicked, evil-hearted   grace goodwill, forgiveness   4 turn . . . contrary report the opposite   5 Misuse abuse   tenor character, nature   6 upon our party on our side   10 true intelligence honest information   11 safety concern for personal safety   14 death execution   15 pause upon think about, consider their fates   16 field battlefield

20   Upon the foot of fear, fled with the rest;
        And falling from a hill, he was so bruised
        That the pursuers took him. At my tent
        The Douglas is, and I beseech your grace
        I may dispose of him.

25 KING HENRY IV   With all my heart.

    PRINCE HENRY   Then, brother John of Lancaster, to you
        This honourable bounty shall belong:
        Go to the Douglas, and deliver him
        Up to his pleasure, ransomless and free:
30   His valour shown upon our crests today
        Hath taught us how to cherish such high deeds
        Even in the bosom of our adversaries.

    KING HENRY IV   Then this remains, that we divide our power.—
        You, son John, and my cousin Westmorland
35   Towards York shall bend you with your dearest speed,
        To meet Northumberland and the prelate Scroop,
        Who, as we hear, are busily in arms.—
        Myself and you, son Harry, will towards Wales,
        To fight with Glendower and the Earl of March.
40   Rebellion in this land shall lose his way,
        Meeting the check of such another day.
        And since this business so fair is done,
        Let us not leave till all our own be won.   *Exeunt*

---

20 Upon . . . fear running away in fear   22 took seized, arrested   24 dispose of decide what
to do with   27 honourable bounty the honor of this act of generosity   29 to his pleasure to
do as he pleases   30 crests helmets   31 high noble   32 Even . . . adversaries in Quarto,
Prince John replies before the king's closing speech: "I thank your grace for this high courtesy, /
Which I shall give away immediately" ("give away": undertake, pass on [to Douglas])
33 power army   35 bend you direct your course   dearest utmost   36 prelate ecclesiastical
dignitary (i.e. the Archbishop of York, Richard Scroop)   37 busily in arms engaged in
preparing for battle   41 check curb, reprimand   such another day another battle like
today's   42 fair successfully   43 leave stop   all . . . won everything that rightfully belongs
to us is under our control (**won** puns on "one")

TEXTUAL NOTES

Q = First Quarto text of 1598
Q5 = Fifth Quarto text of 1613
Q7 = Seventh Quarto text of 1632
F = First Folio text of 1623
F2 = a correction introduced in the Second Folio text of 1632
F3 = a correction introduced in the Third Folio text of 1663–64
Ed = a correction introduced by a later editor
SD = stage direction
SH = speech heading (i.e. speaker's name)

List of Parts = Ed BARDOLPH = F. Q = *Bardoll*
1.1.64 Stained = Q. F = Strain'd **66 welcome** = Q. F = welcomes
76 In . . . is = Ed. F *includes at end of king's speech, making his answer his own rhetorical question*
1.2.0 SD *Falstaff* = Ed. F = *Falstaffe and Pointz (it is conceivable that Poins enters here and remains silently in the background during the first 98 lines of dialogue, but more likely that he enters when his name is mentioned at line 94)* **38 of Hybla** = Q. *Not in* F **72 similes** = Q5. F = smiles
80 for . . . it = F. Q = for wisedome cries out in the streets and no man regards it **94 Poins** *set as a speech heading in* F **110 had been** = Q.
F = had **145 Peto, Bardolph** = Ed. F = *Haruey, Rossill (Shakespeare's original names for these characters)* **195 foil** = Q. F = soyle
1.3.24 name = Q. *Not in* F **27 As . . . son** = F. Q = As is deliuered to your maiestie. / Either enuie therefore, or misprision, / Is guiltie of this fault, and not my sonne (F *is more likely to be purposeful revision than compositorial error*) **43 bore** = Q. F = bare **45 corpse** *spelled* Coarse *in* F
68 this = F. Q = his **78 yet he doth**= Q. F = yet doth **136 downfall** = F.
Q = down-trod **164 wore** = F. Q = weare **239 poisoned him** = F.
Q = him poisoned **256 candy** = Q. F = caudie **303 Lord** = Ed. F = loe
2.1.31 SH FIRST CARRIER = Ed. F = *Car.*
2.2.0 SD *and Bardolph* (*not in* F *but implied by Q's "and Peto &c."*)
10 thief's = Q. F = Theefe **12 square** *spelled* squire *in* F **27 me**
my = Q. F = my **46 SH BARDOLPH** = Ed. F = *Bardolfe*, what newes? (*continuation of Poins' speech*) **47 SH GADSHILL** = Ed. F = *Bar.*

71 **SH FIRST TRAVELLER** = Ed. F = *Tra.* 76 **Ah, whoreson** = Ed.
F = a whorson

2.3.1 **SH HOTSPUR** = Ed. *Not in* F 15 **our friends** = Q. F = our Friend
54 **beads** = Q. F = beds 108 **well believe** = Q. F = will beleeue 110 **far
will** = Q. F = farre wilt

2.4.106 **and foot them** = Q. *Not in* F 114 **with lime in't** F *(uncorrected) reads*
with in't F *(corrected) reads* with lime 132 **SH POINS** = Q. F = *Prin.*
178 **ward** = Q. F = word 208 **the** = F. Q = their 221 **plentiful** = Q.
F = plentie 305 **talon** *spelled* Talent *in* F 308 **Braby** = F. Q = Bracy
309 **That** = Q. F = The 316 **that** = Q. F = the 364 **tristful** = Ed. F =
trustfull 378 **sun** *spelled* Sonne *in* F 444 **most** = Q. F = most most
502 **march** = Q. F = Match

3.1.46 **the** = F. Q = he 67 **sent** = Q. F = hent 135 **on** = Ed. Q/F = an
193 **our** = Q. F = your 220 **'twixt** = Q. F = betwixt 228 **hence** = Q.
F = thence

3.2.113 **swaddling** *spelled* swathing *in* F 154 **heaven . . . survive** = F.
Q = God I promise heere, / The which if he be pleasd I shall performe
*(F alteration due to 1606 Parliamentary "Act to Restrain the Abuses of
Players")* 158 **bonds** *spelled* Bands *in* F.

3.2.20 **my** = Q. F = thy 31 **son** *spelled* Sunne *in* F 49 **tithe** = Ed. F = tight
65 **your** = Q. F = you: 76 **sneak-cup** = F. Q = sneakup 120 **owed**
spelled ought *in* F 156 **and cherish** = F. Q = cherish *(F sets this speech as
verse, though it is prose in Q; seems to have been added in an attempt to create
a pentameter line)* 158 **prithee** = Q. F = I prithee

4.1.21 **I his mind** = F. Q = I my mind. Ed = I, my lord 45 **not. His** = Ed. F =
not his 63 **hair** = Q. F = Heire 81 **our** = Q. F = your 88 **as** = Q. F = At
dream = F. Q = tearme 92 **with him** = Q. F = with 127 **hot** = Q. F = not

4.2.3 **Coldfield** = Ed. F = cop-hill 18 **fowl** = Q. F = Foole 31 **tattered** = F3.
F = totter'd

4.4.0 **SD** ***Michael*** *spelled* Michell *in* F

5.1.47 **swore** = Q. F = sware 72 **your younger** = Q. F = yonger 136 **Is it** = F.
Q = tis

5.2.8 **other** = Q. F = others 31 **news** = Q. F = newe- 52 **talking** = F.
Q = tasking 73 **a liberty** = Q. F = at Liberty 79 **Than** = Q. F = That
89 **are** = Q. F = is 139 **ragamuffins** = Ed. F = rag of Muffins
143 **lies** = Q. F = likes

5.3.6 **Lest your** = Q. F = Least you 63 **that** = F. Q = the 93 **thee dead** = Q7.
Q/F = the dead 127 **with me** = Q. F = me

OATHS FROM THE QUARTO

The following oaths were altered in the Folio text as a result of the Parliamentary Act to Restrain the Abuses of Players (spelling has been modernized in this list):

	QUARTO	FOLIO
1.2.18	No, by my troth, not so much	No, not so much
1.2.36	By the Lord, thou say'st true, lad	Thou say'st true, lad
1.2.58	By the Lord, I'll be a brave judge	I'll be a brave judge
1.2.66	Zblood,* I am as melancholy as a gibcat	I am as melancholy as a gib cat
1.2.74–5	I would to God thou and I knew	I would thou and I knew
1.2.86	By the Lord, an I do not	An I do not
1.2.89	Zounds,** where thou wilt, lad	Where thou wilt, lad
1.2.123	Not I, by my faith	Not I
1.2.130	By the Lord, I'll be traitor then	I'll be a traitor then
1.2.135–6	Well, God give thee the spirit . . . and him the . . .	Well, mayst thou have the spirit . . . and he the . . .

* **Zblood** God's blood.
** **Zounds** God's wounds

	QUARTO	**FOLIO**
1.3.132	Zounds, I will speak of him	Yes, I will speak of him
1.3.219	By God, he shall not have a Scot	By heaven, he shall not have a Scot
1.3.253	Zblood, when you and he came back	When you and he came back
1.3.264	I have done, i'faith	I have done, in sooth
2.1.15	By the mass, there is ne'er a king	There is ne'er a king
2.1.25	God's body, the turkeys	The turkeys
2.1.34	Nay, by God, soft, I know	Nay, soft, I pray ye; I know
2.1.74	and yet, zounds, I lie	And yet, I lie
2.1.83	Nay, by my faith, I think you are	Nay, I think rather you are
2.2.32	Zblood, I'll not bear mine own flesh	I'll not bear mine own flesh
2.2.58	Zounds, will they not rob us	Will they not rob us
2.3.14	By the Lord, our plot	I protest, our plot
2.3.19	Zounds, an I were	By this hand if I were
2.3.77–8	In faith I'll know your business	In sooth, I'll know your business
2.3.85	In faith I'll break	Indeed, I'll break
2.4.8	upon their salvation	upon their confidence
2.4.11	a good boy, by the Lord, so they call me	a good boy
2.4.121	I could sing psalms or anything	I could sing all manner of songs

	QUARTO	FOLIO
2.4.132	Zounds, ye fat paunch	Ye fat paunch
2.4.132	call me coward, by the Lord, I'll stab thee	call me coward, I'll stab thee
2.4.174	Pray God	Pray heaven
2.4.218–9	Zounds, an I were at the strappado	No. Were I at the strappado
2.4.226	Zblood, you starveling	Away, you starveling
2.4.246	By the Lord, I knew ye as well as he	I knew ye as well as he
2.4.253	But by the Lord, lads	But, lads
2.4.261	O Jesu, my lord the prince	My lord the prince
2.4.275	Now sirs, by our lady, you fought fair	Now, sirs: you fought fair
2.4.279	Faith, tell me now	Tell me now
2.4.343	Not a whit, i'faith	Not a whit
2.4.361	O Jesu, this is excellent sport	This is excellent sport
2.4.366	O Jesu, he doth it as like	O, rare, he doth it as like
2.4.409	Zblood, my lord, they are false	I'faith, my lord, they are false
2.4.410	for a young prince, i'faith	for a young prince
2.4.434	God help the wicked	heaven help the wicked
2.4.444	O Jesu, my lord, my lord	O, my lord, my lord
3.2.4	I know not whether God will have it so	. . . whether heaven will . . .
3.2.29	God pardon	Heaven pardon

	QUARTO	FOLIO
3.2.131	And God forgive	And heaven forgive
3.2.154	This, in the name of God, I promise here	. . . in the name of heaven . . .
3.3.30	By this fire, that's God's angel	By this fire
3.3.41	God reward me for it.	Heaven reward me for it!
3.3.42	Zblood, I would my face were	I would my face were
3.3.43	Godamercy,* so should I	So should I
3.3.54	I defy thee: God's light, I was never	I defy thee. I was never
3.3.74	O Jesu, I have heard	I have heard
3.3.76	Zblood and he	An if he
3.3.78	in that door i'faith	in that door
3.3.104	Why a thing to thank God on.	Why, a thing to thank heaven on.
3.3.105	I am no thing to thank God on,	I am no thing to thank heaven on,
3.3.136–7	I pray God my girdle break	let my girdle break
4.1.6	By God I cannot flatter	By heaven, I cannot flatter
4.1.18	Zounds, how has he the leisure	How? Has he the leisure
4.3.44	And God defend,	And heaven defend
4.3.121	Pray God you do	Pray heaven you do

* **Godamercy** God have mercy

	QUARTO	*FOLIO*
5.1.127	Why, thou owest God a death	Why, thou ow'st heaven a death
5.2.137–8	God keep lead out of me	heaven keep lead out of me!
5.2.152	Nay before God Hal, if Percy	Nay, Hal, if Percy
5.3.11	And God forbid	And heaven forbid
5.3.16	for God's sake come	For heaven's sake, come
5.3.17	By God thou hast	By heaven, thou hast
5.3.51	O God, they did me too much injury,	O heaven! They did me too much injury
5.3.70	and would to God,	and would to heaven
5.3.113–4	Zblood, 'twas time to counterfeit	'Twas time to counterfeit
5.3.120–1	Zounds I am afraid of this gunpowder	I am afraid of this gunpowder
5.3.122	by my faith I am afraid he	I am afraid he
5.3.150–1	zounds I would make him eat	I would make him eat
5.3.161	God reward him	heaven reward him!

SCENE-BY-SCENE ANALYSIS

ACT 1 SCENE 1

King Henry despairs at the civil unrest that has dominated his reign. He describes the "civil butchery," establishing the motif of "blood" that highlights both the violent conflict and the theme of lineage and inheritance. He declares his intention to lead a long-planned Crusade to the Holy Land. He talks of the Crucifixion, "fourteen hundred years ago," and of the "twelvemonth" plan he has had to make his Crusade, establishing the motif of time, which functions to place the events of the play in a wider historical context, as well as drawing attention to the brevity of individual man's existence within this.

Westmorland informs Henry that the English forces, led by the "noble Mortimer," have been defeated by the Welsh rebels, led by Glendower. Henry realizes he must put his plans for a Crusade aside, and Westmorland tells him of more fighting between Scottish insurgents and "the gallant Hotspur . . . / Young Harry Percy." Henry updates Westmorland: Hotspur defeated the "bold Scots" and took many noble prisoners: "an honourable spoil." This emphasizes the theme of "honour," further reinforced by Henry's comparisons between Hotspur and his own son, Prince Henry (also called Harry): the shared name establishes the deliberate paralleling and comparison between the two young men.

Lineage and father–son relationships are addressed as the king envies Hotspur's father, Lord Northumberland, whose son is "the theme of honour's tongue," while "riot and dishonour stain the brow" of his own. He also comments, however, on Hotspur's "pride" in only sending one noble prisoner to the king and keeping the rest. Westmorland suggests that this is due to the influence of his uncle, Worcester, who is "Malevolent" toward the king. Henry has sent for Hotspur to explain his actions.

ACT 1 SCENE 2

Lines 1–98: Providing a comic contrast to the political/military concerns of the previous scene, Prince Henry and Falstaff exchange rapid-fire, quick-witted banter. Henry comments on his friend's corrupt lifestyle spent drinking and visiting brothels. Despite the accusation that Falstaff is "fat-witted," his responses show that he can be quick and entertaining in his use of language, although both men speak in prose, reflecting the "low" nature of their subject matter. Falstaff is revealed as a robber and a freeloader, but he appears good-natured and fond of Prince Henry, sometimes addressing him in a paternal tone that serves to highlight the estranged relationship between the prince and his father. Falstaff refers to the future, when Henry will be king, reminding the audience of the obligations of birth and rank that Henry is neglecting.

Lines 99–174: They are joined by Poins, who reveals that he plans to rob a party of traveling pilgrims and traders, all "with fat purses," the next morning. Falstaff agrees to join him, but Henry refuses. Poins asks Falstaff to leave them while he convinces Henry to participate. Poins explains that he has planned "a jest": Falstaff, Peto, Bardolph, and Gadshill will commit the robbery, after which Poins and Henry will rob them of their ill-gotten gains. Henry objects that the others will know them by their horses, "and by every other appointment," raising the question of appearance and identity. Poins suggests they leave their horses and disguise their "outward garments" with outfits of buckram. Henry agrees to the plan and Poins goes to prepare.

Lines 175–197: Henry's soliloquy reveals a different side to his character. Speaking in blank verse, an indication of his noble status, he compares himself to the sun (a repeated image, associated with royalty), which has permitted "the base contagious clouds / To smother up his beauty from the world." Using repeated images of concealment, disguise, and revelation, he explains that he is hiding his true character in order to appear even greater when the world witnesses his "reformation." Despite revealing a strong sense of his social status and responsibility, he is deliberately deceiving his friends and family and seems more concerned with creating a "glittering" appearance than with his obligations.

ACT 1 SCENE 3

Lines 1–124: At court Hotspur has responded to King Henry's summons, accompanied by his father, Northumberland, and his uncle, Worcester. The king announces that he has been too "temperate," and that Hotspur has taken advantage of his "patience." He declares that from now on he will be "Mighty and to be feared." Worcester argues that their family does not deserve to be punished, particularly as they helped Henry to achieve his "greatness." Henry sends Worcester out and Northumberland pleads on his son's behalf, arguing that there has been some "envy or misprision" in the representation of his actions over the prisoners. Hotspur offers an explanation that shows his eloquence, but acknowledges his potentially rash temper. He tells Henry that, "dry with rage and extreme toil" after the lengthy battle, with his wounds still raw and "smarting," he was approached by a courtier, a "popinjay," whose foppish behavior and demands for the prisoners at that moment provoked him into rudeness. Sir Walter Blunt suggests that under such circumstances, Hotspur's actions might be overlooked, but Henry is still angry, revealing that Hotspur retains the prisoners and refuses to return them unless the king ransoms Mortimer, Hotspur's brother-in-law, from Glendower. Citing Mortimer's marriage to Glendower's daughter as evidence of treachery, Henry refuses to ransom "revolted Mortimer." Hotspur furiously defends his brother-in-law, describing his bravery in the "bloody" battle with Glendower and accusing the king of slander. Henry forbids Hotspur to mention Mortimer again and, demanding the immediate delivery of the prisoners, he leaves.

Lines 125–310: Hotspur announces that even if "the devil come and roar for them" he will not hand over the prisoners. His father urges him to calm down as Worcester returns, but Hotspur ignores him, calling Henry an "unthankful king." Hotspur describes Henry's reaction to the mention of Mortimer, and Worcester reveals that Richard II (who was deposed by Henry, and murdered shortly after) named Mortimer as his successor. Hotspur now understands Henry's reluctance to help Mortimer, but is angry with his family for their role in deposing "that sweet lovely rose," Richard, and replacing him with "this thorn, this canker, Bullingbrook," and with Henry for his ingratitude for the "shames" that the family has undergone on his behalf.

Worcester tries to tell Hotspur of a "deep and dangerous" plan, but Hotspur ignores him, continuing to rail against Henry. Northumberland tells his son that he is "wasp-tongued and impatient." Eventually, Worcester is able to outline his plan to ally with the Scottish and Welsh forces against Henry. He advises Hotspur to release his Scottish prisoners without ransom and to form an alliance with the Earl of Douglas. Worcester tells Northumberland to enlist the help of the Archbishop of York, Lord Scroop, whose brother was executed by Henry. Worcester himself will go to Wales to Glendower and Mortimer, promising to arrange a meeting of all of their "powers."

ACT 2 SCENE 1

At an innyard on the London–Canterbury road, two Carriers are preparing their horses. Once again, the motif of time is dominant, establishing the night setting of the scene and reinforcing the wider temporal concerns of the play. The Carriers are interrupted by Gadshill, asking for a lantern but, suspicious of his motives, they refuse and leave. The references to darkness emphasize secrecy and deception: both the comic deception of Falstaff by Poins, and the more serious plotting against King Henry. The inn's chamberlain arrives and informs Gadshill that there are wealthy guests preparing to leave. Gadshill sets off to organize the robbery.

ACT 2 SCENE 2

Farther down the highway, Poins tells Henry, Peto, and Bardolph that he has hidden Falstaff's horse for a joke. They stand aside as Falstaff approaches, angrily calling for Poins. Henry tells Falstaff to be quiet and pretends to go to find Poins, but joins the others in the darkness as they listen to Falstaff complaining and cursing them. They join him again, and Henry teases "fat-guts" Falstaff as he demands the return of his horse. Gadshill arrives with the news that there is "money of the king's" on its way down the hill. Henry says that he and Poins will go further down the lane to catch their victims if they should escape from the others, and they leave, exchanging an aside about their "disguises." Falstaff, Peto, Bardolph, and Gadshill carry out the robbery, leaving with their victims. Henry and Poins return, disguised, and hide as the robbers reenter, dividing up their profits. As Falstaff says that Poins and Henry will get nothing for being "arrant cowards," the prince and his companion set upon them. Frightened, the robbers run away, leaving the loot behind. Henry laughs at the fact that Falstaff must walk home.

ACT 2 SCENE 3

Hotspur's serious plans contrast with the low and essentially comic plotting of the last two scenes, reinforcing the deliberate character contrast with Prince Henry. Hotspur is reading a letter from an unnamed nobleman, who has declined to join the rebellion. Hotspur criticizes the letter writer as a "shallow cowardly hind," showing his quick temper and concerns with honor. Worried that the "frosty-spirited rogue" will reveal the plot to the king, Hotspur decides that he must set off at once to join his fellow conspirators. He is interrupted by his wife, Lady Percy, demanding to know what is wrong. She complains that he has been neglecting her: instead of "pleasure and . . . golden sleep" in bed, he disturbs her with nightmares, talking of "prisoners' ransom and of soldiers slain." She is worried that her brother, Mortimer, intends to stake his claim to the throne, and that Hotspur is involved. Although their exchange reveals a loving relationship, Henry is impatient, saying that he has no time for love. He tells her that she must not question him, as, although he knows her to be "wise" and "constant," she is a woman, and therefore not to be trusted. He consoles her with the promise that she shall soon join him.

ACT 2 SCENE 4

Lines 1–102: Prince Henry continues to lead a disreputable existence, ignoring his noble birth and responsibilities. In the Eastcheap tavern, he boasts to Poins of his drinking exploits. In order to "drive away time" while they wait for Falstaff, he orders Poins to help him tease the young bartender, Francis. The prince mocks Francis for his limited use of language (forcing a contrast with the verbal dexterity of other characters in the play, such as himself, Falstaff, and Hotspur) and for his hardworking nature. He moves on to criticize the similarly industrious character of "the Hotspur of the north," one of his first acknowledgments of the political world outside his current life.

Lines 103–274: The others arrive and, as they drink, Henry and Falstaff banter rudely with each other, demonstrating the mixture of affection and contempt that the prince feels for Falstaff, and Falstaff's simultaneous lack of respect and awareness of Henry's royal status. Falstaff accuses the prince and Poins of being cowards for not taking part in the robbery. When Henry asks where the loot is, Falstaff tells how they were themselves robbed by "a hundred" men. Dramatic irony compounds the humor as Falstaff boasts of how he fought off their attackers and only escaped "by a miracle." Encouraged by Poins and Henry, he continues to exaggerate, contradicting himself and inventing details, until the prince calls him a liar. They exchange insults until Henry reveals the truth: it was he and Poins who robbed them. Falstaff quickly recovers, claiming that he knew this, and that he did not fight back because he did not wish "to kill the heir-apparent." They are interrupted by Hostess Quickly who announces that a nobleman has brought Henry a message from the king. Falstaff goes to "send him packing."

Lines 275–443: Falstaff returns, and the prince immediately starts taunting him again, but Falstaff tells Henry that he has been summoned to court the following morning by his father. Falstaff tells Henry of the rebellion, and Hotspur's alliance with the Welsh and Scottish forces, and urges him to prepare what he is going to say to the king the next day. In a meta-theatrical episode, they "act out" Henry's coming interview with his father. Despite its comic overtones, this episode explores the relationships that Henry has with both Falstaff and his father. The questions that Falstaff puts to him as to whether the "son of England" should "prove a thief and take purses" emphasize the disparity between the prince's rank and duty and his current behavior. When Falstaff uses his "role" as king to recommend that Henry keep Falstaff by him even when he banishes the others, Henry decides that they should swap places. He is playing the role of king, and abusing Falstaff, when a knocking is heard and Bardolph runs in.

Lines 444–507: Bardolph announces that the Watch are at the door. Hostess Quickly adds that they have come to search the house. The prince advises Falstaff to hide while he talks to the sheriff. Henry denies that Falstaff has been there, but promises to find him and send him to the sheriff, who leaves. Peto finds Falstaff snoring behind the arras and Henry goes through his pockets, finding only a bill for food and drink. Henry tells Peto that he will go and see the king in the morning, and warns him that they "must all to the wars," joking that he will put Falstaff in command of an infantry company.

ACT 3 SCENE 1

Lines 1–148: The rebels meet in Wales to discuss their plans. They begin civilly, but Hotspur loses patience with Glendower's beliefs in astrological signs. Glendower claims that King Henry fears him because, at his birth, heaven was "full of fiery shapes" and the earth "Shaked like a coward," but Hotspur is rudely dismissive of these claims and mocks Glendower. Mortimer intervenes and they look at a map showing the potential division of land after the defeat of Henry. Mortimer announces that he, Hotspur, and Worcester will set forth the next day to meet Northumberland and the Scottish armies at Shrewsbury, while Glendower gathers his forces to meet them "in fourteen days." Glendower promises to be with them quickly, and to bring their "ladies" with him (Kate, Lady Percy, and his own daughter, wife of Mortimer). Hotspur, however, is still looking at the map and announces that he is not satisfied that his share is equal. Showing his lack of maturity, he goads Glendower and threatens to divert the course of the River Trent. In contrast to Hotspur, Glendower remains calm and agrees to a minor change in the map before leaving to find the ladies.

Lines 149–193: Mortimer rebukes Hotspur for his rudeness. Hotspur complains that Glendower angers him by talking about myths and magic and "skimble-skamble stuff." Worcester tells Hotspur that he must "amend" his behavior, providing an accurate analysis of his nephew's character: divided between "greatness, courage, blood" and "harsh rage . . . Pride, haughtiness, opinion and disdain."

Lines 194–268: Glendower brings the ladies to bid good-bye. He translates the conversation between his daughter and Mortimer, as husband and wife do not speak each other's language. Their exchange is apparently romantic, however, and she sings him a parting song in Welsh. Hotspur mocks them as he and Lady Percy wrangle affectionately, perhaps showing a more genuine relationship than that of Mortimer and his wife. Mortimer and Hotspur leave.

ACT 3 SCENE 2

King Henry sends his lords away so that he can speak privately with Prince Henry. The king wonders whether God is punishing him through his son for some "displeasing service" he has done in the past. Angry and disappointed, he rebukes Prince Henry for his lifestyle of "barren pleasures [and] rude society." Prince Henry claims that he has not behaved as badly as rumor suggests and asks for his father's pardon, but the king continues, pointing out that the prince's younger brother, Prince John, has had to take on his responsibilities. He argues that if he himself had been "So common-hackneyed in the eyes of men" during his campaign for the throne, he would have lost the good opinion of the public, which was so important to his cause. In an emotional appeal, he compares Prince Henry's behavior to that of Richard II, who "Mingled his royalty with carping fools" and destroyed his popularity by being too much in the public eye. He talks about Hotspur, claiming that he "hath more worthy interest to the state" than Prince Henry does, as he has shown courage and nobility in battle, even in his challenge to the king. He ends by saying that his son is just as likely to fight against him through "fear" and "Base inclination." Moved, Henry begs him not to "think so" and promises to redeem himself "on Percy's head," washing away his own "shame" with the blood of battle. His speech is eloquent and his use of blank verse and stirring imagery form a stark contrast with his speech and behavior in previous scenes.

The king places Prince Henry in charge of the royal forces. Sir Walter Blunt brings news that the rebels are going to meet in Shrewsbury, and King Henry says that he knows this: Prince John has already set out. He announces that Prince Henry will set out "on Wednesday next," that he will follow, and that all their forces shall meet "at Bridgnorth" in twelve days.

ACT 3 SCENE 3

In the Eastcheap tavern, Falstaff and Bardolph are involved in a humorous exchange. Hostess Quickly interrupts and Falstaff demands to know if she has caught whoever picked his pocket. She is indignant at the suggestion that there are thieves in her house, and reminds him that he owes her money. He claims that as well as his money, a seal ring "worth forty mark" has been stolen, but she tells everyone that the prince said that the ring was made of copper. Falstaff denounces Henry as a "sneak-cup" and threatens to "cudgel" him. As they bicker, Prince Henry arrives. They reveal their argument to him, Falstaff claiming that he has had "three or four bonds of forty pound apiece, and a seal-ring" stolen, and the Hostess telling Henry that Falstaff spoke "most vilely of" him and claimed that the prince owes him a thousand pounds. Falstaff jokes his way out of the accusations, and Henry reveals that it was he who went through Falstaff's pockets and found nothing of value. He asks Falstaff if he is "not ashamed," but Falstaff is unrepentant, calling Hostess Quickly to prepare breakfast. Prince Henry reveals that he has paid back the sum taken in the robbery so Falstaff is no longer in trouble, and turns the conversation to the impending conflict, providing a serious conclusion to the boisterous comedy of the scene. Henry tells Falstaff that he has given him command of an infantry company, much to his lazy friend's disgust, but the humor that this generates is swiftly forgotten as the prince sustains his new, more serious character.

ACT 4 SCENE 1

The swift movement between the four scenes of this act emphasizes the increased pace of events.

Lines 1–88: Hotspur and Douglas are interrupted by a Messenger bringing news that Northumberland is "grievous sick" and unable to lead his forces to join them. Northumberland's letter urges them to go into battle: in fact, they have no choice as the king is aware of their intentions and is preparing to fight. Worcester is concerned, but Hotspur remains optimistic, arguing that they will not be using all of their military strength at once, and will have "A rendezvous, a home to fly unto" if they are unsuccessful. Douglas agrees, but Worcester worries that it will seem as though there is a division in the rebel forces, suggesting weakness. Hotspur bravely, if naively, retains his optimism.

Lines 89–143: Vernon brings news that Westmorland and Prince John are marching toward them with an army of seven thousand. The king has also set out "With strong and mighty preparation." Hotspur listens calmly, then mockingly asks about Prince Henry, "The nimble-footed madcap," showing contempt for the prince's lifestyle and reputation. Vernon reports, however, that Henry's forces are "All furnished, all in arms," "Glittering in golden coats," "full of spirit," and "gorgeous as the sun," evoking Henry's own image of himself at the end of Act 1 Scene 2. Vernon recounts how the prince himself is like a "feathered Mercury," riding on "fiery Pegasus." Angry at this praise of Henry, Hotspur declares himself "on fire" to go into battle. He wants to meet the prince in single combat, "Harry to Harry," symbolically emphasizing the dramatic paralleling of the two characters. He asks after Glendower, and Vernon reveals that the Welsh leader is not ready. Worcester and Douglas are disturbed by this news, but Hotspur urges them into battle, to "die all, die merrily."

ACT 4 SCENE 2

On the march to Shrewsbury, Falstaff sends Bardolph to buy wine. Falstaff reveals how he has "misused" the power of conscription, making "in exchange of a hundred and fifty soldiers, three hundred and odd pounds," by recruiting mostly wealthy men who can buy their way back out of service. Consequently, the troops he now has assembled consist of "scarecrows" such as prisoners, "servingmen . . . revolted tapsters and ostlers trade-fallen." While this provides comic relief from the preparations for battle, Falstaff's sustained dishonesty contrasts with Prince Henry's newfound sense of duty and honor. Falstaff is joined by the prince and Westmorland, who criticize his troops. Falstaff comments callously that they are good enough for cannon fodder, and Henry urges him to hurry: the king and Hotspur are already encamped and ready for battle.

ACT 4 SCENE 3

The rebels argue over when to attack. A trumpet sounds a parley and Blunt brings a message from the king. Henry asks that the rebels "name [their] griefs," promising to try to resolve matters and to pardon those who have stood against him. Hotspur launches into a long complaint, revealing the grievances of the Percy family against the king, detailing the help that they gave him in overthrowing Richard II and the king's subsequent ingratitude, such as his refusal to ransom Mortimer. When Blunt offers to relay this, however, Hotspur shows unusual restraint, saying that Worcester will be sent "in the morning early" to talk with the king. He responds graciously to Blunt's wish for a peaceful solution.

ACT 4 SCENE 4

In a scene that foreshadows events in *Henry IV Part II*, the Archbishop of York sends letters to the Lord Marshal and Lord Scroop. He fears the outcome of a battle without Northumberland and Glendower's forces and is strengthening his defenses in readiness against the king, who is aware of his role in the conspiracy.

ACT 5 SCENE 1

The pace of the previous act is sustained into Act 5, reinforcing the rapidity and confusion of the battle.

The king and prince discuss the worsening weather. Worcester is brought in and the king chastises him for deceiving his trust and bringing them to conflict. He gives Worcester the opportunity to "unknit / This churlish knot of all-abhorrèd war," and Worcester responds that he is not the one responsible for the hostilities. He reiterates the complaints made by Hotspur in Act 4 Scene 3, concerning the "unkind usage" of the Percy family by the king. The king responds that this is merely an excuse with which to "face the garment of rebellion." Prince Henry offers to meet Hotspur in single combat to settle the matter, in order to prevent lives being lost in battle. He acknowledges Hotspur's bravery and nobility, and admits his own past failings as a "truant . . . to chivalry." The king forbids this and again offers to pardon the rebels if they surrender now. Worcester goes to deliver this message, and the prince warns his father that the rebels will not accept his offer of peace. The king leaves to prepare. The prince and Falstaff say good-bye, and, once he is alone, Falstaff muses on the futility of honor if it leads to death, reasoning that "honour" is merely "a word."

ACT 5 SCENE 2

Lines 1–42: Worcester tells Vernon that Hotspur must not learn of the king's offer. He argues that, while the king may forgive and forget Hotspur's "trespass" as a youthful misdemeanor, he and Northumberland would be punished by Henry; thus selfishly placing his own concerns before the possibility of averting the war. Hotspur joins them and Worcester announces that the king will engage in battle, dishonestly claiming that he "gently" told Henry of their "grievances" and that the king called them traitors.

Lines 43–102: Douglas returns from sending Westmorland to the king with a message of defiance and Worcester tells Hotspur that Prince Henry offered to meet him in single combat. Hotspur is pleased with this idea, echoing Henry's honorable concern for the lives of his men. Vernon describes how Henry praised Hotspur and confessed his own "truant youth," but Hotspur is unimpressed, expressing his intention to meet Henry on the battlefield. A messenger brings in letters, but Hotspur claims that "the time of life is short" and that he cannot read them now. Another Messenger announces that the king is approaching and Hotspur leads the rebels to battle.

Lines 103–133: Douglas and Blunt enter, Blunt disguised as the king. They fight and Blunt is killed. Hotspur arrives and recognizes Blunt, revealing that Henry has many decoys on the battlefield. They head back to battle.

Lines 134–161: Falstaff enters, alone, and sees Blunt's body, remarking: "There's honour for you!" Prince Henry finds him and demands his sword, chastising him for standing idle. Falstaff offers him a pistol, but the prince finds a bottle of wine in the holster. Disgusted, he leaves, and Falstaff reiterates his point that he would rather live than achieve honor in death.

ACT 5 SCENE 3

Lines 1–24: The king urges an injured Prince Henry to withdraw, accompanied by Prince John, but they refuse. Prince John and Westmorland return to the fight and the king and Prince Henry comment on John's bravery before the prince also returns to battle.

Lines 25–58: Douglas finds the king alone and, although uncertain whether it is another "counterfeit," begins to fight him. The king is in danger of defeat when Prince Henry rejoins them, causing Douglas to flee. King Henry tells his son that he has "redeemed" his "lost opinion" before heading back into battle.

Lines 59–111: Hotspur arrives and the prince declares that one of the Harrys must die: "Two stars keep not their motion in one sphere." As they fight, Falstaff arrives, followed by Douglas. They also fight and Falstaff collapses as if dead. As Douglas leaves, Henry kills Hotspur and eulogizes over his body, acknowledging his bravery. He sees Falstaff, apparently dead, and delivers an ambiguous but fond eulogy, promising to return for both bodies later.

Lines 112–163: In a moment of bathos after the tensions of the scene, Falstaff sits up, revealing that he faked his death to avoid being killed. He decides to claim that Hotspur regained consciousness and that he, Falstaff, killed him. He stabs the body and is interrupted by the two princes, to whom he tells his unlikely tale. Unconvinced, Henry tells Falstaff he will back him in his claims if it will do his friend "grace." They leave as the retreat signals their victory over the rebels.

ACT 5 SCENE 4

The royal party enters, with Worcester and Vernon as prisoners. The king lays responsibility for the day's bloodshed on Worcester for not accepting his offer of peace, and condemns both rebels to death. Prince Henry reveals that he has Douglas prisoner and asks permission to release him in recognition of his bravery. The king agrees and issues his instructions: Prince John and Westmorland are to lead forces against Northumberland and Scroop, while he and Prince Henry march to Wales to fight Glendower. Despite the victory, the play ends as it began: with the country in civil conflict.

SYNOPSIS OF
HENRY IV PART II

In despair at the death of his son Hotspur, the Earl of Northumberland lends his support to a second rebellion, led by the Archbishop of York. As the threat of civil war looms over the country, King Henry IV grows sick, while also fearing that his son Prince Henry (known as Harry and, by Falstaff, as Hal) has returned to his old life with Falstaff and the other disreputable denizens of the Eastcheap tavern. Falstaff is sent on a recruiting expedition and renews old acquaintances in Gloucestershire. The rebel army is met by the King's forces, led this time by Hal's younger brother, Prince John of Lancaster. On his deathbed, King Henry is reconciled with his son, who has begun to distance himself from his former companions. A new, mature Hal accepts the crown as Henry V.

HENRY IV IN PERFORMANCE: THE RSC AND BEYOND

The best way to understand a Shakespeare play is to see it or ideally to participate in it. By examining a range of productions, we may gain a sense of the extraordinary variety of approaches and interpretations that are possible—a variety that gives Shakespeare his unique capacity to be reinvented and made "our contemporary" four centuries after his death.

We begin with a brief overview of the play's theatrical and cinematic life, offering historical perspectives on how it has been performed. We then analyze in more detail a series of productions staged over the last half century by the Royal Shakespeare Company. The sense of dialogue between productions that can only occur when a company is dedicated to the revival and investigation of the Shakespeare canon over a long period, together with the uniquely comprehensive archival resource of promptbooks, program notes, reviews, and interviews held on behalf of the RSC at the Shakespeare Birthplace Trust in Stratford-upon-Avon, allows an "RSC stage history" to become a crucible in which the chemistry of the play can be explored.

We then go to the horse's mouth. Modern theater is dominated by the figure of the director. He or she must hold together the whole play, whereas the actor must concentrate on his or her part. The director's viewpoint is therefore especially valuable. Shakespeare's plasticity is wonderfully revealed when we hear the directors of two highly successful productions answering the same questions in very different ways. And finally, we offer the actor's perspective: a view of the play through the eyes of Prince Hal.

FOUR CENTURIES OF *HENRY IV*: AN OVERVIEW

Henry IV Part I was probably written and performed between 1596 and 1597 with *Part II* following a year later. The first performances of which records survive were at court in 1612–13 when a total of twenty plays were presented to celebrate the marriage of James I's daughter Elizabeth to Frederick, the Elector of Palatine. They are listed as *The Hotspurre* and *Sir John Falstaffe*, and were only later identified as the two parts of Shakespeare's *Henry IV*. These alternative titles suggest that both were originally seen in terms of their star parts rather than as a political study of kingship with Prince Hal at the center. As scholars and theater historians have pointed out:

> That change of emphasis required a change of format. It takes both parts of *Henry IV* followed by *Henry V* to make Prince Hal into a fully-fledged hero, or anti-hero, and it was not until the mid-twentieth century that an influential cycle of these plays . . . was staged in the English theatre.[1]

Until this point the plays were performed individually and, although *Part II* was clearly designed as a sequel to *Part I*—probably in order to capitalize on the enormous and immediate popularity of the first play—there is little evidence to suggest that they were performed in sequence. Numerous contemporary references and reprints of the Quarto editions all point to their popularity and success, however. The writer Nicholas Breton mentions seeing "the play of Ancient Pistol,"[2] and Leonard Digges' prefatory poem to the 1640 edition of Shakespeare's poems provides further evidence of their popularity:

> . . . let but Falstaff come, Hal, Poins,
> the rest, you scarce shall have a room,
> All is so pestered . . .

In his commendatory poem to the Folio edition of Beaumont and Fletcher (1647), Sir Thomas Palmer claims he could "tell how long / Falstaff from cracking nuts have kept the throng."

Falstaff was originally played either by company clown Will Kempe or comic actor Thomas Pope, while Prince Hal was almost certainly played by Richard Burbage, the leading tragedian with Shakespeare's acting company, the Lord Chamberlain's (later the King's) Men. John Lowin took over the role of Falstaff: "before the

Wars Lowin used to act, with mighty applause Falstaff."[3] During the interregnum from 1642 to 1660, the theaters were technically closed, although various means were employed to get around the prohibition on plays, such as the introduction of music and dancing into sketches from popular plays known as drolls; a collection of twenty-seven of these, *The Wits, or Sport Upon Sport*, by Francis Kirkman, was published in 1662 with three featuring episodes from Shakespeare's plays, including *The Bouncing Knight, or the Robbers Robbed*, centered on Falstaff's exploits. The frontispiece illustration places Falstaff and the Hostess in prominent positions.

Henry IV Part I continued to be popular after the Restoration and was one of the first plays performed by Thomas Killigrew's King's Company in 1660. Samuel Pepys' diary records his attendance at no fewer than four performances over the period 1660–68. The play's main attractions were still Hotspur and Falstaff. Thomas Betterton, the great Restoration actor-manager, played Hotspur in 1682, with "wild impatient starts" and "fierce and flashing fire,"[4] but in the 1700 revival he took on the role of Falstaff. Thomas Davies records how "the versatility of Betterton's genius was never more conspicuous than in his resigning the choleric Hotspur, in his declining years, and assuming the humour and gaiety of Falstaff, in which he is said to have been full as acceptable to the public as in the former."[5] In contrast to most Shakespearean revivals in the period, it underwent relatively few changes apart from textual cuts of long political speeches, the Welsh dialogue and song, and much of the mock trial in the tavern. Betterton's continued popularity as Falstaff was largely responsible for a revival of *Part II* during the eighteenth century, in which the star turns were Falstaff and Justice Shallow.

In the next generation, James Quin, who had previously played Hotspur and the king, was the most notable Falstaff. David Garrick played Hotspur on five occasions, dressed "in a laced frock and a Ramilie wig,"[6] but was plainly unsuited to the role, and the part was taken over by Spranger Barry. One of the theatrical highlights seems to have been Falstaff carrying Hotspur offstage:

No joke ever raised such loud and repeated mirth, in the galleries, as Sir John's labour in getting the body of Hotspur on his back . . . Quin had little or no difficulty in perching Garrick upon his shoulders, who looked like a dwarf on the back of a giant. But oh! how he tugged and toiled to raise Barry from the ground![7]

His successor, John Henderson, reportedly had so much difficulty with his Hotspur that a small gang of "Falstaff's ragamuffins" were used instead to bear the body offstage.[8] Other late eighteenth-century Falstaffs included at least one woman, Mrs. Webb, who "excelled in corpulent and grotesque characters" in Norwich in 1786.[9]

John Philip Kemble played Hotspur at Covent Garden in the early nineteenth century and his brother, Stephen, was one of a number of actors to play Falstaff without padding, although William Hazlitt remarked of his performance, "Every fat man cannot represent a great man."[10] The American actor James Henry Hackett played the part in England and America for forty years, and his Hotspurs included John Philip and Charles Kemble, as well as Edmund Kean and William Charles Macready. He received mixed reviews; *The Athenaeum* reported:

His is the best Falstaff that has been seen for many a day,—which, however, is not saying much for it. But it has positive merits that deserve recognition. He did not . . . reach the full conception which Shakespeare has here embodied . . . but he aimed at it, and accomplished much; his soliloquy on honour, in particular, was well delivered, and, take him for all in all, we are disposed to give him a cordial welcome.[11]

His identification with the role was such that he became known as "Falstaff Hackett."

In 1821 a spectacular production of *Henry IV Part II* with Macready as King Henry and Charles Kemble as Prince Hal included a magnificent staging of the coronation procession as a tribute to the coronation of George IV. Kemble's production of *Part I* in 1824 with himself as Hotspur was mainly noted for the historical accuracy of costumes and sets, which included "the King's Chamber in the old Palace of Westminster; the inn-yard at Rochester with the castle, by night; Hotspur's Camp; a distant view of Coventry; and Shrewsbury from the field of battle."[12] Samuel Phelps' production at Sadler's Wells in 1846 was similarly spectacular:

> All has been done with a lavish and judicious hand, without a regard to cost or aught beside, save the desire of gratifying the public. The accoutrements, armour, and trappings worn by the several armies in the fourth and fifth acts are indeed splendid, and the minutest care has been shown in the arrangement of the costumes, even to the very crests of the different parties. The battle was admirably managed—the scenery was entirely new, and elicited much applause.[13]

The 1864 revival at Drury Lane which included the Glendower scene in full for the first time was distinguished by Phelps' Falstaff: "He lays stress not on Falstaff's sensuality, but on the lively intellect that stands for soul as well as mind in his gross body," in a performance marked by "a smooth delicate touch that stamps the knight distinctly as a man well born and bred."[14] Phelps' remarkable doubling of the king and Justice Shallow in *Part II* later that year earned further praise.[15]

Herbert Beerbohm Tree's 1896 production at the Haymarket Theatre used a fuller text of the play and was well received by the critics, with the exception of George Bernard Shaw. William Archer praised the overall conception—"There has been no nearer approach in our day to the complete performance of a Shakespearian drama."[16] Of Tree's performance, *The Athenaeum* reported: "it is the fat knight himself that comes before us."[17] Shaw, however, thought that "Mr Tree only wants one thing to make him an excellent Falstaff, and that is to get born over again as unlike himself as possible."[18]

Victorian spectacle went out of fashion in the early twentieth century, influenced by the ideas of William Poel and the English Stage Society, which favored performances on a thrust stage with minimal scenery and faster-paced, fluid action.

History does not update in the same way as the comedies and tragedies that have lent themselves to a variety of settings, costumes, and periods. The effect on the history plays has been to emphasize

1. Herbert Beerbohm Tree as Falstaff in his 1896 production at the Haymarket Theatre. *The Athenaeum* reported: "it is the fat knight himself that comes before us."

their historicity. Between 1901 and 1906 Frank Benson staged a cycle of Shakespeare's history plays for the first time at the Stratford-upon-Avon festival season which omitted *Henry IV Part I* but included *King John, Richard II, Henry IV Part II, Henry V, Henry VI Part II*, and *Richard III*. W. B. Yeats was impressed by the way in which "play supports play"[19] when presented in this way. *Henry IV Part I* was included in the new cycle in 1905, as was Marlowe's *Edward II*. In 1921 Barry Jackson had staged both parts of *Henry IV* on the same day (23 April) in Birmingham. The two parts of *Henry IV* were the first plays performed after the opening of the New Memorial Theatre in Stratford by the Prince of Wales in 1932—*Part I* in the afternoon and *Part II* in the evening.

In 1935 Robert Atkins and Sydney Carroll staged a production of *Henry IV Part I* with the popular vaudeville comedian George Robey as Falstaff. Despite his lack of classical training many critics were impressed by his performance; Herbert Farjeon reflected that "We learn from Mr Robey's Falstaff many things. One of them is that it is a tremendous advantage to have Shakespeare's clowns . . . played by men who are funny *before they begin* . . . Mr Sydney Carroll's brilliant casting of Falstaff should put an end to the long dreary line of legitimate actors who have made soggy hay of Shakespeare's comics."[20] However, *The New Statesman* regarded Robey's Falstaff as an "old soak rather than the fallen gentleman . . . nothing more than a super-Bardolph."[21]

John Burrell's production a decade later at the New Theatre was warmly received:

> *Feliciter audax* [pleasingly audacious] is, indeed, the phrase for Mr Burrell's production. Choosing not to adopt the uninterrupted flow of the Elizabethan method, he closes each scene with a moment of dumb-show, shadowy and significant. I shall never forget Glendower, standing at the window (the actor is Harcourt Williams, who knows how to stand)—standing and staring after Hotspur as he gallops away, with the two women weeping at his feet while we know what they guess, that they will never see Hotspur again.[22]

Harcourt Williams' performance was not the only one to be widely praised. Ralph Richardson's Falstaff was universally admired:

> a grand buffoon and rapscallion in *Part I*, proceeded in *Part II* to a still richer understanding which could catch the sombre

2. Ralph Richardson as Falstaff and Laurence Olivier as Justice Shallow in John Burrell's 1945 New Theatre production: Ralph Richardson's Falstaff was universally admired, and Laurence Olivier triumphed as Hotspur in *Part I* and Justice Shallow in *Part II*.

illumination of "Do not bid me remember mine end" and suggest, as Falstaffs rarely do, the attraction of the man for the Prince as well as the considerable brain behind the wit. This was a metamorphosis assisted by make-up but by no means entirely dependent on it: for Richardson's greatness—and I think the word is justifiable—in the part was a greatness of spirit that transcended the mere hulk of flesh.[23]

Laurence Olivier, meanwhile, played Hotspur in *Part I* and Justice Shallow in *Part II*, and triumphed in both.

But it was the 1951 presentation of the tetralogy of *Richard II*, *Henry IV Part I*, *Henry IV Part II*, and *Henry V* by Anthony Quayle, John Kidd, and Michael Redgrave at the Shakespeare Memorial Theatre which was to prove decisive in the plays' fortunes. Anthony Quayle explained the thinking behind the productions:

it seemed to us that the great epic theme of the Histories had become obscured through years of presenting the plays single, and many false interpretations had grown up, and come to be accepted, through star actors giving almost too persuasive and

3. The 1951 Shakespeare Memorial Theatre presented *Richard II*, *Henry IV Part I* and *Part II*, and *Henry V* as a tetralogy: with Harry Andrews as Henry IV and Richard Burton as Hal.

dominant performances of parts which the author intended to be by no means sympathetic.[24]

One critic suggested: "One will never again think of these plays as single entities, and when they are played as such we shall feel them to have been lopped."[25] Tanya Moiseiwitsch designed a single set of "plain unvarnished oak" which could be "embellished as the occasion demanded with props or with hangings" and "provided three acting spaces and a large variety of entrances; it allowed the action to move in an uninterrupted flow."[26] There *were* star performances though—"Mr Redgrave's poetic Richard and dazzling Hotspur, Mr Quayle's splendidly rich Falstaff and Mr Richard Burton's sultry intriguing Hal," as well as "Mr Harry Andrews's superb and masterly Bolingbroke";[27] the balance was shifted decisively away from Hotspur and Falstaff toward Hal.

Douglas Seale directed both parts of *Henry IV* at the Old Vic in 1955 in productions admired for being "simple and direct and, while comparatively and mercifully static within each individual scene . . . they are driven with a brilliant sense of the narrative speed over all."[28] Again, a strong cast achieved unanimous praise, from Paul Rogers' Falstaff—"leaner and considerably dilapidated, is already some of the way downhill," to Robert Hardy's Prince—"a very strong and charming performance," while "John Neville makes a fine Hotspur and a whirlwind Pistol, and Paul Daneman an ominous Worcester followed, in a miraculous transformation, by an extremely funny Shallow, withered with senility and malice. Rachel Roberts and Gwen Cherrell draw fruitfully on Hogarth for Mistress Quickly and Doll Tearsheet."[29]

It has become the norm since then for the two plays of *Henry IV* to be performed together, often within the context of a larger cycle of Shakespeare's history plays. The resources required for such ambitious projects are only realistically available to the national subsidized companies, and productions by the RSC (discussed below) have constituted the majority of these. In 1986 Michael Bogdanov and Michael Pennington formed the English Shakespeare Company with the aim of promoting and presenting the works of Shakespeare both nationally and internationally. The inaugural production, *The Hen-*

rys, consisted of *Part I* and *Part II* of *Henry IV* plus *Henry V*. The following year they presented *The Wars of the Roses*, comprising *Richard II*, *Henry IV Part I*, *Henry IV Part II*, *Henry V*, the three plays of *Henry VI* telescoped into two plays (*Henry VI: House of Lancaster*, *Henry VI: House of York*), and *Richard III*. The production toured successfully for two years, both within the UK and internationally. The company deliberately worked against the dominant mode of theatrical realism to present radical and exciting productions, designed to engage a modern audience:

> We would provide a space that would allow the plays to range over the centuries in imagery. We would free our, and the audiences' imaginations by allowing an eclectic mix of costumes and props, choosing a time and a place that was most appropriate for a character or a scene. Modern dress at one moment, medieval, Victorian or Elizabethan the next. We would use a kit of props . . . [which], as far as possible, would remain on stage. The means of transformation from one scene to the next would remain visible. No tricks up our sleeves (until we needed one). We would create a style that was essentially rough theatre, but would add, when we needed it, a degree of sophistication.[30]

The relatively few American productions of *Henry IV* have concentrated historically on *Part I*, focusing on the roles of Hotspur and Falstaff. Stuart Vaughan directed both parts which played in repertory at New York's Phoenix Theater in 1960: the emphasis on Eric Berry's widely praised, compelling Falstaff led to the accusation that it "might accurately be called 'The Decline and Fall of Sir John Falstaff, Fat Old Knight.' "[31] In 1993, Ron Daniels directed back-to-back stagings of *Part I* and *Part II* for the American Repertory Theater, updated to an American Civil War setting which enjoyed a mixed critical reception:

> Mr Daniels has created a wildly anachronistic, culturally mixed salad in which different elements of Shakespeare's epic portrait are accorded theatrical analogues from wholly disparate historical moments. The result, given visual life by John Conklin's

time-traveling, slightly ragged scenic shorthand, is less disjunctive than one might expect.[32]

Barbara Gaines' 1999 production of both plays at Chicago's Shakespeare Repertory Theater was widely praised for its simple staging and strong performances. In 2003 Dakin Matthews conflated the texts of both plays in a production at Lincoln Center's Vivian Beaumont Theater, directed by Jack O'Brien. The resulting adaptation lasted nearly four hours with two intervals, but compressed the action to create a fast-paced, fluid text. Kevin Kline played Falstaff.

> . . . made up to resemble a threadbare Santa Claus with a blimp of a prosthetic belly and a snowy beard, Mr Kline looks like the most traditional Falstaff imaginable. The wonderful surprise is how he deviates from the convention of bluster and braggadocio. Mr Kline has never had more of a chance to make a meal of the scenery. Instead, he delivers a finely measured performance that matches the actor's infinite resourcefulness with that of the character he plays.[33]

Remarkably, London's National Theatre did not stage a performance of *Henry IV* until Nicholas Hytner's production in 2005 played on a "roughly arrow-shaped stage" in the large Olivier Theatre. The production managed "to suggest the mighty sweep of the plays—their oscillation from uptight court to frowsty lowlife, from the frenetically urban to the peacefully pastoral, from the battlefield to the boozer—with depth and definition."[34] Michael Gambon was praised for the way he:

> wonderfully incorporates the contradictions of Falstaff. He looks like the kind of wily, drunken bohemian tramp that Just William would ill-advisedly let into the Brown household, where he would later be found comatose in the wine cellar. In the moveable feast of his accent, you hear the tones of a parvenu whose poshness is pretty precarious and inclined to slip into saloon-bar bravado. This is not a sentimentalised fat

knight. He's utterly out for himself, and the last thing we're treated to in *Part 1* is the sight of him shamelessly robbing two venerable corpses.[35]

Matthew McFadyen made a "shrewd witty prince," and David Bradley played the "haunted cadaverous king," while:

> The scenes in Gloucestershire are delectably comic, thanks to the great John Wood, whose Justice Shallow is a transcendent study in florid, nervously energetic self-delusion about a wild youth that he did not experience. He is delightfully partnered by Adrian Scarborough, who, as Silence, is like a little slip of death inadequately warmed up—until he gets a few glasses inside him, when he cannot be restrained from providing quavering, unwanted cabaret.[36]

The two parts of *Henry IV* with their broad cross section of scenes and characters have come to be regarded as a sort of national epic firmly established at the heart of the Shakespearean repertory. The most remarkable film version is Orson Welles' 1966 film adaptation, *Chimes at Midnight*, in which the entire tetralogy from *Richard II* to *Henry V* is telescoped into less than two hours. In 1938 Welles directed an unsuccessful play called *Five Kings* in which he had gathered all the Falstaff material from the *Henrys* and *The Merry Wives of Windsor*. This formed the basis of Welles' film, shot while he was supposedly making *Treasure Island*. As Scott McMillin suggests, "he was not interested in the historical epic formed by the histories; he was interested in Falstaff—or, perhaps more accurately, in a certain angle of vision which he thought of as Falstaffian."[37] The star-studded cast included Jeanne Moreau, Margaret Rutherford, John Gielgud (as Henry IV), with Ralph Richardson as the narrator. The film's "brilliance" lies in Welles' characteristically bravura film vocabulary and style. As McMillin puts it: "If Falstaff had made films, he would have made something like this one."[38]

The BBC Shakespeare version, by contrast, offers a conventional historical cycle of the second tetralogy (*Richard II*, *Henry IV Part I*, *Henry IV Part II*, *Henry V*) made for television and directed by David

Giles. Anthony Quayle, who had played Falstaff so successfully in 1951, reprised the role. The narrow focus of television does not, however, lend itself easily to the broad sweep of history:

> If cycle-thinking puts the realm and its rulers ahead of Falstaff, and if the performance of Falstaff puts him well ahead of the realm and its rulers, trouble is brewing. Quayle's assured performance as Falstaff is the strongest element of the production, and the separate "sphere of intelligence" provided by his addresses to the audience happily interrupts the dutiful effort to capture history in the space of the television studio. He is in better control of the medium—and this makes Prince Hal's efforts to take better control of the kingdom seem second-rate.[39]

The English Shakespeare Company's highly politicized, eclectic *Wars of the Roses* was recorded for television in 1989.

AT THE RSC

> The stage is the world, as in a mediaeval morality play. It may represent court, camp, tavern, England, France, but it is always the blank slate on which life writes its lessons for [Hal], the bare, mental arena in which the soul of a royal Everyman discovers his destiny and true friends.
>
> (Ronald Bryden)[40]

In mid-twentieth-century postwar Britain, Hal took center stage in productions of *Henry IV Part I*. Caught between the mighty figures of Henry IV and Falstaff and the worlds of court and tavern, his education became the focal point of the play. Directors instilled an ambiguity into the proceedings, with Hal never truly revealing his nature but remaining enigmatic, and therefore slightly dangerous and anti-heroic. An adolescent under the sway of two highly charismatic father figures, manipulative and aware of the power he wields, critics and audiences have often found him a difficult character to like. Sympathy for Hal derives mainly from the portrayal of Henry IV and Falstaff. The prince attempts to learn from two men who are not what they seem to be; who present one face to the world and another to themselves. He inhabits two worlds, different in their emotional propensities and ethos, but equal in their duplicity.

When looking at RSC productions, the resulting influence of these environments on Hal can be seen reflected in the design concept chosen by directors. Pointing to an overarching theme, court and tavern were either designed as stylistically opposed or inextricably linked. With *Henry IV Part I* rarely performed on its own, the design of a production will often be part of a larger scheme, involving *Henry IV Part II*, *Richard II*, and/or *Henry V*. Occasionally, they have been performed as part of the cycle of Shakespeare's histories (produced in 1963–65, 2000–01, and 2006–08), chronologically following through and encompassing the eight plays from *Richard II* to *Richard III*.

In 1964 *Henry IV Part I* and *Part II* were performed as part of a seven-play history cycle called *The Wars of the Roses* that examined the politics, the mechanics of power that moved behind Shakespeare's history plays. These:

> were bleakly anti-heroic, capable of making war seem devastating and inhuman. The younger theatregoers of 1963 did not share the end-of-war patriotism that had motivated the . . . 1951 Stratford series for the Festival of Britain. The sensibilities of the new audience were being shaped by Beckett, Osborne, Pinter, Brecht. This was not a crowd given to what they would have regarded as the sentiment and jingoism of the past . . . Peter Hall saw the dominant image as a mechanism of power:

> > Over the years I became more and more fascinated by the contortions of politicians and by the corrupting seductions experienced by anyone who wields power . . . I realised that the mechanism of power had not changed in centuries.

> . . . [Designer, John] Bury saw the violence and power politics of the cycle as framed in steel:

> > It was a period of armour and a period of the sword: they were plays about warfare, about power, about danger. One spent one's time either in armour, or piercing someone's armour—or being pierced . . . We were trying to make a

world: a dangerous world, a terrible world, in which all these happenings fit.[41]

The hard and heavy oppressive nature of the set complemented a darkly political reading of the play. The fragility of the characters and the dehumanizing effect of war were also reflected in the costumes, which assimilated the metal world:

The stage floor was plated steel. The acting space for all seven plays was defined by two huge triangle-based metal-plated walls, which could be turned to present different faces and shifted to form different angles . . . [For *Henry IV*] the dominant metallic textures were modified here and there by wood and cloth, and banners were used in the battle scenes, but austerity prevailed in the overall visual impression.[42]

When Bury joined the RSC in 1962, he brought with him a revolutionary concept—that a production's design should be based around a central "image" which should be followed on in the costuming and sound of that production. He altered the use of stage space by using real materials that had texture, substance, and a natural sound when the actors worked on them. His style was a rejection of the romantic designs and costumes frequently seen in the 1950s.

As in so many of Shakespeare's plays, the physical and mental condition of the king is reflected in his state. The ill health of the "body politic" was clearly visible in John Napier's design for the 1982 production. Picking up on the idea that "We are all diseased," director Trevor Nunn

contrived to suggest that a whole range of minor figures suffered from the general malaise . . . [The] set consisted of four tall wooden structures, each built like the open-section interior of a three-storey square house . . . each structure could be moved separately backwards or forwards, to build a different "house" for each location. Often the structures were full of people, even as they were moved into place, particularly with the tavern-scenes, which became momentarily large portable pubs. At times, the scene practically seethed with extras, working hoists, trundling kegs, mounting ladders to paint signs, bustling about with sacks or trays of drinks, beating carpets, making beds . . . these sets remained drab. The boards were twisted. They were hung with shields and lances, but all were painted black—the colour of the wood itself—and the dark heavy structures seemed gloomy and overpowering. The effect was enhanced by David Hersey's lighting: often a dim suffused light; at other times a bright overhead spotlight, leaving dingy shadows all around. In addition, Eastcheap extras often remained on the set, lounging up stairs, watching, during the intervening court scenes. The effect was to suggest a political world which was haunted by shabbiness.[43]

In keeping with the idea that *Henry IV* takes its form from the medieval morality play, Adrian Noble's designer, Bob Crowley, strongly marked out the symbolism of faith and sin, heaven and hell, in the set design in 1991. He "sharply juxtaposed the excesses of the tavern with the calculation of the court":[44]

Julian Glover's King Henry and Robert Stephens's Falstaff form the opposing poles of Adrian Noble's production of *Henry IV Part 1*, the King stern, cold and authoritarian in grey and black, Falstaff warm, mercurial, libertarian, and faintly epicene in scarlet . . . The King's bare court is furnished with hard chairs and severe tables; while soft fabrics and yielding sofas in glowing shades of red characterise the tavern scenes. The Eastcheap tavern erupts on us like a mediaeval vision of hell, a lurid maze of private rooms with sex visibly on sale.[45]

We could hardly be reminded more forcibly that Shakespeare's matchless history has its roots in mediaeval drama or that Hal is poised between an angry God in Henry and a ribald Satan in Falstaff.[46]

Meanwhile, the greed, the violence, the humble bustle, the sordid pastimes of ordinary English life go on. Shakespeare's greatness is at its most awesome when he shows you how the politics of the nobility is mirrored, refracted, parodied and complemented by the goings on in Eastcheap and Rochester. Noble has retained Act Two Scene One, in the inn at Rochester, which directors usually cut. Here the robbery is set up when Shakespeare's equivalent of the hotel manager tips off Gadshill as to which guests are carrying the loot. The underworld types are played without a touch of mockery. These are dangerous but ordinary people who have a living to make, and their lives are no laughing matter any more than the Percys'.[47]

When explaining his entrance as Falstaff, Desmond Barrit explained the idea for the design of *Henry IV* in 2000:

Up through the floor I pushed, by way of a sort of rubber flange that we came to know as the sphincter . . . The idea of this curious entrance, of course, was symbolic: our production was part of the RSC's "This England" project to present eight of Shakespeare's history plays, and the subject of those plays was this island, this England, this earth that we live on, and the director wanted Falstaff, as a man of the earth, to be seen to be born from the earth.[48]

In contrast to the history cycle of 1964, no design concept linked the plays. Each was individually conceived by separate directors and designers. This was criticized by some who felt that the continuity of the cycle was less apparent, and confusing, when the same actors in the same roles appeared in completely different times and settings. However, Es Devlin's set design for the two parts of Michael Attenborough's production of *Henry IV* was completely appropriate to the play: "England is basically conceived as an often blood-stained, earthy battleground, with a steep hill at the rear, [conveying] Attenborough's sense that the play intensifies the impression . . . of a country rent asunder."[49] With lights shining up through the floor, the earth appeared primordial and volcanic, as if awaiting a moment of violence. With "its mound of smoke-filled peat [the set] effectively embodies the idea that "the land is burning."[50]

Fathers and Sons

> What the father hath hid cometh out in the son; and oft have I found in the son the father's revealed secret.
>
> (Friedrich Nietzsche)[51]

As Harold C. Goddard points out, it would be hard to find a better illustration of this axiom than Henry IV and Hal: "In his concentration on power the elder Henry has suppressed both the playful and the passionate tendencies of his nature . . . What he has kept under comes out in Hal, who leads a life of abandon under the tutelage of Falstaff."[52] Hal finds in Falstaff a father who embodies the "unrealised half of [Henry's] soul,"[53] providing him with a rough education and emotional warmth.

Of the 1975 production, directed by Terry Hands, John Elsom wrote:

> Alan Howard's Hal is a young prince, growing up. His mind is being formed by two mutually opposing fathers. His natural father, the King, is tortured by guilt and obsessed with ideals of kingship. His debased "father," Falstaff is impervious to guilt, scornful of honour and duty, but relishes the simple pleasures in life, sack, sex and getting away with things.[54]

Hands' production focused on this central relationship, providing "a study in domestic psychopathology, probing the tortured relationship of father and son."[55]

Emrys James, who played Henry IV, portrayed him as a lonely character frustrated by his inability to express emotion in a non-aggressive fashion:

> The play is about the longing a father has for a relationship with his son. It is peculiarly painful to have that figure high above, cut off from his son, but watching. He is a distant father-figure for Hal because this man doesn't, cannot unbend . . .

4. Alan Howard as Prince Hal, "a young prince growing up," and Brewster Mason as Falstaff, who "relishes the simple pleasures in life, sack, sex and getting away with things," in Terry Hands' 1975 RSC production.

Stay, and breathe awhile.
Thou hast redeemed thy lost opinion,
And showed thou mak'st some tender of my life,
In this fair rescue thou hast brought to me.

It's incredible that he is not able to say, "You are a wonderful son to me because you have given yourself in battle with this great beast of a man and fought him off. And it shows without question that you love me." That's not the way he thinks. It's part of his hang-up, part of his trouble. If he had shown emotion to this emotional young man their relationship would have been that much easier.

. . . It isn't accidental that Shakespeare left his wife out of the play. He's a lonely man surrounded by four big, surly, rebellious sons, whom he rules with a rod of iron . . . Here's a man who hasn't learned how to handle his emotions and his solution to the problem is to suppress them completely. Except in moments of extreme stress. Then they come out.[56]

In order to emphasize the relationship between father and son, Hands deliberately merged Eastcheap and the court, with Henry and Hal often present, onlookers in their separate scenes:

> Here both king and prince stray into scenes from which they are usually absent. From the first, Henry IV watches, soft-lit and chorus-like, from the back of the stage as Hal and Falstaff flirt—almost literally flirt—with self-indulgence. From his dallying, Hal strolls off, seeing Henry lambaste the nobles who will turn against him, removed from his father yet linked as he circles the stage.[57]

Props were also used to signify Hal's half existence between two worlds:

> James's Henry treats Hal as a child, takes his hand, pulls him onto the seat . . . beside him, hugs him, kisses him. He tries to supplant the physical affection evident between Hal and Sir John but the boy is only disorientated and reaches out of the scene to take a bottle and goblet from the tavern in which their palace meeting is limboed.[58]

The deliberate merging of court and tavern also prompts us to think of Henry IV and Falstaff as the lords of two realms within England. The device was used to great effect in Michael Attenborough's production in 2000:

> Bolingbroke, now Henry IV, sits on the same throne that serves as Falstaff's perch in downtown Eastcheap. This neatly indicates that the king and the old reprobate serve as competing father figures to Prince Hal.[59]

How the actors physically relate to each other reveals their character and the dimension of their relationships. Of the 1964 production, Scott McMillin observed that

> Falstaff offered what Hal ought to have sought according to a psychological reading, a little fatherly contact. Hal's own

father, the Henry IV of Eric Porter, was remote and unap-
proachable, but Falstaff showed warm feeling and caressed
Hal's face while acting the father's role. [Ian] Holm did not
spurn such gestures.[60]

Holm played Hal in an antiheroic fashion, as an onlooker, never completely engaged or in contact with the people around him, "a cold-
blooded young man who was working his way toward heroism":

in the vital matter of [Henry's] relationship with Hal there
seemed not even the contact of pity between father and son.
Their meeting . . . was played with great physical and emotional distance between the two men. When the time came for
Hal (Ian Holm) to declare his loyalty, he first went over and
closed the door: a telling gesture with its suggestion of guarded
secrecy. He remained inaccessible to his father.[61]

In Adrian Noble's 1990 production:

Caught between King and clown is Michael Maloney's slightly
built Hal, initially an emotionally dependent adolescent. His
relationship with Falstaff is intense: they hold hands affectionately in the opening scene; as the boy taunts Falstaff after the
exposure of his cowardice, Falstaff kisses him on the lips on
"no more of that, Hal, an thou lovest me." And Robert
Stephens' . . . agile Falstaff is dependent on Hal too. There is
introspection behind this bluff exterior; the spaniel eyes seek
affection . . . Hal's determination to conquer Hotspur is motivated by the need to demonstrate his maturity to his father; the
thwarted love behind it seems about to resolve itself with a kiss
from son to father when the King [Julian Glover] holds Hal at
arm's length.[62]

David Troughton, who played Henry in 2000, believed, like
Emrys James, that Henry is aware of his failure as a father and
attempts to redress this in order to win back his son: "with his own
son he has no idea how to behave at all. Hal's search for an alterna-

tive father is a cry for help, because his own father wants him for only one thing: to be his successor."[63] Unable to be demonstrative in his love, Henry's attempts at a bond between father and son are thwarted by awkward moments of unwanted physicality. Unlike Glover's Henry, who chose to remain distant, Troughton's actively sought to embrace his son when the opportunity arose:

> It takes just one speech from Hal to bring them together—metaphorically, anyway, for though I used to put out my arms to him here, he never noticed, and no embrace was achieved. Perhaps Hal doesn't want to notice, or perhaps he simply doesn't see; that ambiguity was important in our production, and I think right. It's like one of those moments when you go to kiss your father—and it turns confusedly into shaking hands. Hal has said that he's sorry; he has said that he will fight along-side his father; but there has been no expression of love of son to father, which is what Henry misses. But whether Henry could achieve the embrace, even if Hal were looking, remains a question. He simply doesn't know how to touch his son properly. So I just used to give him a little push on his shoulder with my fist, and the awkward moment passed.[64]

Troughton thought *Part I* "brilliantly written in its exploration of all the tactics that we use as parents: anger, loving kindness, emotional blackmail, they're all there." The character of Hotspur was key in this production as a means for Henry to get to his son: "he betrays his weird fixation on Hotspur, that son who is the 'theme of honour's tongue' . . . who is so good to his father, such a great soldier."[65] It is clear that this is the son that Henry would wish for, and that Hal, played by William Houston, was made aware of it.

The parental battle between Falstaff and Henry for Hal never comes to a climactic moment when the two characters meet and argue over his emotional and moral education. In 1982 Trevor Nunn contrived

> a moment in which Hal finds himself between his father and Falstaff, with Bolingbroke's look of envious contempt at Sir

John and silent appeal for his son's affections answered by Hal's following his friend's insistent call: "Hal, if thou seest me down in the battle . . . " The king turns away, apparently defeated, an interesting explanation for what in the text is the curious continuation of the estrangement of Hal and his father in *Part 2* in spite of the outcome of the battle. Not until he sees his father dying is this Hal ready to demonstrate any emotional commitment to him.[66]

Similarly, in 2001, "Troughton also gives us the anxious father aware that he is in danger of losing his son to the taverns and the fat knight: there's a great moment when his path crosses that of Falstaff in battle and he shoots him a wounded look."[67] David Troughton recalled how this moment was realized:

[Henry and Falstaff] . . . were symbolically present on stage together for a few moments between the first and second scenes of *Part One* . . . We created a brief moment in our production— after I had rejected (for fear of losing my heir) Hal's offer to take on Hotspur in single combat and as we were all girding up for battle—when I look at him and Falstaff together and thought "O, God, I don't want them meeting any more."[68]

Kingship

Renaissance philosophy believed that the best man was the "fullest" man, the one with the widest experience of the world. Behind this lay the mediaeval theory of elements and humours, whose balance and combination was the key to mastery of oneself and others. A king should not only know the life of his subjects. He should contain in himself an equilibrium of all human passions—anger, pride, melancholy, mercy and love . . . The best education is the world itself, and the best introduction to the elements of one's own nature is other people.

(Ronald Bryden)[69]

Henry IV Part I posits many questions as to the nature of kingship. Shakespeare examines the political theory of the divine right of kings through Henry's gnawing guilt, which stems from a belief that he has sinned against God in the usurpation and murder of Richard II. Regardless of the fact that he believed himself the right man for the job, Henry cannot escape the belief that he is a counterfeit king: "Confirming a change that had long been in incubation, on the day when Henry deposed Richard he became a double man, one thing to the world, another to his own conscience."[70]

Emrys James played Henry in 1975 as the most unregal of men. Erratic in behavior, he was a self-made man, an administrator and clerk, a cunning politician who made his way to kingship when, as Falstaff said (ostensibly of Worcester), "Rebellion lay in his way, and he found it":

> He wants to assert his authority again and again, because kingship doesn't come naturally to him . . . Richard could go through crowds as a golden figure, and you could never ever conceive of Henry IV as a golden figure. Here is an executive, an executive of the state, angrily aware that the kind of chief executive he is is better for the state than the preening vision of majesty that Richard II presents.[71]

In David Troughton's highly acclaimed performance in 2000, he embodied the idea of Henry as a man racked by inner conflict, caught between faith and the necessities of power:

> A dominant Bolingbroke, he now turns into a guilt-wracked Henry IV, ever conscious that he seized the throne by force. Yet, although first seen at prayer in penitent's gown, Troughton's king is still a brutal pragmatist who seeks to pre-empt rebellion by squashing his fractious nobles.[72]

> The opening is heavy with brooding anger, even melancholy . . . Power may be coveted; you may cheat, lie, manipulate, even kill for it; but when it is yours it can become a burden, a prison of responsibility . . . [Troughton's] huge body suggests both brute force and vulnerability. The king is not at ease with himself . . . loyalties come at a heavy price. And over

5. David Troughton as King Henry IV "believes himself cursed by his sin of regicide" in Michael Attenborough's 2000 RSC production.

all this hangs Henry's guilt about the murder of his predecessor, the deposed Richard.[73]

Having achieved power he believes himself cursed by his sin of regicide. If the king is God's emissary on earth, to kill the king is an act against God:

Once he gets the crown, things start to go wrong politically and personally. The guilt has started to eat away at him; it's as though the year that elapses between the plays has hugely changed him. The fulfilment of that one aim of getting the crown was one thing; keeping it is quite another, for once you've got it, the only thing to do with it is to stop anyone else getting it.[74]

In a very different reading of the part, Julian Glover's Henry in *Part I* "was neither infirm nor tired, as so often he has been played, but firmly in control of the political world":[75]

When Glover is present there is no doubt where the power lies, and the daring and monstrosity of the challenge against him is palpable. There is a strong sense of personal ambition and vanity in these confrontations, but essentially they are about political power: great impersonal imperatives which command a man's will and demand his self-sacrifice.[76]

Until struck down with a heart spasm in his moment of victory, he plays with undiminished power throughout: curtly disdainful to Owen Teale's hulking Hotspur, releasing thunderbolts of majestic wrath against Hal, and a match for Angus Wright's fire-breathing Douglas on the battlefield.[77]

[Julian Glover] is like some stern, unforgiving Old Testament patriarch who provokes rebellion by his curt dismissal of the Percys and who alienates his son by treating him as a recalcitrant hooligan. It is a marvellous portrait of a frosty spirit incapable of warmth.[78]

The qualities of kingship are constantly discussed or displayed by various characters in the play, as if Shakespeare were asking us, *What makes a king?* The influence of Falstaff, Hotspur, and Henry offers Hal life's alternatives from which he must choose and discard in his preparation for the throne.

Hotspur so impresses his elders because he embodies the idea of chivalric honor, an exalted view of warfare and armed conflict that is tried and tested on the battlefield. Combining the qualities of military skill and political power, matched with a single-minded determination to promote the rebels' cause, Hotspur drives much of the main plot and is admired by all, despite his occasional outbursts. Although historically older than Hal, Shakespeare makes him a peer to establish a direct rivalry between the two men, especially in Henry's conception of the ideal son. If, as Montaigne suggests, "The reputation and worth of a man consisteth in his heart and will; therein lies true honour"[79] rather than in martial prowess, we can see that Hotspur and Hal are on opposite sides of this maxim. Contrary to Hal, in Hotspur's attractive arrogance we can see the essence of an unbending spirit, especially in the scene with his wife.

In 1964, Roy Dotrice's Hotspur, although capturing his usual inextinguishable humor and vitality, in the words of the *Times*' reviewer, had "the mentality of an amiable psychopath."[80] The scene with Lady Percy took the form of rough foreplay, with "husband and wife pushing over, kissing, tumbling, wrapping-up, kneeling astride or lying on top."[81] In this very antiheroic production, Hotspur's death was in keeping with Dotrice's interpretation and the mood of the production. At war with Hal, he was in his element. Flying at him with a huge sword, laughing aloud, Hotspur's sword jammed into the side of a horse trough, Hal got in quickly to stab him under the ribs. "Hotspur's . . . violent death-throes . . . robbed his death of the last shred of heroic dignity."[82] "Lowering him, dying, into the trough Hal delivered his line 'For worms, brave Percy' [5.3.88]. Now he was dead; and curiously, the man who remained alive seemed to have no zest for life at all."[83]

In 1982, Timothy Dalton's Hotspur emerged

not as a contrast but as a parallel. The warm-hearted side of him was played down, and replaced by moodiness. Many of his more "poetic" lines were cut. His impulsiveness was much like Hal's own. In the first scene with his wife, he knelt, reading, as his wife came creeping downstairs. Played by Harriet Walter as a very submissive lady, she crouched beside him. The two figures became, suddenly, two people talking about their marriage. They looked grim and lugubrious. Hotspur jumped up, to call for his horse. Lady Percy followed, attempting playfully to wheedle his secrets out of him. Quite suddenly he turned on her. The line, "Away, you trifler" was delivered with ferocious force. When he said, "I care not for thee, Kate," there was no doubt that he meant it. If at the end he relented, holding out a hand to her which eventually she took, the patching-up of their marriage was only temporary.[84]

Honor at the expense of the personal, or personal life at the expense of honor? Is there any way that a man in power can maintain a life of duty and keep intact his humanity? Key to Hal's education, and a central concern of Shakespeare's in many plays, is this understanding of "honour." On discussing his portrayal of Falstaff in 2000, Desmond Barrit pointed to this questioning nature of the play in his performance of the famous soliloquy:

> I used to play the "honour" soliloquy as a sort of dialogue with the audience, with them asking the questions: "Can honour set to a leg?," and Falstaff replies "No"; "Or an arm?," and Falstaff replies "No"; "Or take away the grief of a wound?," and again he replies "No" [5.1.131–3]. Falstaff is placing himself, I think, as an intermediary between the war and the audience, forcing them to wonder why men go to war at all, asking, and answering, the questions that are in their minds.[85]

The effectiveness of this delivery was picked up on by most reviewers, and was an appropriately serious reading for the end of the twentieth century: "His beautiful delivery of the famous 'honour' speech here becomes a totally persuasive indictment of the hallow, macho posturing of war."[86]

The question as to whether Hal truly learns the lessons offered by both court and tavern is best discussed in the representation of the prince in *Henry IV Part II*: "Hal must learn to exercise authority with integrity. In *Part I*, this is the path Hal successfully finds for himself, on the way losing nothing in his admiration for Hotspur's shining example and learning something of the warmth of humanity from Falstaff and his cronies."[87]

Despite the upbeat nature of the ending of *Part I*, productions often suggest a certain ambiguity as to Hal's assumption of kingly behavior. What has he learned from these diverse parental figures that will make him a better king? The various workings of the father–son relationship demonstrate the battle in Hal to find a true path to kingship. Hal proves, as he said he would in the "I know you all" speech (1.2.175–97), his abilities to his father and the officials of the court. However, his education is at an early stage. For Shakespeare, honor and integrity do not come from wielding a sword, and Hal has his most difficult of battles yet to face. Only when fathers are lost and cast aside will we see the emergence of the man who will be king.

THE ACTOR'S VOICE AND THE DIRECTOR'S CUT: INTERVIEWS WITH MICHAEL PENNINGTON, ADRIAN NOBLE, AND MICHAEL BOYD

Michael Pennington, born in 1943, was brought up in London and read English at Cambridge University. While at university he appeared with the National Youth Theatre. He went on to join the RSC, playing small parts in *The Wars of the Roses* directed by Peter Hall (1964). He has since returned to the RSC on many occasions, playing Angelo in *Measure for Measure* (1974), Edgar in *King Lear* (1976), Berowne in *Love's Labour's Lost* (1978), Hamlet (1980), and Timon in *Timon of Athens* (2000). He has numerous radio and television parts to his credit, as well as film roles. He has written books on acting Shakespeare and Chekhov. In 1986 he and Michael Bogdanov founded the English Shakespeare Company (ESC), dedicated to taking Shakespeare to new audiences. Their inaugural production, *The Henrys*, comprising the two parts of *Henry IV* plus *Henry V*, in which he played Prince Hal/King Henry V, was enormously successful. *Richard II*, the three *Henry VI* plays, and *Richard III* were subsequently added, and their *Wars of the Roses* toured the world to great acclaim. He launched his one-man show, *Sweet William*, about Shakespeare's life and writing and his own relationship with those works, in 2006. He talks here both about playing the part of Hal and about wider aspects of the ESC staging of the two parts.

Adrian Noble, born in 1950, arrived at the RSC from the Bristol Old Vic, where he had directed several future stars in productions of classic plays. His first production on the main stage of the Royal Shakespeare Theatre in Stratford was the acclaimed 1982 *King Lear*. Two years later, his *Henry V* sowed the seed for Kenneth Branagh's film. Among his other major productions during his two decades at the RSC were *Hamlet*, again with Branagh in the title role; *The Plantagenets*, based on the *Henry VI/Richard III* tetralogy, and the two parts of *Henry IV*. Noble's 1994 *A Midsummer Night's Dream* was made into a film. He was artistic director from 1991 to 2003, since when he has been a freelance director. His production style is characterized by strong use of colors and objects (such as umbrellas), and fluid scenic structure. He talks here about his 1991 production with Robert Stephens as Falstaff, making reference to both *Part I* and *Part II* of *Henry IV*.

Michael Boyd was born in Belfast in 1955, educated in London and Edinburgh, and completed his MA in English literature at Edinburgh University. He trained as a director at the Malaya Bronnaya Theater in Moscow. He then went on to work at the Belgrade Theater in Coventry, joining the Sheffield Crucible as associate director in 1982. In 1985 Boyd became founding artistic director of the Tron Theater in Glasgow, becoming equally acclaimed for staging new writing and innovative productions of the classics. He was drama director of the New Beginnings Festival of Soviet Arts in Glasgow in 1999. He joined the RSC as an associate director in 1996 and has since directed numerous productions of Shakespeare's plays. He won the Laurence Olivier Award for Best Director for his version of the *Henry VI* plays in the RSC's *This England: The Histories* in 2001. He took over as artistic director of the RSC in 2003 and oversaw the extraordinarily successful Complete Works Festival in 2006–07. He followed this up with a cycle of all eight history plays, from *Richard II* through to *Richard III*, with the same company of actors. This transferred to London's Roundhouse Theatre in 2008 and won multiple awards. He talks here about both parts of *Henry IV*.

These plays can be thought of as individual works, as parts of a pair, or of a tetralogy, or even of a longer cycle of English history plays. There are cross-references across the two parts, back to *Richard II* and forward to *Henry V*. Some audience members know the backstory and the forward-story, some don't. How do you cope with all this?

MP: Each of the history plays has to stand alone—that's how Shakespeare planned them—but it's almost as if he had an idea that they might one day be seen in sequence, as they often are now, because each generally "trails" the next episode of the story at its end. So *Part II* closes by looking forward to Henry V's French campaign, and indeed the end of *Henry V* to the reign of Henry VI. With the *Henry IV*s it doesn't really matter if the audience doesn't know *Henry V* since it's in the future, except as general interest as to how Henry V became Henry V. The backstory of *Richard II* is more of a problem: you need to know about the shakiness of Henry IV's claim to the throne and his own conscience—if he has any—about having usurped. The only real answer is to make sure the actors make the audience truly listen to Hotspur's argument against Henry in *Part I* and what the king himself says, so that they miss none of it. It's a matter of emphasis in the acting, of determination to get it across.

AN: In two ways. First of all, one has to start with the very simple premise that people are buying a ticket for one show, therefore it has to stand alone. But from the point of view of the acting company and as somebody involved at the RSC with the history plays for quite some time, it's very hard not to appreciate the wider context, going back to the *Henry VI* plays. It seems to me impossible that Shakespeare did not have an architectural form in his head as he wrote them. The *Henry VI/Richard III* tetralogy was the first time since Sophocles and Euripides that someone had attempted a cycle of interrelated plays for the secular stage. It hadn't happened for two thousand years. Writing it as a man in his mid-to-late twenties, I cannot believe Shakespeare wasn't conscious of that. And of course they were enormously successful, so slightly later in his career, when his gaze cast upon the *Henry IV* plays, I think he must again have had some sort of ghost of the architecture in his mind all the time. But because the first tetralogy tackled events that chronologically took place after those of the second, you get a very strong sense of moving forward toward anarchy and chaos. If you look at all eight, you start with the formality of *Richard II* and end up with the butchery of *Richard III*. It's a divine untidiness. In the second tetralogy you can see the architecture but also a maturity of construction and a depth of characterization within each play, which makes them highly satisfactory as individual plays.

MB: We conceived our *Henry IV*s as part of an eight-play cycle of Shakespeare's history plays, and a large proportion of our audience saw them in this context. Clive Wood had not only played Bullingbrook in *Richard II* but, as Richard of York, had spent three plays trying to take the crown from Henry VI and failing. We staged the plays initially in the order of their writing so York was seen on a Sisyphean journey toward the crown, which faltered in *Henry VI Part III* and began again with renewed vigor and sophistication in *Richard III*. The *Henry IV* plays revealed the eventual fruits of his labors as bitter.

Shakespeare had five very successful histories behind him as he wrote the *Henry IVs*, and *Henry V* was a popular title long before Shakespeare wrote his version, so I think it's fair to say that both author and audience were conscious of context as they experienced the events of *Henry IV*.

These plays move between very distinctive settings: royal court, rebels' castles, Eastcheap tavern, Gloucestershire orchard, battlefield. How did you and your designer set about creating these contrasting worlds?

MP: On their own terms, eclectically. The court wore Edwardian dress, the rebels harked back variously to the eighteenth century and forward to twentieth-century warfare; the tavern was more or less 1980s, the Gloucestershire orchard perhaps a little pre–First World War, the battlefield went back to medieval chain mail and broadsword. All the time we were responding to the temperament of the characters and the atmospherics of each scene and asking the audience to accept unexpected contrasts. The plays are in a sense about the entire history of Britain.

AN: Bob Crowley designed the set and Deirdre Clancy the costumes. We started with a very beautiful wooden floor fringed with gold that both functioned as a practical space and had a strong resonance that could operate as a metaphor. The second thing we decided was that we would spend a lot of our money (because in the end it comes down to that) on the Boar's Head in Eastcheap, because we felt it was an aspect of the play that really needed to jump into the audience's imagination. In any of Shakespeare's plays, some parts require what I would loosely call "social realism" and some don't. *King Lear* does not require much social realism. *The Merry Wives of Windsor* requires a lot, because the plots operate and are triggered by different things. There are certain aspects of *Henry IV Part I* that require that social realism, and the Boar's Head tavern is one of those.

The tavern in *Part I* was a well of life: it absolutely teemed with energy and life. The tavern in *Part II* was a much emptier place. It was a lonely and quite sad place, a place for losers, a place where folk were in danger, so everyone got out very fast when they were told there was another war starting. I used it for Henry IV's great monologue, "How many thousand of my poorest subjects / Are at this hour asleep?" [3.1.4–5]. I had King Henry wander through the tavern, in which the down-and-outs and the losers were all lying drunk and asleep.

This relates to the structure of *Part II*, which is absolutely brilliant. It all works contrapuntally. It's contrapuntal between town and country, between war councils and petty quarrels. And one of the great pieces of counterpoint is at the death of King Henry IV. Henry IV dies in the Jerusalem chamber in the Palace of Westminster and the next scene is in Gloucestershire. From the very beginning of *Part I* he has wanted to go to the Holy Land. He keeps talking about how he wants to go to Jerusalem and eventually he does go there, but he goes there in death. I had his sons and the courtiers lift his body and carry him, and as his bed was lifted aloft and he came weaving downstage then upstage, I did a transformation into the countryside in Gloucestershire. I had a huge canopy with ladders poking up through it and all you saw were the legs of the actors. They were up the ladders, throwing apples down, and the dead body of the king was carried up through the canopy, up through this orchard, the orchard of England. We did this strange picture in slow motion, so it was like he'd gone to heaven, and so we had this fabulous juxtaposition which I think completely fulfilled Shakespeare's purpose. It was a wonderful juxtaposition of the realistic—we had real beekeepers and real apple-pickers in the orchard—and the imagistic, the metaphorical. The man had finally found his way to Jerusalem: it was just eighty miles up the Thames in Gloucestershire. So we found a way in *Part II* of being much freer, much bolder, in the integration of the scenery with the structure of the play.

MB: Henry's court was characterized by a simple silver bowl of water where he tried to wash his hands of the blood of Richard II.

Eastcheap was dominated by a battered old armchair that had

taken the shape of David Warner's Falstaff, and was framed by a large and tattered red velvet drape, which spoke of warmth, theatrical artifice, and backstage assignations. Staff and customers also emerged from and disappeared into a smoky purgatory beneath the stage.

Nearly all the castles from Orleans and Bordeaux in *Henry VI Part I* to Harfleur in *Henry V* were carried by our great rusty Louise Bourgeois–style tower, that rose from its hell mouth gates up past an "I'm the King of the Castle" balcony to an ambiguous spiral stair, which rose to and fell from the grid seven meters above the stage.

Gloucestershire was a bale of hay, some bunting, blossom, and a barbecue.

Our battlefields were the bodies of men fighting over the rusty body of England, which Tom Piper created. Our set suggested arms and legs and a head and viscera.

The plays dramatize the movement from feudalism (with the powerful barons of the north) to the early modern state (with an absolutist idea of monarchy). But they also speak to very Elizabethan concerns, such as the administration of the nation by means of a network of local justices (not all of whom are entirely free from corruption . . .). And at the same time, the idea of the education of a future leader is a timeless theme. So: medieval setting, Elizabethan, modern, or some eclectic mixture of them all?

MP: I'm not so sure about this education of Hal. I think he has a great struggle between his impulses and his duties; he realizes what he will have to sacrifice, and in playing the part I came to think it costs him something. Not that he lets on: in *Henry V* he hardly mentions his past and is completely ruthless about hanging Bardolph for robbing a church, the kind of thing he might once have done himself. So if this is an education, it is not a very inclusive or compassionate one, more a hard lesson in *realpolitik*.

AN: We chose to set it pretty accurately in its period. I think it becomes a nonsense if you take it out of its period, to be absolutely honest, because we all know too much about other periods in which you might set it, and its own period is itself so interesting and resonant. When you've got a wonderful company of actors and you do it reasonably well, relevance jumps out at you.

MB: We found ourselves more interested in Shakespeare as a story-teller for his own age than as medievalist scholar. After the corruption of the old world, the old faith, and the would-be absolutist Richard, comes the cold wind of religious and political reform. Elizabeth may have seen herself characterized as Richard II, but she is also the reforming Protestant ruler beset with a dissenting and unruly populace that we see in *Henry IV*. The Archbishop of York, who "Turns insurrection to religion," can't fail to have reminded Shakespeare's audience of the Pilgrimage of Grace which threatened Elizabeth's father, Henry VIII, with a militarized Catholic backlash from the north.

We opted for three generations: the glamorous remnants of Richard/Elizabeth's golden age; the new black, simple, puritanical broom of Bullingbrook/Elizabeth; and the new generation of Hal and Poins willfully revisiting some of the decadent glamour of the past (with a little help from the saloon glamour of westerns).

Prince Hal is sometimes one of the lads, sometimes coolly detached from his companions. Does this change over the two parts of the drama? Or, to ask the same question in another way: his first soliloquy, "I know you all," is crucial, isn't it? Do you see him speaking it essentially to himself or to the audience in the theater? Does it reveal him as a Machiavellian manipulator from the start, just playing a game in order to improve his own image, always intending to reject his companions when the time is ripe? Or is there much more ambivalence in the progress from "I know you all" early in *Part I* to the rejection speech, "I know thee not," at the end of *Part II*?

MP: Yes, he oscillates—he's tugged in two directions, as anybody might be. He pulls princely rank sometimes in the tavern, and in the court he plays the bad boy. He's quite unresolved.

"I know you all" is a very unusual soliloquy in that it seems not to be addressed to the audience but to his offstage friends and is overheard by the audience. Shakespeare hardly ever does this. A soliloquizer normally confides in the theater audience more intimately than this, more trustingly. The effect here is to make Hal seem a little remote from us.

Playing him as what you call a Machiavellian is possible, but it's not very interesting theatrically, like playing the Duke in *Measure for Measure* simply as a manipulator.

Hal is very monosyllabic when he comes to the point—as in those two cases [his first soliloquy in *Part I* and the rejection speech at the end of *Part II*], and also "I do, I will" when he promises Falstaff he will reject him. I think what keeps the play and the part alive is that he has great difficulty in resolving his conflicting urges. He sets out his program at the start, but he doesn't find it that easy to execute. He leaves the tavern and goes to the court, but is disappointed by his father, who is manipulative and self-absorbed; he goes back to Falstaff, but realizes he can't truly be part of that world either. There is a lot of implied conflict in him.

6. "O polished perturbation! Golden care!" Michael Pennington as Prince Hal and John Castle as Henry IV in the English Shakespeare Company's *Wars of the Roses*, 1986–89.

AN: He is all of those things. He's very complex because if you try and play it as somebody who's being manipulative and Machiavellian, in terms of a great scheme, it doesn't sustain itself. It's un-actable and it's incredible to the audience. The only way it works is if he thoroughly embraces the Eastcheap world and is a protagonist within it. You have to work back from that and from the fact that he says "I know you all." Some people find it necessary to have the character one or the other; I think he's both. I think he's a human being and human beings are extremely complex people. Young people, especially, live several lives: they live the life they live with their parents and they live a completely different life with other people. That's part of growing up and of how you relate to your parents. Hal has, in a way, been very lucky, in the sense that he has two fathers who each represent the two aspects of his character, so again you get this counterpoint which is very creative and very abrasive; it creates intellectual energy. I think Hal embraces that world fully, and the key moment for him is when he finally answers his dad: "Do not think so. You shall not find it so" [3.2.130]. It's a monosyllabic line and you can't rush that line, because there are too many vowels in it. That's a turning point for the character; that's when he realizes he actually has to decide. It's also, interestingly enough, when he finds a voice. I think it's when he finds the voice that will attack Hotspur and will attack the French in *Henry V*. He embraces both worlds happily, and I think that's part of his personality. It's part of the education of the king, but it's more particularly part of the humanity of the king. Another way of looking at it is to think of Hal's time with Falstaff as a time of disguise; the disguise allows him the freedom to explore and develop and thereby achieve wisdom. The character is both with and outside the disguise at one and the same time.

MB: Hal's genuine longing to be a hard-drinking, womanizing Corinthian is in tension from the beginning with his dark understanding that he is heir to the throne and therefore the target of flattery and envious rumor. He starts by flirting with the political theater of the deferred appearance of the sun from behind the cloud, and ends as the leading player in a much darker piece of political theater as he renounces Falstaff, and is groomed for war with France.

The comparison and contrast between Prince Harry and Harry Hotspur is obviously crucial. Did you have particular stylistic or visual devices for establishing and exploring it?

MP: Hotspur seemed like a version of Bonnie Prince Charlie—quite a romantic, eighteenth-century rebel. Hal was completely modern except on the battlefield when he went into chain mail. So as I said above we handled these things not so much conceptually as expressionistically.

AN: It's unavoidable, isn't it? All you have to do is read the play. It's totally and utterly in your face. It's a constant reminder to the audience of what the danger of Prince Hal's behavior is, that he is messing up big-time, because it's a dominating dramatic presence. Hotspur is such a charismatic man. He's a natural leader, he has such command of language, and he has all the other things that audiences want kings to have, like a good wife, a great sense of humor, the ability to deal with his elders in a fair, just, but respectful manner. He's got all of those things; they're there like this great big elephant in the room.

MB: Our Percys were descended from Shakespeare's earlier father-and-son duo in *Henry VI*: the Talbots. By now the honorable code of chivalry of this pairing has become warped. The father caves in horribly in *Part II* and the son is bold but arrogant and reckless. Chivalry is stone dead by *Henry IV*.

Prince Hal moves in the other direction, from selfish, hedonistic criminality to a new contingent morality which will find its fullest paradoxical expression in *Henry V* (and then of course in *Hamlet*).

To answer the question: Geoffrey Streatfeild's Hal was more of a decadent dandy in *Part I* and Lex Shrapnel's Hotspur a glamorized vision of martial prowess.

It's sometimes said that in *Part I* Hal learns the military virtues of the true prince, in *Part II* the civic virtues. So Hotspur is a key opponent in *Part I*, the Lord Chief Justice a key figure in *Part II*. Was that a productive way of looking at it for you?

MP: That didn't occur to me, and I don't think Shakespeare writes that programmatically. The developments in his characters are more

7. "O, Harry, thou hast robbed me of my youth!" Geoffrey Streatfeild as Hal and Lex Shrapnel as Hotspur in Michael Boyd's 2007–08 RSC production.

subtle, less easily explained. And I'm not sure Hal learns any virtues really, only pragmatism—how to handle everybody effectively, in fact. The Lord Chief Justice is his third father figure, after Falstaff and the king—Falstaff is the one that loses out of course.

AN: Not at the time, but yes, that's quite interesting!

MB: No, but it is one template to apply to the plays. It feels more like the Lord Chief Justice's template than Shakespeare's, and it makes the royalist assumption that "becoming a true prince" is Shakespeare's subject.

Having staged all the histories, I began to realize that the drive for power and the yearning for the crown is one big politically acceptable MacGuffin [plot device] that allows Shakespeare to examine the nature of humanity under pressure. Shakespeare is consistently skeptical and critical of those in power, and this famously nonjudgmental author makes an exception for any character showing signs of being over-influenced by *Il Principe*.*

---

*_Il Principe_ (1513) (Italian) *The Prince*: Niccolò Machiavelli's examination of Renaissance *realpolitik*.

In *Part I* Hal wrestles with authority and his father, trying to find/avoid his place in life. In *Part II* Hal confronts the mortality of the very man he has defined himself against and therefore confronts his own mortality. And he kills Falstaff.

Another difference between the two parts is that, simply in terms of size of parts, *Part I* is dominated by Hal, Falstaff, Hotspur, and King Henry, whereas *Part II* has a far larger number of substantial roles. Does that suggest that they are very different kinds of play? *Part I* a star vehicle and *Part II* an ensemble vision?

MP: They're both ensemble pieces—fabulously so. Hotspur's death and Hal's withdrawal from events in *Part II* makes room for Shallow and Silence and the rest, and there's much more Falstaff too. I think *Part II* is just *Part I* rebalanced—not essentially different, except that there's definitely a sense of imminent change, and loss, with the king dying; the tavern scenes have less vitality and Hal generally keeps away from Falstaff, as if he was preparing himself for his future.

AN: The second half is for me the great director's challenge, because it is symphonic. Some plays work as concerti, with a series of solo turns, and some operate more symphonically. This is particularly true of the eight history plays. *Henry VI Part I, Part II,* and *Part III* operate symphonically. My mistake when I did *Richard III,* as the last of that tetralogy, is that until I started rehearsing it I thought it also operated symphonically, but it doesn't: it's written in a completely different manner to the *Henry VI*s. It's written as a series of concerti: one after the other, somebody stands up and plays the violin, plays the viola, plays the cello, plays the trumpet. Edward IV, Clarence, Hastings, one after the other they all stand up. It's not true to such an extent with the two parts of *Henry IV,* but it is to a degree.

I'd wanted to do *Henry IV Part I* and *Part II* for years, but for me you don't even start until you've got Falstaff, which I was very fortunate to get in Robert Stephens. That's the character that not only sets half the agenda of the plays, but is also the person who attracts all the other actors. If you don't have a genius Falstaff, then you won't get a brilliant Henry IV, and if you don't have a brilliant Henry IV, then the spine of the two plays is very shaky. Hal and Hotspur are much easier.

It's for Falstaff, Henry IV, and Shallow that you really need people at the top of their game to fulfill the majesty of those two plays.

MB: Not really. *Part II* was in part conceived as a vehicle for the runaway success of Falstaff as a "turn" in *Part I*.

Does Falstaff change between the two parts?

MP: In *Part I*, Hal and he are wonderfully matched, especially in their capacity for (more or less) friendly insults. Falstaff feels Hal's absence in *Part II* very keenly—he knows in his heart the best times are past. Falstaff talks about him all the time, wistfully.

AN: He matures somehow and gets wiser in the second part. I think the reason he appears to get older in the second part is because he has the Page. That's why Shakespeare gives him a young person to walk about with, so you realize he's old. Also in *Part II* he associates much more with people of his own age, particularly with his fellow students from when he was a law student at Temple. By hanging out with Silence and Shallow, on the one hand, and with a twelve-year-old boy, on the other hand, we get a strong whiff of mortality coming off Falstaff in *Part II*, which we don't so much get in *Part I*.

MB: Falstaff has become a star in *Part II* because of his false success in Shrewsbury, and his real success in the theater in *Henry IV Part I*. Shakespeare promotes him to the courtly world and gives him exchanges with the most powerful people in the land, but then punishes him with cynicism, gout, and mortality.

He's a force of nature in *Part I*, and in *Part II* he's someone clinging on to influence, and opportunity, and life.

What did you learn in the process of rehearsing the great playacting scene in *Part I*—the preenactment by Hal and Falstaff of Hal's confrontation with his father? And did it teach you things that you could use when working on the actual encounters between the prince and his father?

MP: Not so much that, but the two successive scenes are at the center of the part. The scene in the Boar's Head has terrific tension—how far will Hal go in mocking his father? How far will he let Falstaff go? The onlookers don't know how loudly they're allowed to laugh. It's a great relief to Hal to make fun of his father; then he goes to see him for real and is very disappointed. He apologizes to the king and promises to toe the line but gets little thanks for it. Hal is very frustrated by his father. It's interesting that he takes Falstaff into battle with him and even lets him take credit for the death of Hotspur—it's as if he were serving notice that he'll do his duty by his father but he's not giving up his old ways that easily.

AN: Not particularly. It's most important because it stands as a rehearsal of the denial of Falstaff; that seems its main function to me. It was fun and funny—it couldn't not be that and I made it that—and I made it very anarchic, but my main purpose related to the denial of Falstaff. I remember feeling it was profoundly wrong that Hal engaged in this playacting. The whole idea of impersonating the monarch had a slight whiff of danger about it, and I think for an Elizabethan audience it would have been almost obscene: a very dangerous thing to do and very disrespectful. The dice are loaded very heavily against Hal in *Part I* and I think that's why it is such a dramatic piece: it's because he turns the stakes around, he overturns the odds, that it is remarkable.

MB: Clive Wood had already shaped his testosterone-fueled, reforming Bullingbrook in our *Richard II,* so we already knew that Hal's encounters with his father would be bruising and straight out of Eugene O'Neill or Tennessee Williams.

There was a moving mismatch of styles in the playacting scene: David Warner's Falstaff revealing an old-fashioned delicacy that had no place in Bullingbrook's actual cold, pragmatic palace.

It's mostly a male world, but, small as they are, the female parts— Hotspur's wife, Quickly, Doll—seem very significant, don't they? What was your take on the women in these plays?

MP: I think Doll's little scene with Falstaff in *Part II* is a real love scene—both of them at their best; open, honest, and affectionate in ways they aren't elsewhere. Mistress Quickly represents one kind of female constancy in her love of Falstaff, and in a sense, Lady Percy

8. Robert Stephens as Falstaff and Joanne Pearce as Doll Tearsheet at Hostess Quickly's tavern in Eastcheap in *Part II* of Adrian Noble's 1991 RSC production.

the other, in her anger at Hotspur's withdrawing from her and her grief at his loss. They're very good parts, all three of them.

AN: They're wonderful parts and you can do fantastic things with them with the right people. I was very lucky and we did great things with those parts. What Shakespeare does is genuinely present a great portrait of a nation. Look at the language of the scene of the two Carriers in Rochester: it's a couple of lorry drivers at Watford Gap services, it's a couple of guys who have done an overnight stay in a B&B somewhere. What he creates with that language—and of course it's distilled and slightly heightened—is the cadence of Elizabethan England. Shakespeare perfectly captures it: people working in an industrial situation. Now compare that with the sound of Shallow and Silence. Again, the cadence there is extraordinary. It's a remarkable soundscape, probably of Warwickshire when he was a boy, and that's part of the richness of the play. The *Henry VI* plays don't attempt that at all: you get little snippets of them with Cade and Dick the Butcher, but they are only snippets. In *Henry IV* they are in-depth portraits of a nation. You get the clergy, you get the courtiers, you get the tapsters, you get the prostitutes. Doll Tearsheet is an amazing portrait of a prostitute. Shakespeare captures the language in an extraordinary way.

MB: And Glendower's daughter possibly wins the war for Bullingbrook.

Ann Ogbomo's Kate Percy was an intelligent, beautiful, and feisty sketch for Shakespeare's later leading women, Rosalind and Beatrice.

As Mistress Quickly, Maureen Beattie brought her own instinctive understanding of comedic rhythms from Scottish variety to a much-loved character that can trace its ancestry to Noah's wife, the Wife of Bath, and beyond. Together with Alexia Healy's Doll, she maintained a haven of imperfect warmth in the cold world of Bullingbrook, until at last Eastcheap was literally dismantled in *Part II*.

Shakespeare's friend and rival Ben Jonson mocked his history plays for representing battles by means of nothing more than "three rusty swords"—and modern audiences are used to the epic battles of the Hollywood screen, complete with hundreds of extras. In light of this, how do you set about staging the battles convincingly? What balance between stylization and realism?

MP: That was quite snobbish of Jonson—they couldn't afford anything else. And Shakespeare always forestalls that argument, as he does in the first chorus in *Henry V*—the means are limited but, as he knows, his imaginative suggestiveness is great.

I think the battles should be as realistic as possible, especially the Hal/Hotspur—traditional one-to-one combat, sweating it out, like Richard III and Richmond; Hamlet and Laertes, too, if you like. They're cathartic confrontations. The difficulty is greater in the general battle scenes and skirmishes; the rhetoric can be a bit thumpy and there's a lot of rushing around without much character (though when Falstaff is on the battlefield there's terrific comic counterpoint). Sometimes directors stylize Shakespeare's battle scenes—slow motion, banners, mime, and so on. I don't much care for it myself, but I appreciate why it happens. I think you have to create the fog of war as realistically as you can. Interestingly enough, in the ESC version, though we used guns often, the big one-to-one set pieces we always did in chainmail and armor and broadswords, two individuals timelessly slugging it out to the death.

AN: You've answered the question actually: you get a balance between stylization and realism. Very simple technology plus a lot of imagination can lead you to extraordinary things. You first ask the question, "What is the battle about? What is this one saying?" At the end of *Part I* it's Shrewsbury: the subject of that battle is the throne, it's a fight for the throne. There was a piece of technology in the old Royal Shakespeare Theatre that no longer exists, which I discovered when I was doing *King Lear* with Michael Gambon. There were two huge lifts running up to the stage, each one nine meters by four meters, that could hold about seventy people each. On certain occasions like Gad's Hill I used the great hole onstage where the lift shaft was. At the Battle of Shrewsbury there were people talking downstage but the hole was down, and in the trap under the stage I'd loaded the throne surrounded by the whole of King Henry's courtiers, and then, with a huge amount of music and drumming,

9. The battle scenes dramatized the essential qualities of a conflict with "three rusty swords" and the audience as extras in Michael Boyd's 2007–08 RSC history cycle.

this throne came out of the earth. Not only did this trap ascend to stage level, it went above it. So when it hit stage level it was attacked in quite a stylized way by Hotspur's men, with the entire company onstage, and it carried on up into the air until it was about eight feet off the ground, and then it started to descend. Everyone was fighting, but they were actually fighting for the throne, and then when it came down to stage level it went into realistic swordplay. It's a bit unfair of Ben Jonson to say that, but he is absolutely right. What we delivered was a quite spectacular battle based upon the technology of that theater. We were just very lucky that we had it there. I think I used that huge hole in each of the seven history plays I did.

MB: Over eight plays, we worked on the battles employing many approaches, including the following:

1. Shakespeare's battles must serve the play in the same way as a song in a musical: they must move the story forward.
2. Renaissance dance was in part physical training for the men at court for battle. Our battles were to a greater or lesser extent all dances.
3. Our battles often carried a cosmological burden: i.e. they were a battle between heaven and hell fought out on earth. This combined with the spatial excitement of the Courtyard Theatre encouraged us to use four dimensions. Violence burst out from the grid, the stage, and the audience as often as from backstage.
4. Battles were staged with consciously shifting points of view, e.g. Shrewsbury was seen mostly from the rebels' perspective and picked up on the practice of decoy kings. We dramatized the courage it took to challenge an "anointed" king by opposing Hotspur with an army of kings.
5. We wanted to celebrate the chief advantage of theatrical over filmic battles: we were not the slaves of naturalism pursuing ever more plausible wounds and dismemberments. We were free to attempt to dramatize the essential qualities of a conflict. The hundreds of extras were supplied by the audience.

SHAKESPEARE'S CAREER
IN THE THEATER

BEGINNINGS

William Shakespeare was an extraordinarily intelligent man who
was born and died in an ordinary market town in the English Midlands. He lived an uneventful life in an eventful age. Born in April
1564, he was the eldest son of John Shakespeare, a glove maker
who was prominent on the town council until he fell into financial
difficulties. Young William was educated at the local grammar
school in Stratford-upon-Avon, Warwickshire, where he gained a
thorough grounding in the Latin language, the art of rhetoric, and
classical poetry. He married Ann Hathaway and had three children
(Susanna, then the twins Hamnet and Judith) before his twenty-first
birthday: an exceptionally young age for the period. We do not know
how he supported his family in the mid-1580s.

Like many clever country boys, he moved to the city in order to
make his way in the world. Like many creative people, he found a
career in the entertainment business. Public playhouses and profes-
sional full-time acting companies reliant on the market for their
income were born in Shakespeare's childhood. When he arrived in
London as a man, sometime in the late 1580s, a new phenomenon
was in the making: the actor who is so successful that he becomes a
"star." The word did not exist in its modern sense, but the pattern is
recognizable: audiences went to the theater not so much to see a particular show as to witness the comedian Richard Tarlton or the dramatic actor Edward Alleyn.

Shakespeare was an actor before he was a writer. It appears not to
have been long before he realized that he was never going to grow into
a great comedian like Tarlton or a great tragedian like Alleyn. Instead,
he found a role within his company as the man who patched up old
plays, breathing new life, new dramatic twists, into tired repertory
pieces. He paid close attention to the work of the university-educated

dramatists who were writing history plays and tragedies for the public stage in a style more ambitious, sweeping, and poetically grand than anything that had been seen before. But he may also have noted that what his friend and rival Ben Jonson would call "Marlowe's mighty line" sometimes faltered in the mode of comedy. Going to university, as Christopher Marlowe did, was all well and good for honing the arts of rhetorical elaboration and classical allusion, but it could lead to a loss of the common touch. To stay close to a large segment of the potential audience for public theater, it was necessary to write for clowns as well as kings and to intersperse the flights of poetry with the humor of the tavern, the privy, and the brothel: Shakespeare was the first to establish himself early in his career as an equal master of tragedy, comedy, and history. He realized that theater could be the medium to make the national past available to a wider audience than the elite who could afford to read large history books: his signature early works include not only the classical tragedy *Titus Andronicus* but also the sequence of English historical plays on the Wars of the Roses.

He also invented a new role for himself, that of in-house company dramatist. Where his peers and predecessors had to sell their plays to the theater managers on a poorly paid piecework basis, Shakespeare took a percentage of the box-office income. The Lord Chamberlain's Men constituted themselves in 1594 as a joint stock company, with the profits being distributed among the core actors who had invested as sharers. Shakespeare acted himself—he appears in the cast lists of some of Ben Jonson's plays as well as the list of actors' names at the beginning of his own collected works—but his principal duty was to write two or three plays a year for the company. By holding shares, he was effectively earning himself a royalty on his work, something no author had ever done before in England. When the Lord Chamberlain's Men collected their fee for performance at court in the Christmas season of 1594, three of them went along to the Treasurer of the Chamber: not just Richard Burbage the tragedian and Will Kempe the clown, but also Shakespeare the scriptwriter. That was something new.

The next four years were the golden period in Shakespeare's career, though overshadowed by the death of his only son, Hamnet, aged eleven, in 1596. In his early thirties and in full command of both his poetic and his theatrical medium, he perfected his art of comedy, while also developing his tragic and historical writing in new ways. In 1598, Francis Meres, a Cambridge University graduate with his finger on the pulse of the London literary world, praised Shakespeare for his excellence across the genres:

> As Plautus and Seneca are accounted the best for comedy and tragedy among the Latins, so Shakespeare among the English is the most excellent in both kinds for the stage; for comedy, witness his *Gentlemen of Verona*, his *Errors*, his *Love Labours Lost*, his *Love Labours Won*, his *Midsummer Night Dream* and his *Merchant of Venice*: for tragedy his *Richard the 2*, *Richard the 3*, *Henry the 4*, *King John*, *Titus Andronicus* and his *Romeo and Juliet*.

For Meres, as for the many writers who praised the "honey-flowing vein" of *Venus and Adonis* and *Lucrece*, narrative poems written when the theaters were closed due to plague in 1593–94, Shakespeare was marked above all by his linguistic skill, by the gift of turning elegant poetic phrases.

PLAYHOUSES

Elizabethan playhouses were "thrust" or "one-room" theaters. To understand Shakespeare's original theatrical life, we have to forget about the indoor theater of later times, with its proscenium arch and curtain that would be opened at the beginning and closed at the end of each act. In the proscenium arch theater, stage and auditorium are effectively two separate rooms: the audience looks from one world into another as if through the imaginary "fourth wall" framed by the proscenium. The picture-frame stage, together with the elaborate scenic effects and backdrops beyond it, created the illusion of a self-contained world—especially once nineteenth-century developments in the control of artificial lighting meant that the auditorium could be darkened and the spectators made to focus on the lighted stage. Shakespeare, by contrast, wrote for a bare platform stage with a standing audience gathered around it in a courtyard in full daylight. The audience were always conscious of themselves and their fellow spectators, and they shared the same "room" as the actors. A sense of immediate presence and the creation of rapport with the audience were all-important. The actor could not afford to imagine he was in a closed world, with silent witnesses dutifully observing him from the darkness.

Shakespeare's theatrical career began at the Rose Theatre in Southwark. The stage was wide and shallow, trapezoid in shape, like a lozenge. This design had a great deal of potential for the theatrical equivalent of cinematic split-screen effects, whereby one group of characters would enter at the door at one end of the tiring-house wall at the back of the stage and another group through the door at the other end, thus creating two rival tableaux. Many of the battle-heavy and faction-filled plays that premiered at the Rose have scenes of just this sort.

At the rear of the Rose stage, there were three capacious exits, each over ten feet wide. Unfortunately, the very limited excavation of a fragmentary portion of the original Globe site, in 1989, revealed nothing about the stage. The first Globe was built in 1599 with similar proportions to those of another theater, the Fortune, albeit that the former was polygonal and looked circular, whereas the latter was rectangular. The building contract for the Fortune survives and allows us to infer that the stage of the Globe was probably substantially wider than it was deep (perhaps forty-three feet wide and twenty-seven feet deep). It may well have been tapered at the front, like that of the Rose.

The capacity of the Globe was said to have been enormous, perhaps in excess of three thousand. It has been conjectured that about eight hundred people may have stood in the yard, with two thousand or more in the three layers of covered galleries. The other "public" playhouses were also of large capacity, whereas the indoor Blackfriars theater that Shakespeare's company began using in 1608—the former refectory of a monastery—had overall internal dimensions of a mere forty-six by sixty feet. It would have made for a much more intimate theatrical experience and had a much smaller capacity, probably of about six hundred people. Since they paid at least sixpence a head, the Blackfriars attracted a more select or "private" audience. The atmosphere would have been closer to that of an indoor performance before the court in the Whitehall Palace or at Richmond. That Shakespeare always wrote for indoor production at court as well as outdoor performance in the public theater should make us cautious about inferring, as some scholars have, that the opportunity provided by the intimacy of the Blackfriars led to a significant change toward a "chamber" style in his last plays—which, besides, were performed at both the Globe and the Blackfriars. After the occupation of the Blackfriars a five-act structure seems to have become more important to Shakespeare. That was because of artificial lighting: there were musical interludes between the acts, while the candles were trimmed and replaced. Again, though, something similar must have been necessary for indoor court performances throughout his career.

Front of house there were the "gatherers" who collected the money from audience members: a penny to stand in the open-air yard, another penny for a place in the covered galleries, sixpence for the prominent "lord's rooms" to the side of the stage. In the indoor "private" theaters, gallants from the audience who fancied making themselves part of the spectacle sat on stools on the edge of the stage itself. Scholars debate as to how widespread this practice was in the public theaters such as the Globe. Once the audience were in place and the money counted, the gatherers were available to be extras onstage. That is one reason why battles and crowd scenes often come later rather than early in Shakespeare's plays. There was no formal prohibition upon performance by women, and there certainly were women among the gatherers, so it is not beyond the bounds of possibility that female crowd members were played by females.

The play began at two o'clock in the afternoon and the theater had to be cleared by five. After the main show, there would be a jig—which consisted not only of dancing, but also of knockabout comedy (it is the origin of the farcical "afterpiece" in the eighteenth-century theater). So the time available for a Shakespeare play was about two and a half hours, somewhere between the "two hours' traffic" mentioned in the prologue to *Romeo and Juliet* and the "three hours' spectacle" referred to in the preface to the 1647 Folio of Beaumont and Fletcher's plays.

The prologue to a play by Thomas Middleton refers to a thousand lines as "one hour's words," so the likelihood is that about two and a half thousand, or a maximum of three thousand lines, made up the performed text. This is indeed the length of most of Shakespeare's comedies, whereas many of his tragedies and histories are much longer, raising the possibility that he wrote full scripts, possibly with eventual publication in mind, in the full knowledge that the stage version would be heavily cut. The short Quarto texts published in his lifetime—they used to be called "Bad" Quartos—provide fascinating evidence as to the kind of cutting that probably took place. So, for instance, the First Quarto of *Hamlet* neatly merges two occasions when Hamlet is overheard, the "Fishmonger" and the "nunnery" scenes.

The social composition of the audience was mixed. The poet Sir John Davies wrote of "A thousand townsmen, gentlemen and whores, / Porters and servingmen" who would "together throng" at the public playhouses. Though moralists associated female playgoing with adultery and the sex trade, many perfectly respectable citizens' wives were regular attendees. Some, no doubt, resembled the modern groupie: a story attested in two different sources has one citizen's wife making a postshow assignation with Richard Burbage and ending up in bed with Shakespeare—supposedly eliciting from the latter the quip that William the Conqueror was before Richard III. Defenders of theater liked to say that by witnessing the comeuppance of villains on the stage, audience members would repent of their own wrongdoings, but the reality is that most people went to the theater then, as they do now, for entertainment more than moral edification. Besides, it would be foolish to suppose that audiences behaved in a homogeneous way: a pamphlet of the 1630s tells of how two men went to see *Pericles* and one of them laughed while the other wept. Bishop John Hall complained that people went to church for the same reasons that they went to the theater: "for company, for custom, for recreation . . . to feed his eyes or his ears . . . or perhaps for sleep."

Men-about-town and clever young lawyers went to be seen as much as to see. In the modern popular imagination, shaped not least by *Shakespeare in Love* and the opening sequence of Laurence Olivier's *Henry V* film, the penny-paying groundlings stand in the yard hurling abuse or encouragement and hazelnuts or orange peel

at the actors, while the sophisticates in the covered galleries appreciate Shakespeare's soaring poetry. The reality was probably the other
way around. A "groundling" was a kind of fish, so the nickname
suggests the penny audience standing below the level of the stage
and gazing in silent openmouthed wonder at the spectacle unfolding
above them. The more difficult audience members, who kept up a
running commentary of clever remarks on the performance and
who occasionally got into quarrels with players, were the gallants.
Like Hollywood movies in modern times, Elizabethan and Jacobean
plays exercised a powerful influence on the fashion and behavior of
the young. John Marston mocks the lawyers who would open their
lips, perhaps to court a girl, and out would "flow / Naught but pure
Juliet and Romeo."

THE ENSEMBLE AT WORK

In the absence of typewriters and photocopying machines, reading
aloud would have been the means by which the company got to
know a new play. The tradition of the playwright reading his complete script to the assembled company endured for generations. A
copy would then have been taken to the Master of the Revels for
licensing. The theater book-holder or prompter would then have
copied the parts for distribution to the actors. A partbook consisted
of the character's lines, with each speech preceded by the last three
or four words of the speech before, the so-called "cue." These would
have been taken away and studied or "conned." During this period of
learning the parts, an actor might have had some one-to-one
instruction, perhaps from the dramatist, perhaps from a senior actor
who had played the same part before, and, in the case of an apprentice, from his master. A high percentage of Desdemona's lines occur
in dialogue with Othello, of Lady Macbeth's with Macbeth, Cleopatra's with Antony, and Volumnia's with Coriolanus. The roles would
almost certainly have been taken by the apprentice of the lead actor,
usually Burbage, who delivers the majority of the cues. Given that
apprentices lodged with their masters, there would have been ample
opportunity for personal instruction, which may be what made it
possible for young men to play such demanding parts.

10. Hypothetical reconstruction of the interior of an Elizabethan playhouse during a performance.

After the parts were learned, there may have been no more than a single rehearsal before the first performance. With six different plays to be put on every week, there was no time for more. Actors, then, would go into a show with a very limited sense of the whole. The notion of a collective rehearsal process that is itself a process of discovery for the actors is wholly modern and would have been incomprehensible to Shakespeare and his original ensemble. Given the number of parts an actor had to hold in his memory, the forgetting of lines was probably more frequent than in the modern theater. The book-holder was on hand to prompt.

Backstage personnel included the property man, the tire-man who oversaw the costumes, call boys, attendants, and the musicians, who might play at various times from the main stage, the rooms above, and within the tiring-house. Scriptwriters sometimes made a nuisance of themselves backstage. There was often tension between the acting companies and the freelance playwrights from whom they purchased scripts: it was a smart move on the part of

Shakespeare and the Lord Chamberlain's Men to bring the writing process in-house.

Scenery was limited, though sometimes set pieces were brought on (a bank of flowers, a bed, the mouth of hell). The trapdoor from below, the gallery stage above, and the curtained discovery space at the back allowed for an array of special effects: the rising of ghosts and apparitions, the descent of gods, dialogue between a character at a window and another at ground level, the revelation of a statue or a pair of lovers playing at chess. Ingenious use could be made of props, as with the ass's head in *A Midsummer Night's Dream*. In a theater that does not clutter the stage with the material paraphernalia of everyday life, those objects that are deployed may take on powerful symbolic weight, as when Shylock bears his weighing scales in one hand and knife in the other, thus becoming a parody of the figure of Justice who traditionally bears a sword and a balance. Among the more significant items in the property cupboard of Shakespeare's company, there would have been a throne (the "chair of state"), joint stools, books, bottles, coins, purses, letters (which are brought onstage, read or referred to on about eighty occasions in the complete works), maps, gloves, a set of stocks (in which Kent is put in *King Lear*), rings, rapiers, daggers, broadswords, staves, pistols, masks and vizards, heads and skulls, torches and tapers and lanterns which served to signal night scenes on the daylit stage, a buck's head, an ass's head, animal costumes. Live animals also put in appearances, most notably the dog Crab in *The Two Gentlemen of Verona* and possibly a young polar bear in *The Winter's Tale*.

The costumes were the most important visual dimension of the play. Playwrights were paid between £2 and £6 per script, whereas Alleyn was not averse to paying £20 for "a black velvet cloak with sleeves embroidered all with silver and gold." No matter the period of the play, actors always wore contemporary costume. The excitement for the audience came not from any impression of historical accuracy, but from the richness of the attire and perhaps the transgressive thrill of the knowledge that here were commoners like themselves strutting in the costumes of courtiers in effective defiance of the strict sumptuary laws whereby in real life people had to wear the clothes that befitted their social station.

To an even greater degree than props, costumes could carry symbolic importance. Racial characteristics could be suggested: a breastplate and helmet for a Roman soldier, a turban for a Turk, long robes for exotic characters such as Moors, a gabardine for a Jew. The figure of Time, as in *The Winter's Tale*, would be equipped with hourglass, scythe, and wings; Rumour, who speaks the prologue of *Henry IV Part II*, wore a costume adorned with a thousand tongues. The wardrobe in the tiring-house of the Globe would have contained much of the same stock as that of rival manager Philip Henslowe at the Rose: green gowns for outlaws and foresters, black for melancholy men such as Jaques and people in mourning such as the Countess in *All's Well That Ends Well* (at the beginning of *Hamlet*, the prince is still in mourning black when everyone else is in festive garb for the wedding of the new king), a gown and hood for a friar (or a feigned friar like the Duke in *Measure for Measure*), blue coats and tawny to distinguish the followers of rival factions, a leather apron and ruler for a carpenter (as in the opening scene of *Julius Caesar*—and in *A Midsummer Night's Dream*, where this is the only sign that Peter Quince is a carpenter), a cockle hat with staff and a pair of sandals for a pilgrim or palmer (the disguise assumed by Helen in *All's Well*), bodices and kirtles with farthingales beneath for the boys who are to be dressed as girls. A gender switch such as that of Rosalind or Jessica seems to have taken between fifty and eighty lines of dialogue—Viola does not resume her "maiden weeds," but remains in her boy's costume to the end of *Twelfth Night* because a change would have slowed down the action at just the moment it was speeding to a climax. Henslowe's inventory also included "a robe for to go invisible": Oberon, Puck, and Ariel must have had something similar.

As the costumes appealed to the eyes, so there was music for the ears. Comedies included many songs. Desdemona's willow song, perhaps a late addition to the text, is a rare and thus exceptionally poignant example from tragedy. Trumpets and tuckets sounded for ceremonial entrances, drums denoted an army on the march. Background music could create atmosphere, as at the beginning of *Twelfth Night*, during the lovers' dialogue near the end of *The Merchant of Venice*, when the statue seemingly comes to life in *The Winter's Tale*, and for the revival of Pericles and of Lear (in the Quarto text, but not the Folio). The haunting sound of the hautbois sug-gested a realm beyond the human, as when the god Hercules is imag-ined deserting Mark Antony. Dances symbolized the harmony of the end of a comedy—though in Shakespeare's world of mingled joy and sorrow, someone is usually left out of the circle.

The most important resource was, of course, the actors them-selves. They needed many skills: in the words of one contemporary commentator, "dancing, activity, music, song, elocution, ability of body, memory, skill of weapon, pregnancy of wit." Their bodies were as significant as their voices. Hamlet tells the player to "suit the action to the word, the word to the action": moments of strong emotion, known as "passions," relied on a repertoire of dramatic gestures as well as a modulation of the voice. When Titus Andronicus has had his hand chopped off, he asks "How can I grace my talk, / Wanting a hand to give it action?" A pen portrait of "The Character of an Excel-lent Actor" by the dramatist John Webster is almost certainly based on his impression of Shakespeare's leading man, Richard Burbage: "By a full and significant action of body, he charms our attention: sit in a full theater, and you will think you see so many lines drawn from the circumference of so many ears, whiles the actor is the centre. . . ."

Though Burbage was admired above all others, praise was also heaped upon the apprentice players whose alto voices fitted them for the parts of women. A spectator at Oxford in 1610 records how the audience were reduced to tears by the pathos of Desdemona's death. The Puritans who fumed about the biblical prohibition upon cross-dressing and the encouragement to sodomy constituted by the sight of an adult male kissing a teenage boy onstage were a small minority. Little is known, however, about the characteristics of the leading apprentices in Shakespeare's company. It may perhaps be inferred that one was a lot taller than the other, since Shakespeare often wrote for a pair of female friends, one tall and fair, the other short and dark (Helena and Hermia, Rosalind and Celia, Beatrice and Hero).

We know little about Shakespeare's own acting roles—an early allusion indicates that he often took royal parts, and a venerable tra-dition gives him old Adam in *As You Like It* and the ghost of old King Hamlet. Save for Burbage's lead roles and the generic part of the clown, all such castings are mere speculation. We do not even know for sure whether the original Falstaff was Will Kempe or another actor who specialized in comic roles, Thomas Pope.

Kempe left the company in early 1599. Tradition has it that he fell out with Shakespeare over the matter of excessive improvisation. He was replaced by Robert Armin, who was less of a clown and more of a cerebral wit: this explains the difference between such parts as Lancelet Gobbo and Dogberry, which were written for Kempe, and the more verbally sophisticated Feste and Lear's Fool, which were written for Armin.

One thing that is clear from surviving "plots" or storyboards of plays from the period is that a degree of doubling was necessary. *Henry VI Part II* has over sixty speaking parts, but more than half of the characters only appear in a single scene and most scenes have only six to eight speakers. At a stretch, the play could be performed by thirteen actors. When Thomas Platter saw *Julius Caesar* at the Globe in 1599, he noted that there were about fifteen. Why doesn't Paris go to the Capulet ball in *Romeo and Juliet*? Perhaps because he was doubled with Mercutio, who does. In *The Winter's Tale*, Mamillius might have come back as Perdita and Antigonus been doubled by Camillo, making the partnership with Paulina at the end a very neat touch. Titania and Oberon are often played by the same pair as Hippolyta and Theseus, suggesting a symbolic matching of the rulers of the worlds of night and day, but it is questionable whether there would have been time for the necessary costume changes. As so often, one is left in a realm of tantalizing speculation.

THE KING'S MAN

On Queen Elizabeth's death in 1603, the new king, James I, who had held the Scottish throne as James VI since he had been an infant, immediately took the Lord Chamberlain's Men under his direct patronage. Henceforth they would be the King's Men, and for the rest of Shakespeare's career they were favored with far more court performances than any of their rivals. There even seem to have been rumors early in the reign that Shakespeare and Burbage were being considered for knighthoods, an unprecedented honor for mere actors—and one that in the event was not accorded to a member of the profession for nearly three hundred years, when the title was bestowed upon Henry Irving, the leading Shakespearean actor of Queen Victoria's reign.

Shakespeare's productivity rate slowed in the Jacobean years, not because of age or some personal trauma, but because there were frequent outbreaks of plague, causing the theaters to be closed for long periods. The King's Men were forced to spend many months on the road. Between November 1603 and 1608, they were to be found at various towns in the south and Midlands, though Shakespeare probably did not tour with them by this time. He had bought a large house back home in Stratford and was accumulating other property. He may indeed have stopped acting soon after the new king took the throne. With the London theaters closed so much of the time and a large repertoire on the stocks, Shakespeare seems to have focused his energies on writing a few long and complex tragedies that could have been played on demand at court: *Othello*, *King Lear*, *Antony and Cleopatra*, *Coriolanus*, and *Cymbeline* are among his longest and poetically grandest plays. *Macbeth* survives only in a shorter text, which shows signs of adaptation after Shakespeare's death. The bitterly satirical *Timon of Athens*, apparently a collaboration with Thomas Middleton that may have failed on the stage, also belongs to this period. In comedy, too, he wrote longer and morally darker works than in the Elizabethan period, pushing at the very bounds of the form in *Measure for Measure* and *All's Well That Ends Well*.

From 1608 onward, when the King's Men began occupying the indoor Blackfriars playhouse (as a winter house, meaning that they only used the outdoor Globe in summer?), Shakespeare turned to a more romantic style. His company had a great success with a revived and altered version of an old pastoral play called *Mucedorus*. It even featured a bear. The younger dramatist John Fletcher, meanwhile, sometimes working in collaboration with Francis Beaumont, was pioneering a new style of tragicomedy, a mix of romance and royalism laced with intrigue and pastoral excursions. Shakespeare experimented with this idiom in *Cymbeline* and it was presumably with his blessing that Fletcher eventually took over as the King's Men's company dramatist. The two writers apparently collaborated on three plays in the years 1612–14: a lost romance called *Cardenio* (based on the love-madness of a character in Cervantes' *Don Quixote*), *Henry VIII* (originally staged with the title "All Is True"), and *The Two Noble Kinsmen*, a dramatization of Chaucer's "Knight's Tale." These were written after Shakespeare's two final solo-authored plays, *The Winter's Tale*, a self-consciously old-fashioned work dramatizing the pastoral romance of his old enemy Robert Greene, and *The Tempest*, which at one and the same time drew together multiple theatrical traditions, diverse reading, and contemporary interest in the fate of a ship that had been wrecked on the way to the New World.

The collaborations with Fletcher suggest that Shakespeare's career ended with a slow fade rather than the sudden retirement supposed by the nineteenth-century Romantic critics who read Prospero's epilogue to *The Tempest* as Shakespeare's personal farewell to his art. In the last few years of his life Shakespeare certainly spent more of his time in Stratford-upon-Avon, where he became further involved in property dealing and litigation. But his London life also continued. In 1613 he made his first major London property purchase: a freehold house in the Blackfriars district, close to his company's indoor theater. *The Two Noble Kinsmen* may have been written as late as 1614, and Shakespeare was in London on business a little over a year before he died of an unknown cause at home in Stratford-upon-Avon in 1616, probably on his fifty-second birthday.

About half the sum of his works were published in his lifetime, in texts of variable quality. A few years after his death, his fellow actors began putting together an authorized edition of his complete *Comedies, Histories and Tragedies*. It appeared in 1623, in large "Folio" format. This collection of thirty-six plays gave Shakespeare his immortality. In the words of his fellow dramatist Ben Jonson, who contributed two poems of praise at the start of the Folio, the body of his work made him "a monument without a tomb":

> And art alive still while thy book doth live
> And we have wits to read and praise to give . . .
> He was not of an age, but for all time!

SHAKESPEARE'S WORKS:
A CHRONOLOGY

1589–91	*? Arden of Faversham* (possible part authorship)
1589–92	*The Taming of the Shrew*
1589–92	*? Edward the Third* (possible part authorship)
1591	*The Second Part of Henry the Sixth*, originally called *The First Part of the Contention Betwixt the Two Famous Houses of York and Lancaster* (element of coauthorship possible)
1591	*The Third Part of Henry the Sixth*, originally called *The True Tragedy of Richard Duke of York* (element of co-authorship probable)
1591–92	*The Two Gentlemen of Verona*
1591–92; perhaps revised 1594	*The Lamentable Tragedy of Titus Andronicus* (probably cowritten with, or revising an earlier version by, George Peele)
1592	*The First Part of Henry the Sixth*, probably with Thomas Nashe and others
1592/94	*King Richard the Third*
1593	*Venus and Adonis* (poem)
1593–94	*The Rape of Lucrece* (poem)
1593–1608	*Sonnets* (154 poems, published 1609 with *A Lover's Complaint*, a poem of disputed authorship)
1592–94 or 1600–03	*Sir Thomas More* (a single scene for a play originally by Anthony Munday, with other revisions by Henry Chettle, Thomas Dekker, and Thomas Heywood)
1594	*The Comedy of Errors*
1595	*Love's Labour's Lost*

1595–97	*Love's Labour's Won* (a lost play, unless the original title for another comedy)
1595–96	*A Midsummer Night's Dream*
1595–96	*The Tragedy of Romeo and Juliet*
1595–96	*King Richard the Second*
1595–97	*The Life and Death of King John* (possibly earlier)
1596–97	*The Merchant of Venice*
1596–97	*The First Part of Henry the Fourth*
1597–98	*The Second Part of Henry the Fourth*
1598	*Much Ado About Nothing*
1598–99	*The Passionate Pilgrim* (20 poems, some not by Shakespeare)
1599	*The Life of Henry the Fifth*
1599	"To the Queen" (epilogue for a court performance)
1599	*As You Like It*
1599	*The Tragedy of Julius Caesar*
1600–01	*The Tragedy of Hamlet, Prince of Denmark* (perhaps revising an earlier version)
1600–01	*The Merry Wives of Windsor* (perhaps revising version of 1597–99)
1601	"Let the Bird of Loudest Lay" (poem, known since 1807 as "The Phoenix and Turtle" [turtledove])
1601	*Twelfth Night, or What You Will*
1601–02	*The Tragedy of Troilus and Cressida*
1604	*The Tragedy of Othello, the Moor of Venice*
1604	*Measure for Measure*
1605	*All's Well That Ends Well*
1605	*The Life of Timon of Athens*, with Thomas Middleton
1605–06	*The Tragedy of King Lear*
1605–08	? contribution to *The Four Plays in One* (lost, except for *A Yorkshire Tragedy*, mostly by Thomas Middleton)

1606	*The Tragedy of Macbeth* (surviving text has additional scenes by Thomas Middleton)
1606–07	*The Tragedy of Antony and Cleopatra*
1608	*The Tragedy of Coriolanus*
1608	*Pericles, Prince of Tyre*, with George Wilkins
1610	*The Tragedy of Cymbeline*
1611	*The Winter's Tale*
1611	*The Tempest*
1612–13	*Cardenio*, with John Fletcher (survives only in later adaptation called *Double Falsehood* by Lewis Theobald)
1613	*Henry VIII (All Is True)*, with John Fletcher
1613–14	*The Two Noble Kinsmen*, with John Fletcher

KINGS AND QUEENS OF ENGLAND: FROM THE HISTORY PLAYS TO SHAKESPEARE'S LIFETIME

	Lifespan	Reign
Angevins:		
Henry II	1133–1189	1154–1189
Richard I	1157–1199	1189–1199
John	1166–1216	1199–1216
Henry III	1207–1272	1216–1272
Edward I	1239–1307	1272–1307
Edward II	1284–1327	1307–1327 deposed
Edward III	1312–1377	1327–1377
Richard II	1367–1400	1377–1399 deposed
Lancastrians:		
Henry IV	1367–1413	1399–1413
Henry V	1387–1422	1413–1422
Henry VI	1421–1471	1422–1461 and 1470–1471
Yorkists:		
Edward IV	1442–1483	1461–1470 and 1471–1483
Edward V	1470–1483	1483 not crowned: deposed and assassinated
Richard III	1452–1485	1483–1485
Tudors:		
Henry VII	1457–1509	1485–1509
Henry VIII	1491–1547	1509–1547
Edward VI	1537–1553	1547–1553

	Lifespan	*Reign*
Jane	1537–1554	1553 not crowned: deposed and executed
Mary I	1516–1558	1553–1558
Philip of Spain	1527–1598	1554–1558 co-regent with Mary
Elizabeth I	1533–1603	1558–1603
Stuart:		
James I	1566–1625	1603–1625 James VI of Scotland (1567–1625)

THE HISTORY BEHIND THE HISTORIES: A CHRONOLOGY

Square brackets indicate events that happen just outside a play's timescale but are mentioned in the play.

Date	Event	Location	Play
22 May 1200	Truce between King John and Philip Augustus	Le Goulet, Normandy	*King John*
Apr 1203	Death of Arthur	Rouen	*King John*
1209	Pope Innocent III excommunicates King John		*King John*
18/19 Oct 1216	Death of King John	Swineshead, Lincolnshire	*King John*
Apr–Sep 1398	Quarrel, duel, and exile of Bullingbrook and Mowbray	Coventry	*Richard II*
3 Feb 1399	Death of John of Gaunt	Leicester	*Richard II*
Jul 1399	Bullingbrook lands in England	Ravenspur, Yorkshire	*Richard II*
Aug 1399	Richard II captured by Bullingbrook	Wales	*Richard II*
30 Sep 1399	Richard II abdicates	London	*Richard II*
13 Oct 1399	Coronation of Henry IV	London	*Richard II*
Jan–Feb 1400	Death of Richard II	Pontefract Castle	*Richard II*
22 Jun 1402	Owen Glendower captures Edmund Mortimer	Bryn Glas, Wales	*1 Henry IV*
14 Sep 1402	Henry Percy defeats Scottish army	Homildon Hill, Yorkshire	*1 Henry IV*

Date	Event	Location	Play
21 Jul 1403	Battle of Shrewsbury; death of Henry Percy (Hotspur)	Battlefield, near Shrewsbury, Shropshire	*1 & 2 Henry IV*
Feb 1405	Tripartite Indenture between Owen Glendower, Edmund Mortimer, and Northumberland (Henry Percy)	Bangor	*1 Henry IV*
May–Jun 1405	Rebellion of Archbishop of York (Richard Scroop), Earl of Norfolk (Thomas Mowbray), and Lord Bardolph	Yorkshire	*2 Henry IV*
8 Jun 1405	Trial and execution of Archbishop of York and Earl of Norfolk	York	*2 Henry IV*
20 Mar 1413	Death of Henry IV	Westminster Abbey	*2 Henry IV*
9 Apr 1413	Coronation of Henry V	Westminster Abbey	*2 Henry IV*
c.1415–16?	Death of Owen Glendower	Wales?	*2 Henry IV*
Early Aug 1415	Execution of Earl of Cambridge, Lord Scroop, and Sir Thomas Grey	Southampton	*Henry V*
14 Aug–22 Sep 1415	Siege of Harfleur	Harfleur, Normandy	*Henry V*
25 Oct 1415	Battle of Agincourt	Agincourt, Pas de Calais	*Henry V*
31 Aug 1422	Death of Henry V	Bois de Vincennes, near Paris	*1 Henry VI*
18 Jan 1425	Death of Edmund Mortimer	Ireland	*1 Henry VI*
Oct 1428–May 1429	Siege of Orléans	Orléans	*1 Henry VI*
17 Oct 1428	Death of Lord Salisbury	Orléans	*1 Henry VI*

Date	Event	Location	Play
18 Jun 1429	Capture of Lord Talbot at battle of Patay	Patay, near Orléans	*1 Henry VI*
18 Jul 1429	Coronation of Charles VII	Rheims Cathedral	*1 Henry VI*
6 Nov 1429	Coronation of Henry VI as King of England	Westminster Abbey	*[1 Henry VI]*
23 May 1430	Capture of Joan of Arc	Compiègne, near Soissons	*1 Henry VI*
30 May 1431	Execution of Joan of Arc	Saint-Ouen, near Paris	*1 Henry VI*
16 Dec 1431	Coronation of Henry VI as King of France	Notre Dame Cathedral, Paris	*1 Henry VI*
14 Sep 1435	Death of Duke of Bedford	Rouen	*1 Henry VI*
Summer–Autumn 1441	Arrest and trial of Eleanor Cobham and accomplices	London	*2 Henry VI*
20 May 1442	Lord Talbot created Earl of Shrewsbury	Paris	*1 Henry VI*
23 Apr 1445	Marriage of Henry VI and Margaret of Anjou	Titchfield, Hampshire	*2 Henry VI*
23 Feb 1447	Death of Humphrey, Duke of Gloucester	Bury St. Edmunds	*2 Henry VI*
11 Apr 1447	Death of Cardinal Beaufort	Winchester	*2 Henry VI*
2 May 1450	Death of Earl of Suffolk	English Channel	*2 Henry VI*
Jun–Jul 1450	Rebellion of Jack Cade	Kent and London	*2 Henry VI*
Spring 1452	Richard, Duke of York, marches on London	London	*2 Henry VI*
17 Jul 1453	Death of Lord Talbot at battle of Cantillon	Cantillon, Gascony	*1 Henry VI*
22 May 1455	First battle of St. Albans	St. Albans, Hertfordshire	*2 Henry VI*

Date	Event	Location	Play
10 Jul 1460	Battle of Northampton	Northampton	[3 Henry VI]
Oct 1460	Richard, Duke of York, holds Parliament	London	3 Henry VI
30 Dec 1460	Battle of Wakefield	Wakefield, Yorkshire	3 Henry VI
2 Feb 1461	Battle of Mortimer's Cross	Near Wigmore, Herefordshire	3 Henry VI
29 Mar 1461	Battle of Towton	Near Tadcaster, Yorkshire	3 Henry VI
28 Jun 1461	Coronation of Edward IV	Westminster Abbey	3 Henry VI
1 May 1464	Marriage of Edward IV and Elizabeth Woodville	Northamptonshire	3 Henry VI
Jul 1465	Henry VI captured	Lancashire	3 Henry VI
26 Jul 1469	Battle of Edgecote Moor	Near Banbury, Oxfordshire	3 Henry VI
Oct 1470–Apr/ May 1471	Readeption (restoration) of Henry VI	London	3 Henry VI
14 Apr 1471	Battle of Barnet; death of Warwick	Barnet, near London	3 Henry VI
4 May 1471	Battle of Tewkesbury; death of Edward, Prince of Wales	Tewkesbury, Gloucestershire	3 Henry VI
21 May 1471	Death of Henry VI	Tower of London	3 Henry VI
12 Jul 1472	Marriage of Richard, Duke of Gloucester, to Anne	Westminster Abbey	Richard III
18 Feb 1478	Death of Duke of Clarence	Tower of London	Richard III
9 Apr 1483	Death of Edward IV	Westminster	Richard III
Jun 1483	Death of Lord Hastings	Tower of London	Richard III

Date	Event	Location	Play
6 Jul 1483	Coronation of Richard III	Westminster Abbey	*Richard III*
2 Nov 1483	Death of Duke of Buckingham	Salisbury	*Richard III*
16 Mar 1485	Death of Queen Anne	Westminster	*Richard III*
22 Aug 1485	Battle of Bosworth Field	Leicestershire	*Richard III*
30 Oct 1485	Coronation of Henry VII	Westminster Abbey	*[Richard III]*
18 Jan 1486	Marriage of Henry VII and Elizabeth of York	Westminster Abbey	*[Richard III]*
Jun 1520	Meeting of Henry VIII and Francis I	"Field of the Cloth of Gold," near Calais, France	*[Henry VIII]*
17 May 1521	Death of Duke of Buckingham	Tower Hill, London	*Henry VIII*
29 Nov 1530	Death of Wolsey	Leicester	*Henry VIII*
25 Jan 1533	Marriage of Henry VIII and Anne Bullen (Boleyn)	Whitehall	*Henry VIII*
1 Jun 1533	Coronation of Anne Bullen (Boleyn)	Westminster Abbey	*Henry VIII*
7 Sep 1533	Birth of Princess Elizabeth	Greenwich Palace	*Henry VIII*
10 Sep 1533	Christening of Princess Elizabeth	Greenwich Palace	*Henry VIII*

FURTHER READING
AND VIEWING

CRITICAL APPROACHES

Barber, C. L., "Rule and Misrule in *Henry IV*," in his *Shakespeare's Festive Comedy* (1959). Superb linking to the "festive" world.

Bloom, Harold, ed., *Modern Critical Interpretations: William Shakespeare's Henry IV, Part 1* (1987). Extracts from strong twentieth-century critical approaches.

Bristol, Michael D., *Carnival and Theater: Plebeian Culture and the Structure of Authority in Renaissance England* (1985). Provocative Marxist reading.

Bulman, James, "*Henry IV, Parts 1* and *2*," in *The Cambridge Companion to Shakespeare's History Plays*, ed. Michael Hattaway (2002), pp. 158–76. Sensible overview.

Greenblatt, Stephen, "Invisible Bullets: Renaissance Authority and Its Subversion, *Henry IV* and *Henry V*," in *Political Shakespeare: Essays in Cultural Materialism*, ed. Jonathan Dollimore and Alan Sinfield (1985), pp. 18–47. Hugely influential "new historicist" reading. Reprinted in Greenblatt's *Shakespearean Negotiations* (1988).

Hodgdon, Barbara, *The End Crowns All: Closure and Contradiction in Shakespeare's History* (1991). Strong on structure.

Hunter, G. K., ed., *Shakespeare: Henry IV Parts I and II*, Macmillan Casebook series (1970). Invaluable selection of earlier criticism.

Kastan, David Scott, " 'The King Hath Many Marching in His Coats,' or, What Did You Do in the War, Daddy?," in *Shakespeare Left and Right*, ed. Ivo Kamps (1991), pp. 241–58. Good focus on politics, duplicity, and kingship.

McAlindon, Tom, *Shakespeare's Tudor History: A Study of Henry IV Parts 1 and 2* (2000). Excellent account of critical history and cultural context, with good close reading.

McLoughlin, Cathleen T., *Shakespeare, Rabelais, and the Comical-Historical* (2000). Fascinating intertextual reading of *Henry IV* plays with Rabelais' *Gargantua and Pantagruel*.

Morgann, Maurice, *An Essay on the Dramatic Character of Sir John Falstaff* (1777, repr. 2004). Gloriously humane character criticism from the

eighteenth century. Also freely available online, e.g., at www.19.5degs
.com/ebook/essay-the-dramatic-character-of-sir-john-falstaff/466/
read#list

Patterson, Annabel, *Shakespeare and the Popular Voice* (1989) and *Reading Holinshed's Chronicles* (1994). Two books that should be read as a pair.

Rackin, Phyllis, *Stages of History: Shakespeare's English Chronicles* (1990). Attentive to women and social inferiors as well as kings and nobles.

Rossiter, A. P., "Ambivalence: The Dialectic of the History Plays," in his *Angel with Horns: Fifteen Lectures on Shakespeare* (1961). Still one of the best things written on the play.

Saccio, Peter, *Shakespeare's English Kings* (1977). The best practical guide to the relationship between actual historical events in the Middle Ages, the Tudor chronicles, and Shakespeare's dramatic reshaping of history.

Wood, Nigel, ed., *Henry IV Parts One and Two* (1995). Sophisticated collection of theoretically informed essays—not for beginners.

THE PLAY IN PERFORMANCE

Bogdanov, Michael, and Michael Pennington, *The English Shakespeare Company: the Story of the Wars of the Roses, 1986–1989* (1990). Insiders' account.

Callow, Simon, *Actors on Shakespeare: Henry IV Part 1* (2002). Takes the reader through the play "from the point of view of the practitioner"— lucid, intelligent, readable account.

McMillin, Scott, *Shakespeare in Performance: Henry IV Part One* (1991). Discussion of five important modern productions, up to English Shakespeare Company, plus films.

Merlin, Bella, *With the Rogue's Company: Henry IV at the National Theatre* (2005). Detailed account of Nicholas Hytner's production.

Parsons, Keith, and Pamela Mason, eds., *Shakespeare in Performance* (1995). Includes a useful essay on both parts of *Henry IV* by Janet Clare— luxuriously illustrated.

Smallwood, Robert, ed., *Players of Shakespeare 6* (2004). Includes illuminating discussions by David Troughton on playing Bullingbrook/Henry IV and Desmond Barrit on Falstaff.

Wharton, T. F., *Text and Performance: Henry the Fourth Parts 1 & 2* (1983). A good basic introduction to the play and detailed discussions of three RSC productions and the BBC television version.

AVAILABLE ON DVD

Chimes at Midnight, directed by Orson Welles (1965, DVD 2000). Condenses all the Falstaff material from both parts of *Henry IV* plus *Henry V* and *The Merry Wives of Windsor*. Multi-award nominated, with a star-studded cast, as eccentric and brilliant as Welles' own performance as Falstaff. One of the all-time classic Shakespeare films.

Henry the Fourth Parts 1 and 2, directed by David Giles (1979, DVD 2005). Somewhat pedestrian account for the BBC series. Anthony Quayle's Falstaff stands out.

Henry V, directed by Kenneth Branagh (1989, DVD 2002). Incorporated some flashback scenes from *Henry IV* with Robbie Coltrane as Falstaff.

My Own Private Idaho, directed by Gus Van Sant (1991, DVD 2005). Loosely based on the Hal–Falstaff relationship. Stars River Phoenix and Keanu Reeves as a pair of gay hustlers.

The Wars of the Roses, directed by Michael Bogdanov (1989, DVD 2005). Recording of English Shakespeare Company's eclectic and highly political stage production.

REFERENCES

1. Scott McMillin, *Shakespeare in Performance: Henry IV, Part One* (1991), p. 1.
2. A reference to *The Second Part of Henry the Fourth* or *Henry V* in Nicholas Breton's *A Post with a Packet of Mad Letters* (Part I, 1603).
3. James Wright, *Historia Historionica* (1699).
4. Colley Cibber, *An Apology for the Life of Mr Colley Cibber* (1740), p. 87.
5. Thomas Davies, *Dramatic Miscellanies* (1784, repr. 1971), pp. 124–8.
6. Davies, *Dramatic Miscellanies*, pp. 127–8.
7. Davies, *Dramatic Miscellanies*, pp. 136–41.
8. Davies, *Dramatic Miscellanies*, p. 153.
9. Davies Laurence Selenick, *The Changing Room: Sex, Drag and Theatre* (2000), p. 270.
10. William Hazlitt, *Examiner*, 13 October 1816.
11. *The Athenaeum*, No. 902, 8 February 1845, p. 158.
12. Harold Child, "The Stage-History of *King Henry IV*," in *The First Part of the History of Henry IV*, ed. J. Dover Wilson (1946), pp. xxix–xlvi.
13. *Theatrical Journal*, Vol. 7, No. 346, 1 August 1846, pp. 243–4.
14. Henry Morley, diary entry for 14 May 1864 in *The Journal of a London Playgoer from 1851 to 1866* (1866), pp. 330–9.
15. Morley, diary entry for 1 October 1864, pp. 344–5.
16. William Archer, *The Theatrical "World" of 1896* (1897, repr. 1971), pp. 141–50.
17. *The Athenaeum*, No. 3577, 16 May 1896, p. 659.
18. G. B. Shaw, *The Saturday Review*, London, Vol. 81, No. 2116, 16 May 1896, pp. 500–2.
19. William Butler Yeats, "At Stratford-upon-Avon" (1901), in his *Essays and Introductions* (1961), p. 97.
20. Herbert Farjeon, "King Henry the Fourth—Part I: Mr Robey's Falstaff," in his *The Shakespearean Scene: Dramatic Criticisms* (1949), p. 92.
21. Child, "The Stage-History of *King Henry IV*," pp. xxix–xlvi.
22. Stephen Potter, *New Statesman and Nation*, 6 October 1945, p. 227.
23. Audrey Williamson, "The New Triumvirate (1944–47)," in her *Old Vic Drama: A Twelve Years' Study of Plays and Players* (1948), pp. 172–212.
24. Anthony Quayle, in a foreword to *Shakespeare's Histories at Stratford, 1951*, by J. Dover Wilson and T. C. Worsley (1970).

25. T. C. Worsley, *New Statesman and Nation*, 3 November 1951, pp. 489–90.

26. T. C. Worsley, *Shakespeare's Histories at Stratford, 1951* (1970), p. 31.

27. Worsley, *New Statesman and Nation*, 3 November 1951, pp. 489–90.

28. T. C. Worsley, *New Statesman and Nation*, 7 May 1955, p. 646.

29. Eric Keown, *Punch*, 11 May 1955, pp. 593–4.

30. Michael Bogdanov and Michael Pennington, *The English Shakespeare Company: The Story of the Wars of the Roses, 1986–1989* (1990), pp. 28–9, quoted in Barbara Hodgdon, *Shakespeare in Performance: Henry IV, Part Two* (1993), pp. 124–5.

31. Donald Malcolm, *New Yorker*, 30 April 1960, pp. 86–9.

32. Ben Brantley, *New York Times Current Events Edition*, 23 December 1993.

33. Ben Brantley, *New York Times*, 21 November 2003.

34. Paul Taylor, *Independent*, 6 May 2005.

35. Taylor, *Independent*, 6 May 2005.

36. Taylor, *Independent*, 6 May 2005.

37. McMillin, *Shakespeare in Performance*, p. 88.

38. McMillin, *Shakespeare in Performance*, p. 95.

39. McMillin, *Shakespeare in Performance*, p. 100.

40. Ronald Bryden, "The Education of a King," *Henry IV Parts 1 & 2*, RSC Programme notes, 1980.

41. McMillin, *Shakespeare in Performance*, p. 86.

42. McMillin, *Shakespeare in Performance*, p. 86.

43. T. F. Wharton, *Henry the Fourth, Parts 1 & 2: Text and Performance* (1983).

44. David Scott Kastan, ed., Introduction, in *King Henry IV Part 1*, Arden Shakespeare (2002).

45. Stanley Wells, *Times Literary Supplement*, 10 May 1991.

46. Michael Billington, *Guardian*, 18 April 1991.

47. John Peter, *Sunday Times*, London, 21 April 2001.

48. Desmond Barrit, "Falstaff," in Robert Smallwood, ed., *Players of Shakespeare 6* (2004).

49. Nicholas de Jongh, *Evening Standard*, 20 April 2000.

50. Michael Billington, *Guardian*, 21 April 2000.

51. Friedrich Nietzsche, *Thus Spake Zarathustra*, Second Part, 29.

52. Harold C. Goddard, "Henry IV," in Harold Bloom, ed., *William Shakespeare: Histories and Poems* (1986).

53. Goddard, "Henry IV."

54. *Listener*, 3 July 1975.

55. Kastan, *King Henry IV Part 1*, p. 97.
56. Emrys James, "On Playing Henry IV," *Theatre Quarterly*, Vol. 7, 1977.
57. W. Stephen Gilbert, *Plays and Players*, Vol. 22, No. 10, 1975.
58. Gilbert, *Plays and Players*.
59. Michael Coveney, *Daily Mail*, 21 April 2000.
60. McMillin, *Shakespeare in Performance*, p. 42.
61. Wharton, *Henry the Fourth, Parts 1 & 2*.
62. Stanley Wells, *Times Literary Supplement*, 10 May 1991.
63. David Troughton, "Bolingbroke in Richard II, and King Henry IV," in Smallwood, *Players of Shakespeare 6*.
64. Troughton, "Bolingbroke in Richard II, and King Henry IV."
65. Troughton, "Bolingbroke in Richard II, and King Henry IV."
66. Robert Smallwood, *Critical Quarterly*, Vol. 25, No. 1, Spring, 1983.
67. Billington, *Guardian*, 21 April 2000.
68. Troughton, "Bolingbroke in Richard II, and King Henry IV."
69. Bryden, "The Education of a King."
70. Goddard, "Henry IV," p. 33.
71. James, "On Playing Henry IV."
72. Billington, *Guardian*, 21 April 2000.
73. John Peter, *Sunday Times*, 30 April 2000.
74. Troughton, "Bolingbroke in Richard II, and King Henry IV."
75. Kastan, *King Henry IV Part 1*, p. 102.
76. Peter, *Sunday Times*, 21 April 2001.
77. Irving Wardle, *Independent on Sunday*, 21 April 2001.
78. Billington, *Guardian*, 18 April 2001.
79. Michel de Montaigne, *Essays* (trans. Florio, 1603), pp. 1, 30.
80. Unsigned review, *The Times*, London, 17 April 1964.
81. Wharton, *Henry the Fourth Parts 1 & 2*.
82. David E. Jones, *Drama Survey*, Vol. 4, No. 1, Spring 1965.
83. Wharton, *Henry the Fourth, Parts 1 & 2*, p. 67.
84. Wharton, *Henry the Fourth, Parts 1 & 2*.
85. Desmond Barrit, "Falstaff."
86. Charles Spencer, *Daily Telegraph*, 21 April 2000.
87. Peter Davison, "Henry IV," in Mark Hawkins-Dady, ed., *International Dictionary of Theatre—1: Plays* (1992).

ACKNOWLEDGMENTS AND PICTURE CREDITS

Preparation of *"Henry IV* in Performance" was assisted by a generous grant from the CAPITAL Centre (Creativity and Performance in Teaching and Learning) of the University of Warwick for research in the RSC archive at the Shakespeare Birthplace Trust. The Arts and Humanities Research Council (AHRC) funded a term's research leave that enabled Jonathan Bate to work on "The Director's Cut."

Picture research by Michelle Morton. Grateful acknowledgment is made to the Shakespeare Birthplace Trust for assistance with picture research (special thanks to Helen Hargest) and reproduction fees.

Images of RSC productions are supplied by the Shakespeare Centre Library and Archive, Stratford-upon-Avon. This Library, maintained by the Shakespeare Birthplace Trust, holds the most important collection of Shakespeare material in the UK, including the Royal Shakespeare Company's official archive. It is open to the public free of charge.

For more information see www.shakespeare.org.uk.

1. Herbert Beerbohm Tree (1896) Reproduced by permission of the Shakespeare Birthplace Trust
2. Ralph Richardson and Laurence Olivier (1945) John Vickers courtesy of the University of Bristol Theatre Collection
3. Directed by John Kidd and Anthony Quayle (1951) Angus McBean © Royal Shakespeare Company
4. Directed by Terry Hands (1975) Joe Cocks Studio Collection © Shakespeare Birthplace Trust
5. Directed by Michael Attenborough (2000) John Haynes © Royal Shakespeare Company
6. Directed by Michael Bogdanov (1987) © Donald Cooper/photostage.co.uk

The Modern Library presents paperback
editions of individual Shakespeare plays from

The Royal Shakespeare Company

Antony and
Cleopatra

King Lear

Macbeth

The Sonnets and
Other Poems

The Winter's Tale

With new commentary, as well as definitive
text and cutting-edge notes from the RSC's
William Shakespeare: Complete Works,
the first authoritative, modernized edition of
Shakespeare's First Folio in more than 300 years.

Hamlet

Love's Labour's
Lost

A Midsummer
Night's Dream

Richard III

The Tempest

Also available in hardcover
William Shakespeare: Complete Works

**"Timely, original, and beautifully
conceived . . . a remarkable edition."**
—James Shapiro, professor, Columbia
University, bestselling author of *A Year in the
Life of Shakespeare: 1599*